The African Union and African Agency in International Politics

Tshepo Gwatiwa

The African Union and African Agency in International Politics

palgrave
macmillan

Tshepo Gwatiwa
Department of International Relations
African Centre for the Study of the United States
University of the Witwatersrand
Johannesburg, Gauteng Province, South Africa

ISBN 978-3-030-87804-7   ISBN 978-3-030-87805-4   (eBook)
https://doi.org/10.1007/978-3-030-87805-4

© The Editor(s) (if applicable) and The Author(s), under exclusive license to Springer
Nature Switzerland AG 2022
This work is subject to copyright. All rights are solely and exclusively licensed by the
Publisher, whether the whole or part of the material is concerned, specifically the rights
of translation, reprinting, reuse of illustrations, recitation, broadcasting, reproduction on
microfilms or in any other physical way, and transmission or information storage and
retrieval, electronic adaptation, computer software, or by similar or dissimilar methodology
now known or hereafter developed.
The use of general descriptive names, registered names, trademarks, service marks, etc.
in this publication does not imply, even in the absence of a specific statement, that such
names are exempt from the relevant protective laws and regulations and therefore free for
general use.
The publisher, the authors and the editors are safe to assume that the advice and information in this book are believed to be true and accurate at the date of publication. Neither
the publisher nor the authors or the editors give a warranty, expressed or implied, with
respect to the material contained herein or for any errors or omissions that may have been
made. The publisher remains neutral with regard to jurisdictional claims in published maps
and institutional affiliations.

Cover illustration: © Alex Linch shutterstock.com

This Palgrave Macmillan imprint is published by the registered company Springer Nature
Switzerland AG
The registered company address is: Gewerbestrasse 11, 6330 Cham, Switzerland

For all students of African multilateralism and security,
Mary S. Gwatiwa, and the memory of Amon Gwatiwa

PREFACE

My introduction to the notion of African agency was rather strange. Almost a decade ago, when I submitted my research proposal as a PhD candidate my American supervisor remarked: "this is such a European research proposal from an African student". Expectedly, I was offended. Little did I know that like many students from Southern Africa—an unabashedly albinocratic region—I was naively immersed in Eurocentric narratives and interpretations of Africa. The international media was, and is still, dominated by Eurocentric narratives of Africa's regional integration, including in the peace and security domain. I was totally oblivious, and perhaps ignorant, of the extent to which African actors shape events within and beyond their continent.

My research visits to the African Union Commission were eye-openers. With unlimited access to the AUC I had the opportunity to conduct interviews in several departments. I was confounded by the gap between the [African] public's general awareness of the role of the AU and the actual "actorness" of the AU in international politics. Between 2012 and 2016, I interviewed more than sixty diplomats and security experts in several diplomatic cities: Addis Ababa, Pretoria, Gaborone, Geneva, Naples, Lisbon, Washington DC, and Brussels. I gained invaluable insights into not only what was said, but also what was not said by the respondents. By 2016, the biggest challenge was to reconcile narratives of African actions and aspirations with non-African narratives, which were either clothed in scepticism or outright hostility towards African agency.

viii PREFACE

Yet for all these narratives, there is always "fiction in the space between". This fiction became apparent when I reconciled my research findings and the years I spent in one of the world's biggest diplomatic hubs—Geneva, Switzerland.

There was no better place to "discover" African agency than Geneva. As prestigious as the *i Institut de hautes es études internationales et du développement* (IHEID) (or the Graduate Institute of International and Development Studies) is, it often revealed the African problem in international relations. The weekly seminars over a three year period since the completion of the *Maison de la Paix*, always featuring personalities from the echelons of international multilateral, and non-governmental organizations often exhibited both a deliberate and understandable flawed perception of Africa. Pedagogically, there was a dichotomy of impenitent supremacists who did not believe anything good could come out of Africa and those encouraged learners to examine the "African voice" in international affairs. A star player in the latter category was my supervisor Thomas J. Biersteker. He encouraged the study of African (and non-Western) agency in international affairs throughout my stay in Geneva. He made similar calls, in 2016, at seminars at the University of Johannesburg and the University of Stellenbosch. There was a particular seminar that revealed the true *situs* of African agency in international relations. There was an anniversary celebration of humanitarian action hosted by IHEID. There was a panel of exclusively Caucasian men—with neither a woman nor an African—cogitating on what had occurred in Africa for a decade prior, and the way forward. I asked why there was no African in their panel. The then head of the ICRC unabashedly defended the setting, with stoic affirmation from the representative of the UK government. I was shocked given my recent discovery that African organisations were bearing the brunt of finding solutions to problems that were mostly caused by Western and Asian states in Africa, with little acknowledgement from international media and scholars. By then I was not fully exposed to the anti-Africanism embedded in international affairs. But this was my first direct encounter with agents of what was hitherto a rumoured spectre of imperialism, racism and patriarchal misogyny. On the bright side, this spurred me to focus more on African agency in international relations. There is a lot that Africans of diverse backgrounds are doing within and outside the continent in the interest of African agency in international politics, yet there are comparatively very few texts focusing on that. As the saying goes, "until the lions have their own [writers], the story of the hunt will always glorify the hunter". This manuscript is an attempt to contribute to the story of the hunt.

This book is the first among several attempts to make a meaningful contribution to the already ongoing academic discourse on African agency in international security and politics. My differences with the current framing of the general narratives are relayed from a genuine place, and neither a reflection of polemic nor iconoclastic inclinations. I am more interested in a realistic portrayal of the African Union, Africa's international partnerships, and the continent's prospects in international affairs.

Tshepo Gwatiwa
Department of International
Relations
African Centre for the Study
of the United States
University of the Witwatersrand
Johannesburg, South Africa

ACKNOWLEDGEMENTS

I am indebted to so many people as I complete this book. First and foremost, I would like to thank Dr. Mehari Taddele Maru who encouraged me to publish my research as a book at the time when I was preoccupied with other pursuits.

Special gratitude also goes to the following people who helped me get access to various sources for this research: Chedza Molefe (AU), Stephen Mayega (AU), Boitshoko Mokgatlhe (AU/UN), Colonel Jacques Deman (EU-2-AU), Boiki C. Kgetsi (AU), Professor Tim Murithi (IJR), Dr Thomas Thatelo (UNISA), Jose Fernando Costa-Pereira (EEAS, EU), Lieutenant Colonel Antony Gash (EU MS), Sethunyiwe Oitsile (AU) and Abdel-Kader Harieche (then at the UNOAU). I would also like to thank various thinkers and scholars whose ideas have gone into this book. Finally, would like to thank my "brother from another continent" Dr Ueli Matthias Illuminatus Staeger, for providing a critical analysis of most of these chapters and constantly urging me to complete this manuscript.

I also wish to relay deep gratitude to the professors who oversaw this research until its final stage at The Graduate Institute in Geneva, Switzerland: Professor Thomas J. Biersteker and Professor Mohamed Mahmoud Ould Mohamedou. I also wish to thank Professors Keith Krause, Liliana Andonova and Paul Huth (during his visiting professorship) whose pedagogy helped me refine my ideas for this research project. I would also like to appreciate Babui G. Monepe for her support and care when I completed this book under the spell of a COVID-19 infection.

CONTENTS

1	Introduction	1
2	African Agency as Agency Slack: From Fiction to Multilateral Empirics	17
3	African Agency in Historical Perspective: A History of Agency Slack	41
4	Agential Challenges Within African Regionalism and Security	67
5	African Agency in the Early Design of African Security Institutions	103
6	The Africa–EU Partnership and African Agency: Model or Pareidolia?	137
7	Shirking in AU Partnerships: The UN and NATO	153
8	Slippage in AU Partnerships: The US Africa Command	183
9	Conclusion	201
Index		219

Acronyms

ACP	African, Caribbean, and Pacific Group of States
ACRIC	African Capacity for the Immediate Response to Crises
AFRICOM	United States Africa Command
AHSG	Assembly of Heads of State and Government
AMISOM	African Union Mission in Somalia
APF	Africa Peace Facility
APSA	African Peace and Security Architecture
ASEAN	Association of South Eastern Asian Nations
ASF	African Standby Force
AU MSC	African Union Military Staff Committee
AU	African Union
AUC	African Union Commission
BDF	Botswana Defence Force
CADSP	Common African Defence and Security Policy
CEWS	Continental Early Warning Systems
CFSP	Common Foreign and Security Policy
COE	Contingent-Owned Equipment
COPS	*Comite Politique et Securite*
CSSDCA	Conference on Security, Stability, Development and Cooperation in Africa
DPKO	Department of Peacekeeping Operations
ECCAS	Economic Community of Central African States
ECOMOG	Economic Community of West African States Monitoring Group
ECOWAS	Economic Organization of West African States
EU MS	European Union Military Staff
EU	European Union

xv

xvi ACRONYMS

EUCOM	United States European Command
FOCAC	Forum for China-Africa Cooperation
G77	Group of 77 (UN)
IGAD	Inter-Governmental Authority on Development
IMF	International Monetary Fund
IPSS	Institute for Peace and Security Studies
ISAF	International Security Assistance Force
ISS	Institute for Security Studies
JAHC	Joint African High Command
NAC	North Atlantic Council
NATO MD	NATO Mediterranean Dialogue
NATO	North Atlantic Treaty Organization
OAU	Organisation of African Unity
OAU-DF	OAU Defence Force
ODC	Office of Defence Cooperation
OIF	Organization Internationale de la Francophonie
PACOM	United States Pacific Command
PANWISE	Panel of the Wise
PRC	Permanent Representatives Committee (AU)
PSC	Peace and Security Council (AU)
PSD	Peace and Security Directorate/Department (AU)
PSO	Peace Support Operation
PSOD	Peace Support Operations Division
RECs	Regional Economic Communities
RI4P	Regional Infrastructure for Peace
SACEUR	Supreme Allied Command Europe (NATO)
SADC	Southern African Development Community
SAIIA	South African Institute for International Affairs
SANDF	South African National Defence Force
SFOR	Special Force (NATO)
SI	Strategic Indicatives
SIPRI	Stockholm International Peace Research Institute
SMLO	Senior Military Liaison Officer[s]
TCC	Troop Contributing Countries
UK	United Kingdom
UN SC	United Nations Security Council
UN	United Nations
UNDP	United Nations Development Programme
UNOAU	United Nations Office to the African Union
US	United States of America

LIST OF TABLES

Table 4.1 Capabilities of major African states according to AU/UN
peace operations requirements 76
Table 4.2 African Union peace support operations, 2003–2013 80

CHAPTER 1

Introduction

There are different conceptions of the notion of agency. The most often used definition is derived from Colin Wight, as cited in Brown, which posits agency as the ability to do something.[1] This notion is rooted in the idea of "intentionality", accountability and subjectivity.[2] My own conception of agency, from which I place the idea of "agency slack", is more nuanced but more at great variance with this conception (discussed later). However, it is imperative to highlight that the African Union (hereafter the AU) has an agential role which cannot be overemphasised. The controversies and calamities visited by the AU's international partners in Libya, as well as discoveries that the AU Commission building "donated freely" by China was bugged and sending computational data to servers in Shanghai every day after midnight for almost a decade, were a slap in the face of the union. Questions arose in public and intellectual circles as to whether the AU had any agential value in international affairs.

Indeed, the AU has a legally and politically mandated agential role in African internationalism. This agency is partially envisaged in the form of international partnerships. Article 3(e) of the AU Constitutive Act vests that obligation on the AU in that it "encourage[s] international cooperation, taking due account of the Charter of the United Nations...".[3] Giving the AU this onus makes it easier for both Africa and the international community to relate since it reduces the transaction cost of having to deal on a bilateral basis.[4] But this also helps situate this empirical

© The Author(s), under exclusive license to Springer Nature Switzerland AG 2022
T. Gwatiwa, *The African Union and African Agency in International Politics*, https://doi.org/10.1007/978-3-030-87805-4_1

1

dynamic within the conceptualization of African agency as something that possibly "influence Africa's structural and relational power".[5] In this light, the African Union's mandate in global politics through international partnerships centralises the concept of "agency" as an empirical element in the overall function of the continental body. Consequently, it has been a "partnerships galore" at the African Union Commission.

Over the last two decades, the AU entered signed different partnerships under unique terms. The union gravitated towards partnerships that are amenable to African agency. Nearly each of the so-called "strategic partnership" agreements, as well as their evaluative documents, contain(s) clauses on "African leadership and ownership" and African "agenda setting".[6] These notions were injected into the post-Lomé negotiations in the late 1990s when African negotiators first challenged Eurocentrism in international partnerships.[7] There are currently nine of these "strategic partnerships".[8] Yet, the AU has several other partnerships with entities such as the North Atlantic Treaty Organization (NATO), Brazil and others.[9]

To be sure, Africa's experience with partnerships dates to the early days of the Organization of African Unity (OAU), during which African political and technocratic elites thought that it would be wise to develop Africa through a "tripartite approach...involving Arab money, African resources and Western technology".[10] As a result, the OAU signed its earliest partnership with the League of Arab States (LAS) in 1977.[11] So coveted are these partnerships that the LAS sought to resuscitate the strategic partnership in 2010, after thirty-three years of dormancy. Russia became the latest entrants into the partnership milieu when it hosted forty heads of state and government to its first Russia-Africa summit in October 2019.[13] Even after similar requests were denied to Vietnam and Australia, the likes of Switzerland are so hopeful that they have developed a "Africa strategy".[14] Yet, this partnerships historicity obscures a major issue in this international foray—the extent to which African agency is under challenge and how African actors deal with it.

Libya and That Other Thing: An Agential Cudgel

In 2011, the African Union evinced its agential and structural limitations when it failed to convince and inhibit its key strategic partners—the US and NATO—from launching a scandalous and potentially disastrous military intervention in Libya. NATO launched Operation United

Protector which toppled Libyan leader, Muammar Gaddafi, and rendered the country into impotence as forewarned by various African scholars and practitioners.[15] The NATO operation was preceded by the US Africa Command (AFRICOM)'s Operation Odyssey Dawn, 19 days' prior.[16] Much of the publicity criticised the inefficacy of the African Union. To most people it seemed as if the "inaction" of the AU warranted the intervention of the United Nations (UN) and NATO. Little attention was paid to the backroom and shuttle diplomacy that the AU had attempted between Addis Ababa, Brussels, and New York prior to the intervention. The AU had put forward a proposal that consisted of one of the power sharing models between belligerents, known as "government of national unity" which had previously been experimented in Burundi, Kenya and Zimbabwe. The US, the European Union (EU) and NATO turned down the proposal and proceeded with the military intervention. But there was another side of the events that are not equally popular in public discourse.

In January 2016, the former president of South Africa, Thabo Mbeki, was asked about the "African voice" in the international system. He responded, "where is the voice? And people feel that somehow it's disappeared…" He illustrated his point using the foreign military intervention in Libya:

> There was this panel of five heads of state chosen by the AU to go and mediate that Libyan conflict…From Mauritania; they were going to go to Libya [sic]. By they were stopped by NATO [which told them]: 'if you come now, your plane might be shot down…because we are beginning our military operations'…Romano Prodi had been in contact with the Libyan factions—the Gaddafi and Bengazi people, the tribal chiefs—and all of them were saying 'Let's find a solution, we are ready to meet'… I contacted the UN and said: 'This is the possibility, personally I support it and I'm sure that if I talk to other former heads of state on the continent, they will support this. So, let's stop all this bombing and let the Libyans sit down' and so on. They said, 'Yes, yes, yes, we will come back to you, Mr. President'. But they never did.[17]

Far from being conspiratorial, the above statement reflects the state of African agency (or voice) in international affairs. Africa's institutional and fiscal shortcomings put it in a position where it depends on external support. The AU might have announced reforms, which could ostensibly reduce foreign influence and domination, but it is too early to tell.

Africa's fiscal fortunes have also dwindled considering the COVID-19 global pandemic. So, the idea of African capabilities will once again come to the fore.

The Problem of African Agency in International Affairs: From Fiction to "Agency Slack"

The main argument in this book is that what is often considered perennial misfortunes of the African continent in international politics, especially under the auspices of the African Union, is a dire manifestation of "agency slack" that has been in place since the formation of the OAU. This is a situation wherein an actor—such as the AU, takes independent action to produce [otherwise] undesirable or unexpected outcomes (defined below). In other words, "agency slack" is a manifestation of a deliberate, relational and inevitable action in a constrained environment. This slack makes use of two techniques. The first is *shirking*, which is a form of agency slack wherein an actor minimises the effort it is capable of exerting.[18] The second is *slippage*, whereby an agent shifts policy away from a preferred outcome to its own preferences.[19] This slack is caused by two intertwined factors that are found at the regional and international levels.

At the regional level, the AU is limited in its ability to project African agency in international affairs by the role and heterogeneity of its member states. First, the lack of political will among member states undermines the role and potential of the AU Commission and its agents. The main problem with principals is that they lack the political will to contribute various public goods to the course of African regional security encapsulated in the African Peace and Security Architecture (APSA)—which is the main project implemented by various AU partners. The AU is dependent on the inputs of member states: the AU can only do so much as it is enabled by its constituencies. These inputs comprise of the role of head of states, security and foreign ministers, technical experts who are supposed to steer the institutionalisation of the APSA. Second, the APSA is a complex project that brings together various regional security systems which comprise of dissimilar political and security histories; different security threats; as well as different visions of regional security.[20] Therefore, the AU cannot act with fortitude because a vastly heterogeneously group of states lack political will. This undermines the capacity of Africa in international affairs.

At an international level, and related to the above, an African organisation that is unable to augment its own position, identity and vision is unable to produce desired outcomes. Different partners contributing to APSA and African security, also face different dynamics. Among other things, they have different visions of security; have different levels of commitment to partnership with the AU; have different preferences and interests at heart; and most importantly, they have varying bandwidth to accommodate African ownership and leadership (read: agency). Within the continent, the AU is a pivotal institution in world politics. The AU plays a critical role that cannot be substituted by any single country. Due to Africa's massive size, sundry demarcations, intricate problems, nuances and inexplicable contradictions, the AU plays a pivotal role. To an extent, the advent of the AU changed Africa's fortunes in international affairs.

It is important to preface a discussion of African agency with a contextual exegesis. Africa's structural vulnerability is intricately weaved into the fabric of international security, which is steeped in the empire.

Empire is pervasive, and Africa is in constant contest with it. Michael Mann describes empire as follows, "an empire is a centralized, hierarchical system of rule acquired and maintained by coercion through which a core territory dominates peripheral territories, serves as the intermediary for their main interactions, and channels resources from and between the peripheries".[21] This implies that the world is virtually controlled by a small fraction of states. Hardt and Negri aptly capture this concept within the idea of "order". Order is a potentially discordant term that implies subjugation. Africa has been subjugated at varying levels of pressure throughout history, and none of those were pleasant. The manifestation of empire in Africa has been mostly at the hands of Britain, France and almost the US.

The irony is that the imperial ferocity that Africa contends with is enabled by the voting populations in these states. Most Westerners are either unaware or deny that their governments or organisations (such as the EU) are in pursuit of empires abroad. British, American and French are the usual suspects in this rancorous act. Various surveys have found that the British believed that colonialism was a good thing – they believed that they were "civilizing savages" in the hinterlands.[22] This is a subtle augmentation of the "order" (read: empire) because in their participation, which masquerades as ignorance, they are just as complicit as the interest groups that lobby for one-dimensional self-serving interests which often undermine African preferences or upset trajectories. For instance, when Barak Obama was still a senator, he was among a group of senators who made various demands such as Nigeria's surrender of Charles Taylor, an undertaking that undermined a component of the Conference on Security, Stability, Development and Cooperation in Africa (CSSDCA) which promoted negotiated exits of autocrats.[23] This was not only myopic but selfish of Barack Obama. As a matter of fact, Barack Obama's speech act is a single unit in a trajectory of highly deceptive and nifty imperial figures who undermined Africa.

The idea of increasing fortunes for Africa agency should not be overstated. The current optimism about growing African influence in international politics[24] is a fiction (also see the next chapter). Not only Africa, but the rest of the world, is designed and operates within an "American imperium".[25] Africa's material weakness leaves it with little options beyond ephemeral flashpoints in international politics, such as the practice of declarations and collective positions designated as indications agency in international affairs.[26] Even where rhetorical statements and texts are considered a form of agency, the picture is more disturbing when viewed from both ends. Africa's so-called gains and ability to control a portion of extraversion[27] is as misguided conceptually misguided as its failure of the empirical test. That narrative fails to capture why that "agency" appears to be growing.

African agency and influence appear to grow in proportion to the extent to which non-African actors are willing to abandon an operational model without necessarily changing the material benefits. Wai aptly explains the imperial core's sudden transformation by pointing to the nuances of global politics. He highlights the subtlety of the changing architecture of the West's imperial strategy which is not real transformation but adjustments that are meant to retain the imperial domination over Africa an other parts of the developing world.[28] So, while Africa may be rapidly transforming economically, its situs in international politics may not change significantly. Hence, the notion that African agency may be changing with development opportunities is misguided. Correspondingly, it is important to also note that:

> To say that the subordinate economies do not develop does not mean that they do not change or grow; it means, rather, that they remain subordinate in the global system and thus never achieve the promised form of a dominant, developed economy. In some cases, individual countries or

regions may be able to change their position in the hierarchy, but the point is that, regardless of who fills which position, the hierarchy remains the determining factor.[29]

Hence it is imperative to grasp the powerful effect of this hierarchy despite some gains in other areas. This applies particularly in international politics where power and structure are defining elements of the systems. For this discussion it is imperative to reiterate that, in the early 1990s, Barry Buzan predicted that African security would constitute the periphery of a Western-centred global security order.[30] The resultant accurate fulfilment of this prophecy derives from the fact that international security is structured in such a way that Africa's fortunes in international cooperation will remain unchanged. Until the nature and exigences of the international structure change, prospects for African agency will remain dim. The idea that Africa, especially in its collective formation, can successfully bargain "in a manner that benefits Africans themselves",[31] will remain in the domain of hope. That is why I turn to the notion of "agency slack" (discussed in detail in Chapter 2).

THE AFRICAN UNION AND AFRICAN AGENCY

This book examines why and how the African Union uses agency slack in international politics. It seeks to highlight and examine the role of the organisation in trying to protect as well as exercise African agency. It focuses on an area that is responsible for Africa's battered image in international affairs—international security.

The historical "image" of Africa has largely been attributed to poverty, starvation, health pandemics and conflicts.[32] However, it is stories of wars and genocide in the media, as well as concomitant multilateral alleviation efforts (peacekeeping and peacebuilding), that have fuelled the idea of African barbarism and impotence.[33] To that end, the book focuses on the AU's international security partnerships. The rationale is binary. On the one hand, prior to the effectuation of the AU (Kagame) reforms, the budget of the Peace and Security Department far exceeded that of the entire AU Commission. This was because the AU's international partners channelled a lot of funding to the department. Second, and related to the first, during the research for this book it was evident there was a general conceptual policy consensus between African bureaucrats and their international counterparts that peace, security and political stability is a prerequisite for [African] development. However, the imperative for such a book is both an intellectual and pragmatic one.

There is a cognitive gap regarding African agency within and beyond the continent. Many Africans, including academics and policymakers, seem unaware of the processes underlying what they perceive as an inability to deal with African [continental] problems. The criticism levelled against the AU and its agents in seminars and conversations often reflects a limited understanding of the empirical efforts of AU, including within the continent. However, this is not surprising. There is an informational problem wherein African agency is deliberately or unwittingly pushed to the backwater of mediated narratives. More so, the international media—such as CNN, NHK, CCTV and the BBC—have romanticised the idea of an impotent continent, dependent on the charitable acts of its erstwhile and emerging colonisers. As a resultant most observers and students of international studies, view Africa with such disdain and contempt. To be sure, the AU is not a perfect organisation. However, to dismiss its capability based on media reportage which promotes Afro pessimism is simplistic. Yet, the media narrative is an incomplete description of the actual picture. That is why I make a stronger case for the notion of "agency slack" in the next chapter.

African Agency as an Inside-Out Dynamic

The decline of African agency under the AU is a function of continental and external factors. If we accept that continental politics are the driving force of such agency, then it is imperative to take note of several factors related to the African multilateralism that undermine African agency. First, the quality and fortitude of Africa's collective diplomacy and engagement with the rest of the world have waned. The fortitude shown by the political cadres consisting of the likes of Olusegun Obasanjo, Thabo Mbeki, Abdelaziz Bouteflika, Abdoulaye Wade, Muammar Gaddafi, Hosni Mubarak and others waned from the start of the 2010s. Equally, the role of the Chairperson of the AU Commission, commissioners, and their special envoys has borne less fruits in the 2010s compared to prior years (discussed in detail in Chapters 2 and 4). Second, and a corollary of the first, is that these cadres failed to institutionalise the informal networks that the African Union used to earn and increase its agency in international affairs.[36] Worse, despite an array of wishes,[37] there is no promise for hegemonic leadership on the continent. Third, the African Union has failed to reify strategic citizenship[38] as well as transform its collective decision-making institutions. Strategic citizenship consists of role playing and burden sharing whereby larger member states are expected to bear a disproportionate burden for regional security.[39] Contrarily, the African regional security order managed by the AU is unrepentantly enshrined in an egalitarianism system[40] which has effectivity stalled over the last two decades.[41]

This book focuses on major AU security partnerships. It does not examine other partnerships because they are either nascent or do not yet qualify as strategic partnerships. Strategic partnerships are all encompassing of the AU's strategic indicatives,[42] of which peace and security are just a part. There is a criterion, consisting of necessary and sufficient conditions, for classifying a partnership as strategic. First and foremost, the partnership agreement should designate the partnership as such. Second, there should be a high level of institutionalisation of the partnership at different levels of corresponding structures between the two partners. Such institutionalisation typically reflects decentralised networks as opposed to bureaucracies. Third, although there is no or soft legalisation, there should be evident political will. Such will should not only be at the echelons (i.e. summitry level) but also identifiable at the expert and technology levels. Fourth, the partnerships exhibit an element of stability and continuity that is akin to those of multilateral institutions.[43] The selected partnerships qualify, except for the NATO partnership which's status is more nuanced.

The AU has other partnerships which are not strategic partnerships of note in the peace and security dimension. Strategic partnerships without noteworthy peace and security components are those with China, Japan, South America, Turkey, the Organisation of Islamic Cooperation (OIC) and the Africa-Arab League partnership, even though these have been growing in significance since this research was last completed.[44]

OUTLINE OF THE CHAPTERS

The next chapters seek to capture different aspects of the manifestation of agency slack in the AU's international security partnerships.

The next, and second, chapter seeks to contextualise the idea of agency slack in the broader domain of African agency. It operationalizes the concept of "agency" as an empirical element and dimension of the continent's foreign relations. It mainly focuses on how the AU's projection of agency falls short of what is popularly considered a manifestation of

African agency. It argues that present conceptions are either a work of fiction or phantoms attending to ephemeral intellectual satisfactions which have no lasting effect in policy terms, or credible empirical resonance. It unfolds in three parts. It contextualises the notion of agency, operationalises the concept at both the abstract and empirical level in the AU's international processes, thereby elucidating the historical and structural context in which Africa's multilateral agency obtains. Second, it pays special attention to the role of summitry through which agents seek to give African agency meaning and intentionality. It also shows the bounded limitations of what is considered an African agency. A third part looks at African agency in the AU's international partnerships and demonstrate how African multilateralism has been an act of agency slack since the early 1960s. Finally, it makes a strong case for AU agency to be understood as an act of agency slack.

The third chapter illustrates the origins of agency slack in African multilateralism and international cooperation. It does this by situating African multilateralism in the context of "postcoloniality" and the "postcolonial condition". It uses a conceptual delineation that highlights the power disparity between African and other regions. It highlights a path-dependency and power differential that constrains the AU—often a junior partner in international partnerships—and its desire to do something new or often different from its partners. This power differential helps clarify why Africa appears to be always in the defensive and likely to remain in that position for a foreseeable period.

Chapter 4 outlines and explains the conditions, within the continent, which place the AU in a chronic condition of agency slack in international security partnerships. It mostly examines political and institutional factors that inhibit the AU's ability to express intentionality and power. Thereafter it narrows into the multifaceted issues that affect African regional security. These include lack of hegemonic leadership, decimated political will, unreliable financial contributions, mutual suspicion between member states, and overall lack of coercive power in African multilateralism. The chapter sums the argument with a demonstration of how these factors make agency slack an integral part of African multilateralism.

The fifth chapter chronicles an attempt to transcend agency slack during the first decade of the African Union. It closely examines why the initial decade is different from those that preceded and succeeded it. The chapter highlights temporal lacunas in global affairs that permitted and thereafter stunted African agency to the level of agency slack. It does this by examining developments within each of the four partnerships under study. Particular attention is paid to the patterns of rise-and-fall as well as rise-and-stagnate in each partnership.

The sixth chapter uses the case of the Africa-EU partnership, often touted as a model, to interrogate whether African agency really existed. The chapter delves deeper into how the EU partnership turned out differently from the rest. Most importantly, it shows how this partnership—at an empirical level, was the genesis for attempts to push for greater African agency in international affairs. The chapter explores both institutional and political dynamics that resulted in a rise-and-stagnate effect which pushed the AU to a general attitude of scepticism which rationalised the resuscitation of agency slack.

Chapters 7 and 8 explore instances of the two manifestations of agency slack. Chapter 7 explores the notion of shirking in the AU's partnerships with the UN and NATO. It examines how each partnership moved from promise to outright scepticism. Most importantly, the chapter examines how the African Union responded to the strategic manoeuvres of these powerful partners. The eighth chapter examines slippage in the AU's partnership with the US Africa Command. It examines the nature and politics of this partnership and why it stands askance from the rest of the partnerships. Importantly, the chapter captures how the African Union exercised slippage.

The final chapter provides a nuanced conclusion. It concludes that the AU's agency slack is, first and foremost, a response to the internal pressures exerted by a huge, complex and constitutively irreconcilable regional security order. These pressures are a preliminary limiting factor in the AU's ability to project intentionality and configurational power in international affairs. The chapter also concludes that the AU's agency slack is also a response to the interconnectedness of African states to imperialism which grossly affects African multilateralism considering the partnerships.

NOTES

1. William Brown, "A Question of Agency: Africa in International Politics", *Third World Quarterly* 33, no. 10 (2012): 1900.
2. Lesly Blaauw, "African Agency in International Relations: Challenging Great Power Politics?" in eds. Paul-Henri Bishoff, Kwesi

Aning, and Amitav Acharya, *Africa in Global International Relations: Emerging Approaches to Theory and Practice* (London: Routledge, 2015), 90.

3. African Union, *Constitutive Act* (Addis Ababa: AU Commission 2000), 5; also see African Union, *Protocol Relating to the Establishment of the Peace and Security Council of the African Union* (Addis Ababa: AU Commission, 2002).

4. see Kenneth Abbott and Duncan Snidal, "Why States Act through Formal International Organizations", *The Journal of Conflict Resolution* 42, no. 1 (1998): 3–32.

5. Elijah Munyi et al., "Conceptualizing Agency and Influence in African International Relations", in *Beyond History: African Agency in Development, Diplomacy and Conflict Resolution*, eds. Elijah Munyi, David Mwambari, and Aleksi Ylonen (London: Rowman & Littlefield International, 2020), 4.

6. European Commission, "Cotonou Agreement", Brussels (2000); Council of the European Union, "The Africa-EU Strategic Partnership: A Joint Africa-EU Strategy", Lisbon: (2007), 4; Ministry of Foreign Affairs of Japan, "Fifth Tokyo International Conference on Development (TICAD V)", (2013), http://www.mofa.go.jp/region/page6e_000075.html.

7. See Organization of African Unity, "Key Issues in the Current ACP-EU Negotiations", Technical Report No.1, prepared for *African Negotiators by OAU Advisory Panel of Experts on ACP-EU Negotiations* (Addis Ababa: OAU, February 1999).

8. African Union, "Evaluation of the Africa's Strategic Partnerships" Draft Final Revised Report, UNDP/AU: Addis Ababa, (November 2014). These are as follows: Africa-European Union (EU) partnership; the Africa-South America Summit (ASA) Partnership; the Africa-League of Arab States; the Africa-India Forum; the Africa-Japan Partnership (TICAD-Tokyo Conference on Africa's Development)) Partnership; the Forum for China-Africa Cooperation (FOCAC); the Africa-Turkey Partnership; the Africa-Korea Partnership; and the Africa-US Partnership.

9. The most common of these agreements are often labelled "strategic partnerships"—which are wider in scope and far-reaching in ambit; while others are simply labelled "partnership agreements"—usually specialized and limited to portions of the continent.

10. Muhammad Gassama, *From the OAU to the AU: The Odyssey of a Continental Organization* (Gambia: Fulladu Publishers, 2013), 25.
11. Olusola Ojo, "The Relationship between the Organization of African Unity and the League of Arab States", *Africa Spectrum* 16:2 (1981): 131–141.
12. Department of International Relations and Cooperation (October 5, 2010), "Deputy President of the Republic, H.E. Kgalema Motlanthe, to Lead a South African Delegation to the 2nd Afro-Arab Summit to be Held in Sirte, Libya, from 6 to 11 October 2010", DIRCO South Africa, http://www.dirco.gov.za/docs/2010/afro-arab1006.html.
13. PSC Report, "How to Rationalise Africa's Many Partnerships?", Institute for Security Studies, December 13, 2019, https://issafr ica.org/pscreport/psc-insights/how-to-rationalise-africas-many-partnerships.
14. Federal Department of Foreign Affairs, "New opportunities are emerging in sub-Saharan Africa", FDFA Swiss Conferedation, January 01, 2021 https://www.eda.admin.ch/eda/en/fdfa/fdfa/aktuell/newsuebersicht/2021/01/subsahara-afrika-strategie.html.
15. see Laurie Nathan, "AFRICOM: A Threat to Africa's Security", *Contemporary Security Policy* 30, no. 1 (2009): 58–61.
16. Colonel William C. Wyatt, personal communication, US AFRICOM Strategic Advisor to the AU, Addis Ababa, November 2014.
17. Thabo Mbeki, "Where Is the Voice of Africa?", *The Africa Report* no. 76 (January 2016): 42–44.
18. Darren G. Hawkins, David A. Lake, Daniel L. Nielson and Michael J. Tierney, "Delegation under Anarchy: States, International Organizations, and Principal-Agent Theory", in *Delegation and Agency in International Organizations*, eds. Darren G. Hawkins, David A. Lake, Daniel L. Nielson and Michael J. Tierney (Cambridge and New York: Cambridge University Press, 2006), 3–38 [pp. 7–10].
19. Ibid.
20. See Zacarias Agostinho, *Security and the State in Southern Africa* (London and New York: Tauris Academic Studies, 1999).
21. Michael Mann, "American Empires: Past and Present", *Canadian Review of Sociology* 45, no. 1 (2008): 7–50.

22. Martin Thomas, Bob Moore and Larry J. Butler, *Crises of Empire: Decolonization and Europe's Imperial States* 2nd ed. (London, NY and Sydney: Bloomsbury, 2015).
23. See John P. Cerone, "US Attitudes toward International Criminal Courts and Tribunals", in *The Sword and the Scales: the US and International Courts and Tribunals*, ed. Cesare P.R. Romano (Cambridge: Cambridge University Press, 2009), 131–184.
24. Munyi et al., "Conceptualizing Agency"; Sophie Harman and William Brown, "In from the Margins? The Changing Place of Africa in International Relations", *International Affairs* 89, no. 1 (2013): 69–87.
25. Peter J. Katzenstein. *A World of Regions: Asia and Europe in the American Imperium* (Ithaca and London: Cornell University Press, 2014).
26. Siphamandla Zondi, "Common Positions as African Agency in International Negotiations: An Appraisal", in *African Agency in International Politics*, eds. William Brown and Sophie Harman (Oxon: Routledge, 2018), 19–33.
27. Blaauw, "African Agency", 91.
28. Zubairo Wai, "The Empire's New Clothes: Africa, Liberal Interventionism and Contemporary World Order", *Review of African Political Economy* 41, no. 142 (2014): 483–499.
29. Michael Hardt and Antonio Negri, *Empire* (USA: Harvard University Press, 2000), 283.
30. Barry Buzan, "New Patterns of Global Security in the Twenty-First Century", *International Affairs* 67, no. 3 (1991): 431–451.
31. Munyi et al., "Conceptualizing Agency", 6.
32. George Ayittey, *Africa Betrayed* (US and UK: Palgrave Macmillan, 1992).
33. Ibid.
34. Moreover, Nigeria like Zambia has lately been plagued by presidents who either die or become ill while in office.
35. Sean Jacobs and Richard Calland, "Thabo Mbeki: Myth and Context", in *Thabo Mbeki's World: The Politics and Ideology of the South African President*, eds. Sean Jacobs and Richard Calland (Pietermaritzburg: University of Natal Press, 2002).
36. Khadija Bah, "Africa's G4 Network", in *Networks of Influence? Developing Countries in a Networked Global Order*, eds. Leonardo

Martinez-Diaz and Ngaire Woods (Oxford: Oxford University Press, 2009).

37. Adeyeke Adebajo and Chris Landsberg, "Nigeria and South Africa as Regional Hegemons", in *From Cape to Congo: Southern Africa's Evolving Security*, eds. Mwesiga Baregu and Chris Landsberg (Colorado: Lynne Rienner, 2003), 171–203.

38. This term is an extrapolation of Eckstein (1992)'s exegesis of the concept of citizenship. See Harry Eckstein, *Regarding Politics: Essays on Political Theory, Stability, and Change* (Berkeley and Oxford: University of California Press, 1992), Chapter 10.

39. Mancur Olson and Richard Zeckhauser, "An Economic Theory of Alliance", *Review of Economics and Statistics* 48 (1966): 266–279; Jolyon Howorth, *Security and Defence Policy in the European Union* (New York: Palgrave Macmillan, 2007).

40. African Union (AU), *Banjul Formula*, Addis Ababa, 2006.

41. Ambassador Sangqu Basu, personal communication, Special Advisor to the Chairperson of the AU Commission: November 2015.

42. These are peace and security, trade, development, energy, technology, infrastructure, science and technology, education, etc.

43. Lilian B. Andonova, "Boomerangs to Partnerships? Explaining State Participation in Partnerships for Sustainability", *Comparative Political Studies* 47, no. 3 (2014): 481–515 [p. 8].

44. Jacob Nyoyo, personal communication, Partnerships Management and Coordination Division, Addis Ababa, July 2015.

CHAPTER 2

African Agency as Agency Slack: From Fiction to Multilateral Empirics

The agency that an African multilateral institution projects deserves contextualization. At best, it requires operationalisation. Although part of the existing discourse has identified African agency within the African Union,[1] the unfortunate part is that some of those core assumptions are based on agential conceptions either situated at or extrapolated from the state level.

To be sure, states and organisation operate in an agent-principal model and clearly have motives for cooperating within multilateral fora.[2] Yet it is imperative to note that organisational secretariats such as the AU Commission, gradually develops expertise and competences which confer a certain level of legal and political authority which grants them a degree of leverage in international politics[3]; with the corollary that such an organisation or institution can partially, yet significantly, insulate themselves from states' intrusion.[4] Certainly, such potency implies a certain degree of agency. Several scholarly treatises[5] have shown how the AU, especially around peace and security, has garnered more expertise that exceeds that of individual states. However, it is important to apply this discussion to the empirical situation at the AU.

The AU primarily engages in two forms of agency slack—"slippage" and "shirking". Hereunder is a delineation and operationalization of these two aspects of agency slack. Prior to an exegesis of these forms of slack, it is important to highlight that collation, augmentation and articulation of preferences is a necessary condition for exercising agency slack. However,

© The Author(s), under exclusive license to Springer Nature   17
Switzerland AG 2022
T. Gwatiwa, *The African Union and African Agency in International Politics*, https://doi.org/10.1007/978-3-030-87805-4_2

the stimuli—internal and external—exert pressure on the potentiality of reifying those preferences that will stimulate appropriate responses.

"Shirking" is a form of agency slack wherein an actor minimises the effort it is capable of exerting.[6] The rationale behind effort minimization is to keep the other party engaged while the shirker seeks other alternatives. In the case of the AU, there are greater risks of disengaging with international partners whose preferences are misaligned with theirs. Historicity of imperialism and political jingoism shows that foreign actors are quite capable of acting outside these partnerships and potentially undermine African agency.[7] But the AU is aware of the foregoing and finds it useful to keep such actors within partnerships because partnership agreements commit actors to certain discourses that limit or shape their choices and actions in the continent. At an empirical level, shirking in these partnerships entails Africans making perfunctory commitments to programmatic proposals and processes. For instance, the AU often employs lackadaisical approaches to proposals from partners such as the EU, UN and NATO with greater risks to African leadership and agenda setting (read: agency) in partnerships. Normally those proposals, especially in the case of the EU, would be additions or adjustments to existing programmatic frameworks, which are either one-dimensional or jingoistic.

The other form of slack, known as slippage, involves a process whereby an agent shifts policy away from a preferred outcome to its own preferences[8] This is also an act of self-preservation. Similar to shirking, slippage does not entail drastic or radical divergence. The shift is not calculated to alienate the other partner. On the larger part, the effect is self-serving and protects the initiator against unfavourable outcomes. The shift is also partial and not whole. For instance, the instigator can decide to shift only a certain portion of the broader programmatic arrangement, which it deems problematic to its agential standing. The partial response is both an appreciation of the expediency of the overall partnership as well as fear of the possible ramifications of full disengagement. A primary example, as will evince in the eighth chapter, is the way the AU engages the US on security issues. On the one hand, it appreciates the overall sophistication of the US, but frowns on its characteristically self-indulgent approach to security cooperation. On the other hand, it is fully aware of the way the US can expand and dominate the continent if kept in askance.[9] Therefore, slippage is neither radical nor entirely antagonistic. It is calculated in the same way that shirking is.

From the abovementioned, it is clear that agency slack is an agential projection that is more reactive than proactive. Indeed, there is both a push and pull effect, but the external stimulus is stronger than the internal. Yet, more importantly, there is another phenomenon that provides an overarching triangulating node for these two methods of slack—forum shopping.

Forum shopping is, at least empirically, a sufficient condition for agency slack. A forum shopping actor makes use of available options to obtain favourable policy outcomes.[10] Typical actors engage in different international forums with overlapping functions to maximise their material benefits. The same logic applies to the AU's partnership milieu. As argued by Harman and Brown, a new form of scramble for Africa opens opportunities for the continent to exercise agency in international affairs.[11] Hence, the AU is fully aware that the multiplicity as well as the functional duplication of international partnerships provides a safety catch-net in a fragile environment. In fact, the scramble engenders a competitive environment which very few, if any, are willing to abandon. This environment provides a tensity for both the AU and its partners. It is a "me against the world" situation for the AU. If the AU wholly ignores this set of actors (stylized as partners) it risks bandwagoning. If it acts, it also must act cautiously in a heavily constrained environment. Shirking and slippages require such an environment.

Both start from the premise that the AU has got certain policy preferences but is materially limited to implement them. So whatever form of slack is applied, it is in relation to well-defined, or at least known, policy or programmatic preferences. Minimising action in one partnership usually means that the same resources can be harvested in another partnership. If the AU does that, it keeps partner A in check, while also making partner B aware that it can obtain favourable but temporal actorness. Moreover, partner A will be aware of the risk of being replaced by partner B, and then adjusts its demands with the hope of maximising them at a later stage. Slippage also takes a similar format. It entails shifting from partner A to partner B who is more aligned to the AU's own preferences. Even in this case partner A is aware of the risk of walking away from engagement.

The foregoing enables us to appreciate agency in the context of a multilateral organisation. However, it only describes agency slack and its two primary manifestations without placing it in the broader conceptions of African agency. Hereunder is a further clarification of why agency slack is a better characterisation of African agency than existing narratives.

Agency Slack as African Agency: From Fiction and Phantoms to Realities

The invocation of the notion of *agency slack* speaks directly to several oddities in the current conception of African agency. The present conceptions of African agency resemble a fictitious attempt to convey notions that do not necessarily meet conditions for conceptualizations in the fullest sense.

Concept-explication should at least meet a five-point criterion. For the purposes of this discussion, three stand out: namely that a concept should "remain reasonably close to ordinary language", "should not preclude empirical investigation by making true 'by definition' what should be open to empirical inquiry", and that "concepts should be operational in the broadest sense".[12] To understand this submission, it is important to examine what has recently been written about African agency.

The appetite for oversimplified conceptions African agency in international politics emanates from a general concern about Africa's subaltern position in international affairs. In this position, Africa lacks "access to mobility" and without "identity".[13] Undeniably, the study and practice of international relations remain Western.[14] However, Africa, like other developing regions of the world, has also made strides in escaping its subaltern position. However, the subliminal desperation to be free from domination somewhat obscures several issues I wish to address regarding African agency.

The main argument here is that *African agency* is *agency slack*. This emanates from empirical cogency. African agency, for the most part, has never engendered agency as an inside-out process, but has always been a response to external circumstances. Munyi et al., identify agency as a process of production and reproduction which includes "the capacity to act while an actor is the body...to which that capacity is ascribed".[15] They also argue that Africa is "not just impacted but impacting others as well".[16] They draw on examples of how Africa influenced "international law through the ICC" as well as how Rwanda "used genocide memory to advance interests". More importantly, they qualify the performative and relational nature of African agency by invoking Chipaike and Knowledge's description of this agency as "an African actor's ability to negotiate and bargain with external actors in a manner that benefits Africans themselves".[17] They also argue that this agency entails the "capacity for **formation of preferences** and capacity for acting creatively to **fulfil those**

preferences" (emphasis mine).[18] They, rightly and perhaps beautifully, proceed to posit African agency as emblematic of influence—the power to shift or influence outcomes; creativity and initiative in international behaviour and norm development; as well as institutionalisation or deepening of identity and "actorness".[19] However, the aforementioned issues are more apparent in fiction than empirical reality.

In reality, African agency manifest more in breach than observation by external actors. It is more evident as a reaction than fortitudinous action by African actors. For instance, Africa's first international efforts, between the 1950s and 1970s, were a reaction to the external pressure from a myriad of external forces including erstwhile colonisers, aspiring imperialists and their lethal institutions—primarily intelligence agencies.[20] Moreover, the Organization of African Unity (OAU) also faced similar challenges in dealing with the United Nations as well as the League of Arab States.[21] There is no denying the apparent limitations in African states' ability to assert their sovereignty in the present epoch (discussed below). However in essence, African agency has largely been a question of slack since the earliest days of African statism and multilateralism. The same applies to the purported post-Cold War transformation.

The post-Cold War, as well as post-OAU, changes did not enable substantial changes such as to warrant significant African agency in international affairs. Largely drawing on recent (i.e. post-Cold War) developments, Harman and Brown posit African agency as a function of combined opportunism and relative weakness. They argue that a "new scramble for Africa" opens up potential for agency to African states themselves, offering them opportunities to play such interests off against each other and use shifts in power to pursue their own interests.[22] This implies that this agency is not necessarily an endogenous process, but an opportunistic undertaking that relies on perforated lapses in an existing system. They also argue, like most African Sinophiles, that China offers more space and opportunities for African agency.[23] In other words, this form of agency is not engendered from within but bequeathed by an external party, much like the "extraversion" that characterised the African gains made in the aftermath of World War II which had weakened colonial metropoles.[24] This then implies that this form of agency is weak, parasitic, uncertain and at worst it is ephemeral. These narrow and overly optimistic characterizations ignore many developments between most of Africa's partners which will undermine African agency in the short-term (as will be argued in subsequent chapters). Considering the above, African agency is essentially a fiction and phantom, without proper agential characteristics.

A Case for African Multilateral Agency as Agency Slack

For the purposes of the discussion in this book, African agency *de jure* must, like all other forms of actual agency, at least exhibit three traits. It should entail unfettered choice, unmediated interaction and uninhibited freedom.

Unfettered choice is a primary element of agency. Agency must reflect unhindered choice that is entrenched in the history of an entity as opposed to a perennial response to structural constraints. This is primarily the case when it comes to political agency. Political agency at the international level can be extrapolated from the domestic level. Mamdani argues that there are three elements of agency within the political sphere: a context where an entity or citizen is bearer of rights; the existence of a civil society; and a domain where political majorities are an outcome of democratic rights[25] The international sphere, as a society, is considered less democratic than the ordinary statist context,[26] but most states bear rights based on juridical and empirical sovereignty, but the role of African actors is subject to political limitations.

Unmediated interaction is also a principal element of agency. Although African actors have more latitude in international affairs today, they have no actual power. The historical and present undertakings of African states, organisations and transnational actors are mediated by a ceiling of actors tied to Africa's limitations. The AU and other African actors follow an agenda set by more powerful institutions such as the UN, the EU, and other rich states (currently stylized as partners). These states, organisations and transnational actors have not abandoned the post-coloniality. What changed is the perimeters of the latitude of African actors yet remaining in a subaltern position. This is not different from the illusory form African agency that existed in colonial Africa. In this context, African agency seemed fortitudinous but was encapsulated in a perforation of dualistic system wherein the coloniser negotiated and imposed preferences via a local organic elite, to whom the masses were beholden.[27] Even in the present context, African actors barely have or exercise any actual agency except in the responsive. This means that Africa is yet to transcend the agential limitations that characterised the continent in the 1950s and 1970s. Thus, present agential ascriptions under this context are merely aphoristic, obscuring the empirical incorporation, co-optation and marginalisation.

Uninhibited freedom is another essential aspect of agency. This might as well be the most principal element of agency. This freedom is based on credible membership, participation, and the ability to undertake multifaceted actions. As Sen notes, "free and sustainable agency...contributes to the strengthening of free agencies of other kinds".[28] He also argues that free agency enables a referent party's ability to help themselves and influence the world and subsequent achievements made on that party's own values and objectives.[29] If this is taken as a critical element of African agency, then there is no irrefutable empirical evidence that African actors have managed to manoeuvre international affairs on their own terms. Africa's free agency would ideally be independent of European, Asian, Arab or American interests and intrusions.

Even if one is to generously consider African agency in the post-OAU domain, it has not changed much (as subsequent chapters demonstrate). African collectivism is still held together by antagonism of external forces than intra-continental considerations. Pan-Africanism still driven by sentimentalism, characterised by both positive self-consciousness of shared experiences; as well as a negative self-consciousness of rejecting external control.[30] This implies that Africa has limited power to effectuate meaningful change in international relations. This also applies to cosmetic and choreographed agency bequeathed by the less violent Eastern forces such as China,[31] Japan,[32] and South Korea. Considering all the aforementioned, there are no convincing frameworks of African agency apart from agency slack. If agency is dialectic, it makes more sense to speak of agency slack because it is innately responsive.

Moreover, a sober assessment of Africa's approach to African agency in international politics still retains a position of slack. If the subaltern position from which we sympathise with Africa's agential position is both a function of lack of mobility and lack of identity, it suffices that Africa still lacks identity and mobility. First, Africa struggles with the question of identity. Mudimbe once posited that there are two types of Africa: the real and the Westernised. In this dichotomy, agency was primarily given to imperially compliant actors.[33] What is Africa? While this may be interpreted as a geographical region, there are states whose social and foreign policies are more aligned with the Middle East or Europe than the continent. Similarly, international partners often package their programmes according to such demarcations. What is African in international politics? Some issues in international politics, such as those in the Horn of Africa, Mediterranean or West African coast, may be rhetorically framed as African but they are essentially transnational, transregional or international in control. The foregoing issues complexify an important question hanging over the discussion of African agency: *who is an African and what is an African actor*? Is it one that identifies with the region, based in the region, or one that is completely free from external membership, control and exclusively has the freedom to project preferences aligned with African objectives and values? A close examination of speeches at the inaugural OAU conference reveals a lack of clarity on this question. States such as Madagascar or Ethiopia and those from the Maghreb strongly emphasised the uniqueness of their own experiences by differentiating them from those of black Africa.[34] This implied cognitive fissures on who is an African, and ipso facto an African actor.

Africa's identity crisis is closely tied to its immobility. It is a state of impotence based on warped consciousness and self-perception. It is a system wherein African actors cannot envision mobility without external patronage. Gassama, a veteran OAU and AU official, argues that external dependence was ingrained into African multilateral thinking in 1960s.[35] This means that the forty years of African regionalism were steeped in dependency which lent an institutional and cognitive rigour mortis. This explains why Africans have failed to achieve the full agential capacity, as normative expected, in spite of numerous rhetorical statements calling for African self-sufficiency, independence and freedom of action. This anomaly is better described by Frantz Fanon.

To paraphrase Fanon, a myriad of African "problems" are seemingly complex, but they are a matter of perception, exaggeration and lack of awareness. The African is victim to a priori perceptions at three levels. First, if they are assisted, they are not given active treatment due to existing misgiving (read: prejudices) about the African's problems. Subsequently, assistance is rendered insincerely on the basis of "restoratives". Second, the prescriptions make the African so dependent that when due for discharge they believe that they have more problems than they actually do. This results in a situation where the African is afraid to leave the hospital.[36] The third is pointedly related to African agency. Any helper, like a doctor is to neo-Hippocraticism, is beholden to help based on political, philosophical, and professional (read: institutional) obligations.[37] The assisted is preoccupied by their malady, often exaggerating the symptoms, and has little input in the diagnosis of the problem, which could lead to a better prescription.

It suffices to argue that the problem of African agential challenges is attributable to an identity crisis and reluctant mobility. The mobility is underwritten by another international entity. The African actor robs herself of free agency both by subscribing to stereotypes about his limitations as well as exaggerating his problems. The referent actor does not admit their exaggeration but misconstrues symptomatic treatment by her "helpers" for wellbeing.

Foreign Policy as African Agency and African Agency as Foreign Policy

The African Union (AU) is a complex organisation at the interstices of bilateral and multilateral foreign policy execution in Africa. In the first instance, the African continent's future largely rests in the hands of the AU Commission (or AUC). The AU is the face of Africa as well as represents the continental interest when it negotiates and implements [international] agreements on issues such as international trade, international law, international security, and other important issues. The primary challenge for the AU is to reconcile external support with African preferences and interests. This epitomises an organisation that finds itself in the perennial quest to protect African agency in international politics, while impelled to forges a unique and actionable course for African multilateralism and regionalism. This obtains in the form of collation of foreign policy processes.

Foreign policy is typically ascribed to states as opposed to multilateral institutions. However, in recent decades, regional organisations such as the European Union (EU), the North Atlantic Treaty Organization (NATO) and others, have all pursued a foreign policy of sorts. The most salient example is the EU which has its "Common Foreign and Security Policy" enforced by the European External Action Service (EEAS). As a supranational organisation, it has assumed many characteristics of a hybrid of a state and a multilateral organisation. Although the EU has been keen to export its model of regionalism to other organisations, especially its protégé, the African Union, such an approach as regards foreign policy is yet to manifest at the AU.[39] However, to understand foreign policy agency, it is important to first consider and extrapolate it from the state level.

Foreign policy is difficult to define, but mostly identifiable in the way decision makers—such as heads of state and government, ministers and diplomats—conduct diplomacy in an international milieu. Elman posits that "a state's behaviour is viewed as a response to the constraints and incentives of its aggregate power relative to others (i.e. the distribution of capabilities) or the degree of aggressive intent on the part of external actors [i.e., the balance of threat]".[40] This means that foreign policy is, among other things, primarily concerned with survival pursued in relation to existing resources and capabilities. These capabilities are harnessed to carefully influence other elements of diplomacy such as norm suasion and entrepreneurship.[41] In order for states (or more recently regions) to play a meaningful role in international affairs, their "national interest"—defined as "the perceived needs and desires of one sovereign state in relation to other sovereign states comprising the external environment"—play a crucial part in defining the nature and extent of foreign policy pursued by that actor.[42] For the national interest to be relevant and achievable, it ideally should be matched with domestic policy[43] because the dichotomous policy must embody the values espoused by the referent polity.[44]

The design and implementation of a foreign policy is the preserve of a set of decision makers—or foreign policy elites.[45] When elites collate their preferences to form a robust policy, they do that based on their perception of the existing international milieu. To have a meaningful role in international affairs, states often adopt a unique rhetoric laced with subjective meanings, as well as interpretations of world politics or "the linguistic construction of reality".[46] For instance, this has been a particularly useful technique in African multilateralism at the United Nations, especially when it dealt with sensitive or controversial subjects such as colonialism, apartheid and other issues related to African sovereignty. This construction is typically based on the preferences and interest of the referent states or institutions.

Preferences and interests form a key component of foreign policy. These interests can be categorised into: (a) those that relate to survival, (b) those that are vital or important and (c), those that are peripheral in order to determine how to allocate resources.[47] In most cases, when elites design foreign policies, they consider military and economic capabilities as well the competing interests of the elites and other constituents within that polity.[48] Although military and economic capabilities are not easily identifiable at the level of the AU, there is evidence (as argued in subsequent chapters) that the AU ranks its preference in order to adequately allocate resources.

The notion of elites designing foreign policy implies that these are social agents acting within a structure. Brown argues that human agents such as individuals, groups and organisations inject meaning and intentionality into structure.[49] In the case of the AU, this includes heads of state and government, ministers (especially of foreign affairs), the Chairperson of the AU Commission, the Commissioner of Peace and Security, African diplomats and others. During a highlight period, of what Landsberg calls the "golden age of African diplomacy" [i.e. circa.1998–2008] in which the role of political elites in advancing African agency had great effect and prominence, there were key human agents. They included President Thabo Mbeki (South Africa), President Olusegun Obasanjo (Nigeria), Abdelaziz Bouteflika (Algeria), Muammar Gaddafi (Libya), Abdoulaye Wade (Senegal), and the then Chairperson of the AU Commission Alpha Konare, among others. Mbeki was arguably the most vocal promoter of African agency in global politics to promote African agency. Theirs was a constant battle against post-coloniality to forge a unique African identity with intentionality and meaning.

Solidarity is a very important aspect of Africa's ability to carry out its regional projects with or against the international community. A careful examination of Mazrui and Zondi suggests that common positions promoting solidarity among AU member states aim at fostering collective diplomacy initiatives at the AU level.[50] Examples include the Solemn Declaration on Common African Defence and Security Policy and the African Union Non-Aggression and Common Defence Pact, both of which address solidarity within the continent to secure the territorial and juridical integrity of the continent.[51] African states' compliance with these positions is debatable but their existence is an indication of an attempt to lay a threshold for agency in international politics.

African Union: Foreign Policy Actor and Foreign Policy Maker

The African Union occupies an important role and position in (African) foreign policy agency. As the primary multilateral institution in Africa, it focuses on collective diplomacy in the continent. This foreign policy mandate derives from the Constitutive Act [of the AU], which states that the AU shall "promote and defend African common positions on issues of interest to the continent and its peoples" as well as "encourage international cooperation" and "establish the necessary conditions which enable the continent to play its rightful role in the global economy and in international negotiations".[52]

There is no rigid template as to who can conceive common African positions. However, most of what results as common positions often emanates from the preferences designed prior at the national level, or from those proposed by an incumbent AU Commission Chairperson.[53] Thereafter, various heads of state and government and ministers (the Executive Council) convene to forge common positions for the entire continent.[54] Finally, implementation is the preserve of the AU Commission Chairperson's cabinet [comprising of his/her deputy and commissioners], working closely with the Permanent Representatives Committee (PRC) to focus on the implementation of those common positions. However, once the AU has codified its position, the AUC Chairperson, often works closely with the AU Chairperson (a nominated head of state or government) who acts as the diplomatic face of the AU in international affairs.

As such, the AU's Constitutive Act gives the AU foreign policy agency with the Chairperson of the AU Commission as the de facto chief diplomatic figure. Nevertheless, several other foreign policy actors are found across the AU's structure and attendant procedures. The primary actors include the Assembly of Heads of State and Government (AHSG), the Executive Council (of Ministers), the PRC and commissioners in various tiers of the AU Commission. All these actors are responsible for coordinating and reconciling interests and preferences between subregional organisations (or Regional Economic Communities/Regional Mechanisms), member states, civil society organisations, business entities and other interest groups.

This task of harmonisation and reconciliation of the various interests and preferences amounts to an act of framing and implementing the foreign policy positions for the continent. At the same time, being an organisation driven by its members states, its collective foreign policy is determined by which member states enjoy influence at any given time and to what extent they can be successful in forging a common and durable consensus across particular issues. However, an incumbent AU chairperson and/or Chairperson of the AU Commission does not necessarily influence these positions, but they are often a result of consensus building between all member states.[55] This consensus creates buy-in for various common positions.

The AU's quest for African agency is not only a question of solidarity and collective action but also one of overcoming coloniality and of making positive contributions to international cooperation.

The Context of Africa's Agency Slack in International Affairs: Post-Coloniality, Identity and Ideology

Africa's agency in international relations obtains under the shadow of empire, post-coloniality and networks of patronage.[56] "Postcoloniality" or the "postcolonial condition' refers to "a global phenomenon of interactions based on unequal power relations in an era that goes beyond the world of colonialism but that has been (and continues to be) decisively shaped by the logic of coloniality".[57] The power differential lent by the logic of coloniality incites a form of political resistance—through rhetoric, shirking and slippage—amounting to agency. This resistance is mostly a result of the incompatibilities between the former colonisers and relatively underdeveloped postcolonial states where both sides differ on the meaning of politics and security.[58]

In light of the above disparities, African agents and organisations frequently invoke the practice of agency slack (i.e., shirking and slippage). This is particularly the case at the UN, which is largely controlled by former colonisers and neo-imperial nations such as France, Italy, the United Kingdom, Germany and the US—despite most UN missions being in Africa. Yet, ironically, African states rely on UN normative leadership and funding on development and security programmes.[59] This implies that African actors resultantly remain in a constrained position, hence without a choice apart from agency slack.[60]

The need to overcome post-coloniality and assert influence requires structural reform and further institutionalisation. Typically, regions are built on the basis of shared identity and ideology.[61] Once states have agreed on this, they embark on a process of institutionalisation aimed at ensuring predictability and growing actorness in international affairs.[62] This involves a process of bureaucratisation and structuration that involves mimicry, coercion and normative suasion.[63] Ideally, such an agglomeration of identity, ideology and structuration produces a scenario where an entity can project a bigger agential role. Correspondingly, Africa has made serious efforts to improve its agential standing and role. However, the lack of authenticity in African multilateralism compels African bureaucrats into a rather passive role. Even where common African positions are held to be signifiers of agency,[64] these are often mimicked. For instance, the Common African Defence and Security Policy (CADSP), strikingly resembles the European Security Defence Policy (ESDP). As will be demonstrated in the various chapters, this is a result of a combination of various factors: coercion, mimicry, lassitude and outright lack of imagination.

The subaltern place of African multilateralism has also rendered it less able to be driven by ideologies developed within the continent. For starters, Pan-Africanism, the hallmark of African discourse and rhetoric, is an imported ideology. The concept was articulated by Henri Sylvester-William—a Trinidadian—and later developed by others in the historical African diaspora.[65] Yet, the power and reach of the ideology of Pan-Africanism and its political movement should not be underestimated. It effectively served as a rallying point for greater African agency in the struggle for independence as well as drove early African multilateralism.[66] It also provided an African-centred view of the world to a plethora of disenfranchised communities across the world. This ideology also provided a threshold of the more fortitudinous notion of "African Renaissance".

African Renaissance became a rallying call at a pan-African conference held in Senegal and was later popularised by South African President Thabo Mbeki. Given the prominent role of South African, Nigerian, Senegalese and East African leaders, this idea became a popular ideology. It was used to drive the inception and institutionalisation of the African Union, the New Partnership for African Development (NEPAD), and other multilateral initiatives.[67] African Renaissance, like, pan-Africanism, reinforced the notion of African agency. However, like pan-Africanism it was more reactive than fortitudinous. However, there was higher level of fortitude where states—particularly South Africa and Nigeria—designed continental or regional institutions in the image of their national development or security programmes. This might have seemed fortitudinous, but the overbearing spectre of colonialism and imperialism was undeniable between the late 1990s and early 2000s.

2 AFRICAN AGENCY AS AGENCY SLACK: FROM FICTION ... 31

Agents, Elites and African Summitry as Drivers of African Agency

African agency, when captured in a regional context, derives from intergovernmental cooperation on the continent. Ideally, regional agency depends on the role of regional powers. For instance, over the years European regional security depended on the leadership of the United Kingdom and France.[68] Some scholars use the problematic notion of hegemons or powers in the context of African regionalism.[69] Typically, Nigeria and South Africa through their heads of state have remained the two main legitimate, de facto agentic pivots linking Africa with the rest of the world; yet African regional agency always constitutes several states. Arguably, it is easier for a charismatic leader of one of the "pivotal states" to be an effective Africa agent. However, leadership in Africa shifts periodically. African agency has centred on different states such as Algeria (Bouteflika), Uganda (Museveni), Rwanda (Kagame), Ethiopia (Zenawi), Libya (Gaddafi) and others, depending on the issue area at hand—and there was hardly a time when any of them acted alone. Herein summitry has often determined which country's head of state would lead a regional project.

The quest for African agency at a continental level began in earnest in the 1980s through elite-driven summitry. The push for overall agency is normally attributed to the "Kampala Movement". In 1991, Olusegun Obasanjo (Nigeria), Arap Moi (Kenya), Omar Al-Bashir (Sudan), and other elites promulgated a range of security and governance prescription dubbed the Conference on Security, Stability, Development and Cooperation in Africa (CSSDCA).[70] The OAU grudgingly endorsed these reforms into its programmatic efforts, but they eventually found a place in the current organisational architecture. In fact, the CSSDCA only gained buy-in after the Rwandan genocide of 1994.

Libyan leader, Muammar Gaddafi, also helped reify the current continental organisation in the late 1990s. According to Francis, several African states were opposed to the idea of transition from the OAU to the AU, to espouse the ideals enshrined in the CSSDCA.[71] Gaddafi made concessions and side-payments to 32 African states that were either opposed or ambivalent to the transition. It took two years of backroom negotiation and bargaining which involved making "economic and financial concessions to opponents of the AU project as promoted by Gaddafi and the pivotal states of Nigeria, South Africa and Algeria".[72] However, Gaddafi was such a controversial figure with sub-imperial ambitions that in later

32   T. GWATIWA

years AU member states came up with rules to limit financial influence within the AU Commission.[73] However, Gaddafi continued to play a pivot role in boosting African agency.

Constituting Actors and Processes at AU: African Foreign Policy Making

Collective positions and diplomacy are the pivot for Africa's engagement with the rest of the world. The echelon of African collective diplomacy is the Assembly of Heads of State and Government (AHSG). International partnerships with the EU, the UN, the US and South America, most of which were signed between 2000 and 2010, were a result of the leadership of two heads of state—President Thabo Mbeki (South Africa) and President Olusegun Obasanjo (Nigeria) working alongside a handful others. According to Landsberg, "...while South Africa under Mbeki brought a sense of urgency to African diplomacy, Nigeria...brought history and diplomatic experience, as well as a sense of legitimacy to South Africa's post-apartheid role in Africa".[74] However, the bargaining also requires the active involvement of the Chairperson of the AU Commission.

The agential role of the AU Commission chairperson is very important. The chairperson of the Commission is essentially its chief diplomat. According to Gassama, the capability of the OAU/AU largely depends on the diplomatic fortitude of the chief of the AUC.[75] In the early days of the AU, heads of state worked closely with then Chairperson Alpha Konare to ensure more African agency. Konare, a former head of state, astutely oversaw the framing and signing of robust partnerships with NATO and the EU. This evident in the wording of both partnerships, where the notions of "African leadership" and "African ownership" was expressly included in the partnership agreements. The AU Protocol on the Peace and Security Council (of 2002) mandates the Chairperson of the AU Commission to initiate and pursue partnerships for peace and security. Correspondingly, Alpha Konare worked with the then NATO Secretary General, Jaap de Hoop Scheffer, to sign the first AU-NATO partnership in 2005. Years later, AU Commission Chairperson, Nkosazana Dlamini-Zuma, as invoked the same privilege to incept and sign a new strategic partnership with Norway; even though the AU had imposed a moratorium on new partnerships. Herein different offices and their holders can enhance agency.

Different chairpersons of the AU—rotational presidencies by heads of state—can also enhance African agency. Lately, President Paul Kagame, of Rwanda, injected new energy and urgency into promoting collective African agency when Rwanda played a meaningful role in actualising the African Continental Free Trade Agreement.[76] Although he is often criticised for authoritarian rule in his country, he has shown immense capabilities in mobilising other African heads of states as well as expediting and overseeing continental projects. One of his key traits is his independent mindedness, his fearless rhetoric and deep belief in African agency. His, is perhaps, much bolder than that of his predecessor such as Thabo Mbeki and Olusegun Obasanjo.

Notes

1. Siphamandla Zondi, "Common Positions as African Agency in International Negotiations: An Appraisal", in *African Agency in International Politics*, eds. William Brown and Sophie Harman (Oxon and New York: Routledge, 2012), 19–33; Tshepo Gwatiwa, "The African Union as a Foreign Policy Player: African Agency in International Cooperation", in *African Foreign Policies: Selecting Signifiers to Explain Agency*, ed. Paul-Henri Bischoff (London: Routledge, 2020), 30–51.
2. Kenneth Abbott and Duncan Snidal, "Why States Act through Formal International Organizations", *The Journal of Conflict Resolution* 42, no. 1 (1998): 3–32.
3. See Michael Barnett and Martha Finnemore, *Rules for the World: International Organizations in Global Politics* (Ithaca and London: Cornell University Press, 2004), 16–44.
4. Tana Johnson, *Organizational Progeny: Why Governments Are Losing Control Over the Proliferating Structures of Global Governance* (Oxford: Oxford University Press, 2014).
5. For an overall overview, see Ulf Engel and Joào Gomes Porto (eds), *Africa's New Peace and Security Architecture: Promoting Norms, Institutionalizing Solutions* (England and USA: Ashgate, 2013); also see Haastrup Toni, "Africa-EU Partnership on Peace and Security", *Africa and the European Union: A Strategic Partnership*, ed. Jack Mangala (New York: Palgrave Macmillan, 2013), 47–67; Haastrup Toni, "EU as Mentor? Promoting Regionalism

as External Relations Practice in EU-Africa Relations", *Journal of European Integration* 35, no. 7 (2013), 785–800.

6. Darren G. Hawkins, David A. Lake, Daniel L. Nielson and Michael J. Tierney, "Delegation Under Anarchy: States, International Organizations, and Principal-Agent Theory", *Delegation and Agency in International Organizations*, eds. Darren G. Hawkins, David A. Lake, Daniel L. Nielson and Michael J. Tierney (Cambridge and New York: Cambridge University Press, 2006), 3–38 [pp. 7–10].

7. Elizabeth Schmidt, *Foreign Intervention in Africa: From the Cold War to the Present* (Cambridge: Cambridge University Press, 2013).

8. Hawkins et al., "Delegation under Anarchy".

9. Tshepo Gwatiwa and Justin van der Merwe (eds), *Expanding the US Military Command in Africa: Elites, Networks, and Grand Strategy* (Oxon and New York: Routledge, 2021).

10. Marc L. Busch, "Overlapping Institutions, Forum Shopping, and Dispute Settlement in International Trade", *International Organization* 61, no. 4 (2007): 735–761.

11. Sophie Harman and William Brown, "In from the Margins? The Changing Place of Africa in International Relations", *International Affairs* 89, no. 1 (2013): 69–87.

12. David A. Baldwin, "The Concept of Security", *Review of International Studies* 23 (1997): 5–26.

13. Gayatri Chakravorty Spivak, "Scattered Speculations on the Subaltern and the Popular", *Postcolonial Studies* 8, no. 4 (2005): 475–486.

14. Arlene B. Tickner, "Core, Periphery and (Neo)imperialist International Relations", *European Journal of International Relations* 19, no. 3 (2013): 627–646.

15. Elijah N. Munyi, David Mwambari and Aleksi Ylonen, eds. *Beyond History: African Agency in Development, Diplomacy, and Conflict Resolution* (London: Rowman & Littlefield, 2020), 5.

16. Ibid., 3.

17. Ibid., 6.

18. Ibid.

19. Ibid.

20. Devlin Larry, *Chief of Station, Congo: A Memoir of 1960–67* (New York: Public Affairs, 2007); Roy Pateman, "Intelligence Agencies

in Africa: A Preliminary Assessment", *The Journal of Modern African Studies* 30, no. 4 (1992): 569–585; John Stockwell, *In Search of Enemies: A CIA Story* (New York: W.W. Norton and Company Inc, 1978); William Blum, *Killing Hope: US Military and C.I.A. Interventions Since World War II* (London: Zed Books, 2004); Seymour M. Hersh, "C.I.A. Said to Have Aided Plotters Who Overthrew Nkrumah in Ghana", *The New York Times*, May 9, 1978, https://www.nytimes.com/1978/05/09/archives/cia-said-to-have-aided-plotters-who-overthrew-nkrumah-in-ghana.html.

21. Olusola Ojo, "The Relationship Between the Organization of African Unity and the League of Arab States", *Africa Spectrum* 16, no. 2 (1981): 131–141; Smith Hempstone, *Rebels, Mercenaries and Dividends: The Katanga Story* (New York: Praeger, 1962).

22. Harman and Brown, "In from the Margins?", 79.

23. Ibid.

24. Jean-François Bayart and Stephen Ellis, "Africa in the World: A History of Extraversion", *African Affairs* 99, no. 395 (2000): 217–267.

25. Mahmood Mamdani, "African States, Citizenship, and War: A Case Study", *International Affairs* 78, no. 3 (2002): 493–506, 503.

26. Magdalena Bexell, Jonas Tallberg, and Anders Uhlin, "Democracy in Global Governance: The Promises and Pitfalls of Transnational Actors", *Global Governance* 16 (2010): 81–101.

27. Mahmood Mamdani, "Historicizing Power and Responses to Power: Indirect Rule and Its Reform", *Social Research* 66, no. 3 (1999): 859–886.

28. Amartya Sen, *Development as Freedom* (Oxford and New York: Oxford University Press, 1999), 4.

29. Ibid., 18–19.

30. William I. Zartman, "Africa as a Subordinate State System in International Relations", *International Organization* 21, no. 3 (1967): 545–564.

31. Harman and Brown, "In From the Margins?".

32. Khadija Bah, "Africa's G4 Network", in *Networks of Influence? Developing Countries in a Networked Global Order*, eds. Leonardo

Martinez-Diaz and Ngaire Woods (Oxford and New York: Oxford University Press, 2009), 147–170.

33. V.Y. Mudimbe, *The Invention of Africa: Gnosis, Philosophy, and the Order of Knowledge* (Bloomington and Indianapolis: Indiana University Press, 1988), 10.

34. See OAU, "Proceedings of the Summit Conference of Independent African States" (Addis Ababa: OAU Secretariat, 1963).

35. Muhammad Gassama, *From the OAU to the AU: The Odyssey of a Continental Organization* (The Gambia: Fulladu Publishers, 2013), 25.

36. Frantz Fanon, *Toward the African Revolution: Political Essays* (New York: Grove Press, 1964), 1–16.

37. Ibid., 7.

38. Caterina Carta, *The European Union Diplomatic Service: Ideas, Preferences and Identities* (London and New York: Routledge, 2013).

39. Jürgen Rüland, Heiner Hanggi and Ralf Roloff, "Interregionalism: A New Phenomenon in International Relations", in *Interregionalism and International Relations*, eds. Jürgen Rüland, Heiner Hanggi and Ralf Roloff (Oxon and NY: Routledge, 2006).

40. Miriam F. Elman, "The Foreign Policies of Small States: Challenging Neorealism in Its Own Backyard", *British Journal of Political Science* 25, no. 2 (1995): 171–217 [p. 172].

41. Rodger A. Payne, "Persuasion, Frames and Norm Construction", *European Journal of International Relations* 7, no. 1 (2001): 37–61.

42. Donald E. Nuechterlein, "National Interests and Foreign Policy: A Conceptual Framework for Analysis and Decision-making", *British Journal of International Studies* 2, no. 3 (1976): 247.

43. Herbert A. Simon, "Human Nature in Politics: Dialogue of Psychology and Political Science," *American Political Science Review* 79, no. 2 (1985): 293–304.

44. Walter Russel Mead, Scott Erwin and Eitan Goldstein, "The United States: Inextricably Linked with Nations across the Globe", *Foreign Policy Agenda* (2006): 5–8, https://usa.usembassy.de/ete xts/ijpe0406.pdf.

45. Emilie M. Hafner-Burton, D. Alex Hughes and David G. Victor, "The Cognitive Revolution and the Political Psychology of Elite Decision Making", *Perspectives on Politics* 11, no. 2 (2013): 368–386, 369.

46. Roxanne Lynn Doty, "Foreign Policy as Social Construction: A Post-Positivist Analysis of U.S. Counterinsurgency Policy in the Philippines", *International Studies Quarterly* 37, no. 3 (1993): 302–305.
47. Mead, "The United States".
48. Michael Brecher, Blema Steinberg and Janice Stein, "A Framework for Research on Foreign Policy Behaviour", *Journal of Conflict Resolution* 13, no. 1 (1969): 75–94.
49. William Brown, "A Question of Agency: Africa in International Politics" *Third World Quarterly* 33, no. 10 (2012): 1889–1908.
50. Siphamandla Zondi, "Common Positions as African Agency in International Negotiations: An Appraisal", in *African Agency in International Politics*, eds. William Brown and Sophie Harman (London and New York: Routledge, 2012), 19–33; Ali Mazrui, "Global Africa: From Abolitionists to Reparations," in *Pan Africanism: Politics, Economy and Social Change in the Twenty-First Century*, ed. Tajudeen Abdul-Raheem (New York: New York University Press, 2006), 123–143.
51. African Union, *Solemn Declaration on a Common African Defence and Security Policy* (Addis Ababa: AU Commission, 2004).
52. African Union, *Constitutive Act* (Addis Ababa: AU Commission, 2000) 5–6.
53. It is important to differentiate the African experience from a phenomenon described by Tana Johnson (2013) and other scholars (Barnett and Finnemore 2004) whereby some intergovernmental organisations, although created by states, tend to assume a life of their own wherein international bureaucrats can insulate those organisations from state control. In Africa, states still exercise tight control of intergovernmental organisations. As a matter of fact, if an AUC Chairperson is perceived as too strong, they are voted out in the next election (Gasamma 2013).
54. Alhaji Sarjoh Bah, Elizabeth Choge-Nyangoro, Solomon Dersso, Brenda Mofya and Timothy Murithi, eds. *The Africa Peace and Security Architecture: A Handbook* (Addis Ababa: Friedrich-Ebert-Stiftung, 2014).
55. Heidi Hardt, *Time to React; The Efficiency of International Organizations in Crisis Response* (Oxford and New York: Oxford University Press, 2014), 47.
56. The literature is awash with explanations of the formation of the African state as a postcolonial entity (Clapham 1996). It also explains how coloniality influenced the way the African state approaches international relations (Mbembe 1992, 2006). Galtung

(1971) insists that there are networks between elites in the developed and developing states which support a political economy of patronage.

57. Jana Hönke and Markus-Michael Müller, "Governing (In)security in a Postcolonial World: Transnational Entanglements and the Worldliness of 'Local' Practice", *Security Dialogue* 43, no. 5 (2012): 383–401 [385].

58. Mohammed Ayoob, "Defining Security: A Subaltern Realist Perspective", in *Critical Security Studies: Concepts and Cases*, eds. Keith Krause and Williams (Minneapolis: University of Minnesota Press, 1997), 121–146; Amitav Acharya, "The Periphery as the Core: The Third World and Security Studies", in *Critical Security Studies: Concepts and Cases*, eds. Keith Krause and Williams (Minneapolis: University of Minnesota Press, 1997), 299–327; Tarak Barkawi and Mark Laffey, "The Postcolonial Moment in Security Studies", *Review of International Studies* 32 (2006): 329–352; Benedikt Franke and Stefan Ganzle, "How 'African' Is the African Peace and Security Architecture? Conceptual and Practical Constraints of Regional Security Cooperation in Africa", *African Security* 5, no. 2 (2012): 88–104.

59. Vinod Aggarwal, "Reconciling Multiple Institutions: Bargaining, Linkages and Nesting", in *Institutional Designs for a Complex World: Bargaining, Linkages and Nesting*, ed. V. Aggarwal (Ithaca and London: Cornell University Press, 1998); Malte Brosig, "The African Union: A Partner for Security", in *The Routledge Handbook on European Security*, eds. Sven Biscop and Richard G. Whitman (Oxon: Routledge, 2013), 292–301; Malte Brosig, *Cooperative Peacekeeping in Africa* (London and New York: Routledge), 2015.

60. Even today, due to its uniqueness, African regionalism is treated as an oddity and a source of intrigue to enterprising theorists. Mbembe (2006: 2) argues that: "It is in relation to Africa that the notion of 'absolute otherness' has been taken farthest. It is now widely acknowledged that Africa as an idea, a concept, has historically served, and continues to serve, as a polemical argument for the West's desperate desire to assert its difference from the rest of the world. In several respects, Africa still constitutes one of the metaphors through which the West represents the origin of its own norms, develops a self-image, and integrates this image into the set of signifiers asserting what is supposes to be its identity".

61. Frank Schimmelfennig, "NATO Enlargement: A Constructivist Explanation", *Security Studies* 8, no. 3 (1998): 198–234.

62. Sociologically, the process of institutionalisation is an isomorphic process that involves a myriad of inputs because "in practice, the distinction between a political institution and a social force is not a clear-cut one..." and "the power and influence of social forces varies considerably" (Huntington 1968: 9).
63. Paul J. DiMaggio and Walter W. Powell, "The Iron Cage Revisited: Institutional Isomporhism and Collective Rationality in Organizational Fields", *American Sociological Review* 48, no. 2 (1983): 147–160.
64. Zondi, "Common Positions".
65. See Shepperson, 1962. Other progenitors or advocates of pan-Africanism include Kwame Nkrumah, Marcus Garvey, Sékou Toure, W.E. du Bois, Julius Nyerere and others.
66. See Mazrui, "Global Africa".
67. Mzobanzi Mboya, "Mbeki and the Peace Process in Africa: A Contribution to Africa's Renaissance", *International Journal of African Renaissance Studies* 1, no. 1 (2006): 80–90; Andre Mangu, "Democracy, African Intellectuals and African Renaissance", *International Journal of African Renaissance Studies, Multi, Inter- and Transdisciplinarity* 1, no. 1 (2006): 147–163; Paul-Henri Bischoff, "Pan-African Multilateralism: Transformative or Disconnected?" *Politikon* 32, no. 2 (2008): 177–195.
68. Jolyon Howorth, *Security and Defence Policy in the European Union* (New York: Palgrave Macmillan, 2007).
69. See Chris Alden and Mills Soko, "South Africa's Economic Relations with Africa: Hegemony and Its Discontents", *Journal of Modern African Studies* 43, no. 3 (2005): 367–392; Chris Alden and Maxi Schoeman, "South Africa's Symbolic Hegemony in Africa", *International Politics* 52 (2015): 239–254.
70. Edward Ansah Akuffo, "Human Security and Interregional Cooperation Between NATO and the African Union", *Global Change, Peace and Security* 23, no. 2 (2011): 223–237.
71. David J. Francis, *Uniting Africa: Building Regional Peace and Security Systems* (London and New York: Routledge, 2006).
72. Francis, *Uniting Africa*, 29.
73. Maphoi Komanyane, personal interview, former member of the AU Permanent Representatives Committee Finance Committee, Geneva: May 2013.
74. Chris Landsberg, "An African 'Concert of Powers?' Nigeria and South Africa's Construction of the AU and NEPAD", in *Gulliver's*

*Troubles: Nigeria's Foreign Policy After the Cold War,*eds. Adeyeke Adebajo and Abdul Raufu Mustapha (Pietermaritzburg: University of Kwazulu Natal Press, 2008), 205.

75. Gassama, *From the OAU*.
76. Paul Kagame, *The Imperative to Strengthen our Union: Report on the Proposed Recommendations for the Institutional Reform of the African Union*, January 29, 2017 (Addis Ababa: African Union Commission, 2017).

CHAPTER 3

African Agency in Historical Perspective: A History of Agency Slack

The legacy of colonialism has had a strong influence on Africa's relations with other world regions. Anti-colonial rhetoric is so pervasive that some (Afro-pessimists) see African regional agency as "anti-imperial phantoms".[1] However, the potency of colonialism cannot be undermined or understated. The underlying theme in this chapter is that African agency is largely a contest with the legacy of colonialism or "postcoloniality". It is from that argumentative standpoint that we can satisfactorily trace the origins of agency slack in African multilateralism.

To put it into perspective, the "postcolonial condition", or "postcoloniality" refers to "a global phenomenon of interactions based on unequal power relations in an era that goes beyond the world of colonialism but that has been (and continues to be) decisively shaped by the logic of coloniality".[2] This delineation highlights the power disparity between African and other regions. This power differential reveals an inadvertent cognitive and practical discrepancy between Africa and its erstwhile or aspiring dominators. Thus, Africa appears to be positioned as a weakling and serial dependent, and its main sponsors are primarily colonisers and their allies. This situation is enabled, sustained and compounded by the fact that erstwhile colonisers and their allies dominate and control international institutions that mentor and bankroll the development of African multilateralism and regional integration.[3] This implies that the system retains

© The Author(s), under exclusive license to Springer Nature Switzerland AG 2022
T. Gwatiwa, *The African Union and African Agency in International Politics*, https://doi.org/10.1007/978-3-030-87805-4_3

41

42   T. GWATIWA

Africa's situs in the subaltern and subordinate position. The concomitant politics and processes inadvertently lend processes and choices that fall within the scope of shirking and slippage in order to protect African agency.

Despite the above submissions, it is imperative to note that shirking and slippage are not limited to transregional interactions between Africa and the rest of the world. Sometimes these processes are observed between regions within Africa. The subsequent sections will show that intra-continental fissures also exhibit some elements of slippage and shirking. However, shirking is more common because all parties would be aware that there would be no continental position unless all African regions reach a compromise of a conclusion. This may be a continental level of Agency slack, yet it is imperative to highlight that the inter-regional differences that invite shirking are usually caused by external influence from unabashed erstwhile colonisers such as France and imperial states such as the US. The origins of such occurrences are explained in historical perspective below.

AFRICAN AGENCY IN THE FACE OF IMPERIALISM AND PATRONAGE, 1950S–1990S

Modes of decolonisation laid foundations for the present agitation for greater agency in international. Decolonization was never about total disengagement. While there was some form of disengagement—varying between the British, Spanish, Italian and French systems—the colonial enterprise was rehinged to Europe which had always been the economic nucleus. While the empire crumbled in the post-WWII period, some states insured their economies against African economic agency through conditions for signing certain treaties. For instance, when the signing of the Treaty of Rome, some erstwhile colonisers emphasised the strategic efficacy of their former African colonies. In 1957, twelve years after the war…

> …France, Belgium, the Netherlands and even Italy all still had some colonial ties, described euphemistically in the Treaty as "special relations" … It had not been envisaged, however, that the new democratic Europe should have colonial entanglements associated with the past era of aggressive nationalism, least of all by the Dutch (who had already lost Indonesia) and by the newly democratic Germans who saw empire as

one more trapping to the Wilhelmine and Prussian past. Thus, a relationship with a few parts of what was to be described as the developing world was wished on the Community almost as an afterthought, but a very French afterthought...Still *it was important enough for the French government of Guy Mollet to make it, in February 1957, a condition of signing up to the Rome Treaty.* The key elements were trade access to the EEC with reciprocity—for these were still colonies and protectorates— and a European Development Fund to which Germany and France were to contribute one-third each, even though the principal beneficiaries were French territories".[4]

The foregoing set the postcolonial framework of Africa's relations with Europe. The abovementioned logic underlay the negotiation and signing of the Lomé Convention of 1974. The same states that set those conditions are the primary drivers of the current African Union partnerships. This implies that these partners were the primary instigators of the current agency slack. This is particularly the case given that France and Britain were the doyens of European regional security through the Saint-Malo Declaration.[5] This means that the same states that signed to uphold African ownership, agenda setting and leadership in the partnerships are expected to sponsor or support what they caused. Indeed, Africans are complicit in the present problems in African regional security, but the European causative is even higher. The present setting of European regional security and foreign policy permit and encourage the logic of 1957.

To be sure, the collation of the European Union's Common Defence and Security Policy (CDSP) in the early 2000s attempted to limit the influence of European major security powers.[6] However, the dominance of France and Britain in Africa resurfaced through the notion of "structured cooperation".[7] The use of structured cooperation in the implementation of the Common Foreign and Security Policy (CFSP) reified postcolonial jingoism in an unprecedented fashion.

The resurgence of European jingoism is attributable to developments within the EU, as nations harmonised their foreign policies with the CDSP. At the turn of the century, previous colonial powers began to "Europeanise" their Africa security policies. "Europeanisation" can be defined as an "ongoing, interactive and mutually constitutive process of change linking national and European levels, where the responses of the member states to the integration process feed back into EU institutions and policy processes and vice versa".[8]

44   T. GWATIWA

According to Bagoyoko and Gibert, key former colonial powers managed to do this with varying degrees of success.[9] France fully ceded its RECAMP[10] security programme to the EU—now known as EURO RECAMP. In 2001, Britain transformed its British Peace Support Teams (BPST) into the Africa Conflict Prevention Pool (ACPP). It was funded through the Africa Pool although not fully ceded to the EU. Portugal also "Europeanised" the PAMPA,[11] which was an Africa-oriented security programme.[12] These programmes were then repackaged into a European security package that would be sent back to the continent through the partnership. This implies that the present security programmes and assistance rendered under the partnership (discussed in the next chapters) are an unadulterated reincarnation of policies that the erstwhile colonisers implemented in various parts of the continent.

The trans-Atlantic security partnership between Europe and the US also casts a shadow on Africa. Following slight frictions between the US and European states in the early days of the European Security Defence Policy (ESDP), the EU and NATO made a joint declaration (in 2002) which tied the two organisations.[13] This EU-NATO pact, which officials often do not want to acknowledge, is one of the enablers for foreign policy jingoism by former colonial states. However, France is the biggest benefactor and benefiter from this tapestry of postcoloniality.

FRANCE'S UNMASKED COLONIALISM: AN UNABASHED ON AFRICAN AGENCY

French foreign and security policy towards Africa deserves a candid discussion. This is the most atrocious legacy of colonialism and imperialism that heavily punctuates the African security landscape.

France's imperial architecture in Africa comes from unparalleled historical brutality and strategic jingoism. It began with Charles De Gaulle orchestrating the strategic neutering of fourteen African states in a set of political and economic terms that he appended as conditions for decolonization. Those conditions, among others, included deposited fifty per cent of their GDP revenues into the French treasury.[14] This also involves the assigning of two French advisors to the foreign affairs ministries of all those countries. Worse, the cabinets of these states are required to send talking heads to Paris prior to their meetings as well as sending minutes of those meetings thereafter.[15] From the Gaullist era the control of African states has been based on "ad hoc structures in Paris...[Rather] than allow them to be managed though normal diplomatic channels...many aspects were kept out of public or parliamentary view and entrusted to de Gaulle's networks of acting and former army and intelligence officers".[16] However, the security dimension was even more grotesque.

The politico-security dimension of this "postcolonial" settlement was designed such that France-Afrique was divided into the "Active Zone"— a top priority zone stretching from Senegal to the DRC; the "Passive Zone"—comprising small former Belgian colonies; and the 'Mixed Zone', comprising former colonies along the Mediterranean Sea and the Red Sea, where French foreign policy is opportunistic.[17] This marked different security arrangements for various parts of the continent. They also define the enthusiasm that France exudes for European interventions in Africa, including with the use of structured cooperation.

The abovementioned enabled French influence in the AU partnerships with the EU, UN (as one of the P3) and NATO. Since RECAMP was designed for these three zones, EURO-RECAMP perfectly fit into strategic interests when it was introduced into EU-Africa relations. Given that most African conflicts are in the Francophonie, this has given France ample influence in Addis Ababa. It does this through the satellite office of the *Organization Internationale de la Francophonie* (OIF) in Addis Ababa as well as the (influential role of the) French strategic advisor to the African Union. Moreover, key EU and NATO officials assigned to African security are always of French nationality.[18] This is not surprising given that seventy-five per cent of the discussions at the EU Peace and Security Committee (PSC) are on African security issues. At some point the EU promulgated a policy wherein member states could lead missions in Africa if they could fund them.[19] By default, France—the country with a brutal uptake on African agency—has become the star of the interventionist show.

Hereunder I focus on intra-continental attempts to protect African agency. The main objective was to counter external influence. The fear of external influence was real. It can also be gleaned from international responses to the formation of the Organization of African Unity (OAU). Archival material shows that the OAU mainly received hortatory moral support from those currently stylized as "partners". The US, the United Kingdom, France, China, Russia, Mongolia and Latin American states all sent terse and vague congratulatory messages.[20]

46 T. GWATIWA

The next sections show that all agential manoeuvres in Africa occurred in negative self-consciousness—i.e. countering external influence. There was little by way of positive consciousness, where there was autonomous action independent of the spectre of imperialism and colonialism.

FROM MONROVIA TO KHARTOUM AND SIRTE (1960–1999)

Regional institutional design was heavily contested in the 1960s. African political elites were preoccupied with the notion of territorial integrity and sovereignty. In their calculation, the optimum instrument for the total liberation of Africa was through the creation of an army and other security institutions. Expectedly, these were aimed at countering colonialism. The envisaged army had little to do with maintaining order and promoting justice within the continent. It was also envisaged in negative self-consciousness.

The inter-regional disagreements, or at least caucuses at the time, compounded Africa's ability to promulgate a strong agential position as early as the 1960s. The design and function of the first African anti-imperial instrument were contested by two groups—the Casablanca Group and the Monrovia Group. The Casablanca Group was led by the then Ghanaian leader, President Kwame Nkrumah; while President Tubman of Liberia led the Brazzaville (later called Monrovia) Group. (The etymology referred to places where those groups previously caucused prior to main conference.) They differed over the type of regional security mechanisms to be instituted under what later became known as the Organisation of African Unity (OAU). In principle, they agreed on the creation of such an instrument but differed over the degree of authority to be bequeathed on the type of proposed institutions.

The Casablanca Group proposed creating a political union with sweeping authority in security matters. Article 2 of *African Charter of Casablanca* proposed the creation of a Joint African High Command (JAHC) as one of the four specialised committees of the Union. The JAHC would set up a "viable unified military structure capable of freeing all African territories that were still under foreign rule".[21] The Monrovia Group, more conservative and gradualist in its approach, opted for a simple Joint Defence Command (with a purely supervisory role) to be based in Ouagadougou. In the resulting compromise the two groups settled on an OAU Defence Commission. According to [the then] Article 2(f) of the OAU charter, the Office of Defence Cooperation (ODC) was assigned a defence role, tasked with working out a formula for coordinating and harmonising the defence policies of member states.[22] The idea of a JAHC was repeatedly reintroduced to the ODC under new names such as the "Africa Defence Organization", "African Defence Force" and the "Africa Peace Force". The abovementioned evinces the difficulty of balancing a continental negative consciousness with various national positive self-consciousness. It points to an agential intricacy wherein states are unwilling to subscribe to ideals that seem to corrode their sovereign legitimacy.

Surprisingly, there was general ambivalence to the notion of interventionism despite the then security landscape and threats. Some states were still under colonialism or apartheid. Western mercenary activity was also on the increase. Asian (read: Chinese) intelligence activities also increased in the 1960s. Some states faced internal upheavals—often supported by erstwhile colonisers or newly interested foreign powers. Yet, despite of all these, most African states rejected the idea of an interventionism by an African multilateral organisation. This ambivalence enabled intrastate insecurity such as the internal mutinies in Tanzania in 1964.[23] In 1970, Portugal also launched military action in Guinea without possible opposition from OAU member states.[24] In same year, the OAU was also unable to stop Western mercenaries in Kisangani, DRC (then Congo).[25] The lack of agreement generally weakened Africa's agential capacity. However, these incidents inspired more conversation on how to improve Africa's institutional agency.

Discussions of increased institutional responses resumed in the 1970s. In the absence of Kwame Nkrumah (of Ghana), Nigeria emerged as a strong voice in West Africa. Initially, Nigeria was strongly opposed to the idea of an empowered continental security arrangement because of its civil war.[26] However, Nigeria changed its stance when its civil war came to an end.[27] At an ODC meeting held in Freetown in February 1965, the Sierra Leone submitted a proposal for an African Defence Organisation (ADO), calling for a "continental clearinghouse for national armies" earmarked within countries and available on request by the OAU.[28] The idea was rejected. However, it is important to realise that rejected ideas do not necessarily disappear in African multilateralism. The framework of the ADO is the same logic that was used in the short-lived African Capacity for the Immediate Response to Crises (ACRIC) and regional standby brigades (RSF) that make up the African Standby Force (ASF). There is one key issue that accounts for such resuscitations.

African regional projects improved when the agential locus shifted from heads of states to ministers and technical experts. In the late 1970s, the OAU made provisions for ministerial dialogue on several issues relating to political and security challenges in the continent. During the Council of Ministers' 31st Ordinary Session in Khartoum in July 1978, the Front Line States (FLS)—the forerunner to the Southern African Development Community (SADC)—facing challenges of a bullish apartheid regime in South Africa, a racist and bullish regime in Rhodesia, and a mercenary infested Zaire, proposed the idea of a more powerful African army. This idea gained support from prominent African political leaders such as Julius Nyerere (of Tanzania).[29] In April 1979, the 6th Ordinary Session of the Defence Commission formed the OAU Defence Force (OAU-DF). Although the Summit of heads of states, held in 1980, referred the OAU-DF "proposal back to the Commission for further study" (a shirking tactic), the OAU-DF would become the blueprint for key elements of the African Peace and Security Architecture (APSA), around which the AU's international partners coalesced.

The OAU-DF was a crucial step towards what is currently considered the cornerstone of African security. The mandate of the OAU-DF was to: (a) support member states in the event of external aggression; (b) assist liberation movements in their struggles; (c) provide peacekeeping and observer forces in the event of conflict between member states; and (d) cooperate with the UN in matters of defence and security affecting member states. The foregoing strongly resemble the principles of the Constitutive Act (2000), PSC Protocol (2002). The first three elements of the OAU-DF are found in Article 13 of the PSC Protocol.[30] The fourth element is also found in Article 13(21),[31] which also exists in the Constitutive Act. It suffices to argue that African agency was reified in 1980 but did not exist in full expression until the early 2000s.

It is important to highlight the effects of Africa's failure to balance positive self-consciousness and negative self-consciousness which put it in a chronic agential quandary. As Zartman argued in his seminal exegesis of early African regionalism, African multilateralism was driven by pan-African sentimentalism, positive self-consciousness of shared experiences and negative self-consciousness of rejecting external control.[32] This might have been ideal at a macro-level, but it was problematic in the sense that it was not accompanied by a candid conversation and institutionalisation of a specific form of African regional identity. This does not imply ethno-nationalist identity, but a form of identity based on shared values, norms and aspirations that would drive African regionalism.[33] Such an intra-regional augmentation not only strengthen the region but also gives it a stronger agential standi in international affairs. Africa's failure in this regard was self-defeating.

Historically, there was no explicit mention of identity and cognitive regionalism in the conferences of the 1950s and 1960s,[34] although it was known that most African heads of state and government largely subscribed to Pan-Africanism. Yet, since some of the OAU's primary objectives were to "promote unity and solidarity of the African States", "...defend their sovereignty, their territorial integrity and independence" ... and "...to eradicate all forms of colonialism from Africa", any newly independent state could join the OAU without explicitly subscribing to pan-Africanism. The question of the North African (Arab) states, which currently beleaguers African regionalism and agency, was taken for granted. The same applies to the case of the multiracial and multi-cultural islands. Yet, as early as 1963, several African states sought to emphasise how they were not "African" enough. At the inaugural OAU conference, Maghreb states, Madagascar and Ethiopia emphasised the uniqueness of their own experiences from those of what was largely perceived black Africa.[35] This was a manifestation of the problem of African identity which Frantz Fanon articulated in his essay on "West Indians and Africans". In that essay he seeks to deconstruct the issues of anti-African identity sentiments among Africans based on a Eurocentric references, which are only abandoned once all parties eventually face the same challenges from the European.[36] This is exactly what happened in the early days of African regionalism. Many OAU member states, including the one hosting its headquarters, paid lip service to the issue of African regionalism. As a result, African regionalism lacked agential substance for decades. Given this context, African regional receded into some form dependency and agential impotence.

As an international weakling Africa developed an appetite for imported ideas and expertise. This should not be a surprise at all. Africa is often bereft of authentic thinking. There is hardly any "African ideology" that is authentically African. For instance, pan-Africanism does not have African roots. The term was coined by (Trinidadian) Henri Sylvester-William, and as Shepperson argued, "[the] concept of continental unity which matters for all-Africanism…seems to have been the creation of New World Negroes—if not 'foreigners' to Africa, certainly 'outsiders'".[37] This resulted in complexities that led to confusion and alienation.[38] The same applies to the idea of African Renaissance, which seems to be a transplantation of elements of European Renaissance, but more so the Harlem Renaissance. Steve Biko's black consciousness was also influenced by the works of Martin Delany, W.E. Du Bois and Frantz Fanon, all of whom wrote from different contexts.[39] Desmond Tutu and Nelson Mandela's idea of the "Rainbow Nation", which was ostensibly supposed to promote multiculturalism also had a striking resemblance of Fred Hampton's notion of the "Rainbow Coalition".[40] This is not to say Africans are not supposed to be inspired by anybody outside the continent, what is at issue here is the fact that none of these ideologies derive from the empirical dynamics of indigenous Africans. This appetite for non-continental ideologies also affected early African multilateral institutionalisation.

It is surprising that the OAU Charter was drafted by a retired Irish general.[41] From the 1970s, the OAU also took a decision to develop Africa using a "tripartite approach…involving Arab money, African resources and Western technology".[42] How does an organisation with a starkly different history commit itself to mimicry from the onset? Imported expertise by international consultants continued from 1963 until the late 1990s. As a corollary, the organisation resorts to the mimicry that most conventions simply resembled those of the UN. Even the much-vaunted increased actorness of the late 1990s, was that the OAU brought in Western-educated and diasporic Africans as consultants to chart a new path for African regionalism. This meant that the resultant ideas remained non-African. There was little by of using indigenous expertise, as reflected in most AU documents.

To be fair, Africans working in the continent (but Western educated) and in the diaspora collectively contributed to the drawing of the Constitutive Act and the African Peace and Security Architecture (APSA). Yet from the perspective of sociological institutionalism, this enabled the prevalence of Western ideas in the blueprints of African regional aspirations.[43] From another vantage point, this may seem acceptable given the interconnectedness of international affairs.[44] However, it is imperative to note that in the present era of increased Afrocentric regionalism, these Western blueprints are a major source of contestation in the partnerships. However, there have been attempts, at least since the early 2000s, to promote positive self-consciousness in African regionalism and actorness.

African positive self-consciousness can be found in key African regional agreements although they are still empirically juxtaposed against the negative self-consciousness of rejecting or limiting foreign influence. Article 4 of the Common African Defence and Security Policy (CADSP) states that "[the] adoption of a Common Defence and Security Policy for Africa is premised on common African perception of what is required to be done collectively by African states to ensure that Africa's common defence and security interests and goals...are safeguarded in the face of common threats to the continent as a whole".[45] The "common African perceptions" were collated through "various efforts made at the sub-regional level...to establish common policies on defence and security issues...".[46] African regional security gives primacy to subregional organisation when identifying and collating such security issues through a memorandum of understanding governing relations between subregional entities and the continental organisation.[47] In this regard, perceptions and prescribed solutions are eclectic—both autonomous as well as linked to external regions and actors. They are autonomous in the sense that some preferences and interests are purely decided by African actors. They are, in other cases, external in that not only were those "African problems" a result of colonial fuckups, but they may still be subject to imperial meddling, especially in the so-called Francophonie. But it is useful to view most post-OAU corrective measures as mostly a product of African agential aspirations. For instance, Nigeria has sought to dominate West African regional security mechanisms as a way of limiting French influence in the region, as well as revive African approaches to conflict resolution. Rwanda also shifted from the OIF to the Commonwealth as a way of shielding itself from French meddling. Similarly, most states have generally sought to improve their agency by focussing on autonomous African ownership, leadership and agenda setting—notion that eventually punctuated most of the partnerships.

REGIONALISM AND AGENCY: AFRICA'S MULTILATERAL ARTHRITIS

While the foregoing section dealt with the issue of identity, the phenomenon also has a debilitating effect on African agency when it manifests in the form of intra-continental regionalism. The different regions of Africa have coalesced into ethnolinguistic enclaves. The northern region, called the Maghreb, consists of countries with an Arab heritage and have strong ties to the Middle East, hence named the Arab Maghreb Union (AMU). The southern region largely consists of states which trace their pre-colonial migration from various parts of modern-day

South Africa, now called the Southern African Development Community (SADC). The western region—called the Economic Community of West African States (ECOWAS)—consists of predominantly French-speaking, or Francophonie, states; except for Nigeria, Ghana and Guinea-Bissau—English and Portuguese, respectively. The eastern region, predictably named the East African Community, is adjacent to the Afro-Arabic region often called the Horn of Africa, which is institutionalised in the Inter-Governmental Authority on Development (IGAD). The strong link between ethnicity, language and geopolitics often engenders regionalist politics at the multilateral level.

Regionalist politics at the AU, which started under the OAU, are a competition for influence and dominion. Actors understand that Africa is a large and highly heterogenous continent with lots of opportunity. As a result, they compete for dominion by seeking to influence the processes of institutionalisation from within and outside of the AU Commission.[48] Geopolitical enclaves thus seek to influence the process through duplication of subregional institutions at the continental level, coercing other regions to favour their positions, and fielding candidates for leadership position.[49] For instance, Gassama's argues that:

> ...regionalism still remains a factor as well, particularly when it comes to matters such as the hosting of new institutions, offices and projects and the election of the Chairperson, his/her Deputy and Commissioners as well as selection of candidates for positions in the UN System.[50]

Why is regionalism an issue in a continent with the biggest imperative to be the most united? It is because African states and subregional organisations are fully aware that "in practice, the distinction between a political institution and a social force is not a clear-cut one..." and "the power and influence of social forces varies considerably...".[51] That is why in the OAU era, the OAU Secretary General had about five deputies drawn from each sub-region. It is surprising that the AU did not retain this arrangement. However, what is most concerning, as highlighted by Gassama, is that even with this arrangement, African multilateralism was still not cogently functional at an agential level. This plays out in the way major states, or the so-called regional hegemons, approach their roles and burdens in the AU systems.

African lead-states' competition for influence within the AU Commission is telling in this regard. While the issue of hegemonic leadership was somewhat mute in the OAU era, it is not so under the AU. To be sure, most states vie for influence within their sub-regions because there are shared identities, histories, political and security threats, values as well doctrinal restoratives.[52] However, some seek more influence. The most ambitious and notorious in this regard has been Nigeria and South Africa. While there was a decision to nullify hegemonic imperialism within Africa,[53] ostensibly aimed at plucking Gaddafi's hegemonic ambitions, these two states and Egypt have been competing for influence. However, Egypt is not, by any measure, considered a serious contender for hegemonic leadership. There has been limited gains for both Nigeria and South Africa.

Nigeria used its influence in ECOWAS to gain a greater political standing within the AU. Nigeria finances about seventy-five per cent of the ECOWAS budget, and always fields most ECOWAS directors. Nigeria used that to bargain with fellow states that it should permanently occupy one of the four seats assigned to the West Africa region in the AU Peace and Security Council.[54] This effectively made Nigeria the only permanent member of the AU PSC! South Africa negotiated with fellow southern African states for the same privilege in the PSC, but without success.[55] However, the stakes would never be in any other aspiring hegemon's favour because the western region is the only one with four seats, while the rest occupy four. It is much worse for Egypt because the northern region has only two seats. This competition, while seemingly natural for a burgeoning organisation, it has enervating effects at an agential level.

The competition between these lead countries has little to do with African regionalism itself. They are tied to greater influence in the international system under the auspices of the United Nations. When the then UN Secretary General, Kofi Annan, first proposed UNSC reforms, AU member states could not agree on which state would represent Africa as a non-veto permanent member of the UNSC. As Adebajo observed, the three states "entered a Byzantine contest...Cynics dismissed Nigeria as too 'anarchic', Egypt as too 'Arab' and South Africa as too 'albinocratic'".[56] African states adopted the *Ezuwlini Consensus* of 2005, which demanded "full representation of Africa in the Security Council...[with] no less than two permanent seats with all prerogatives and privileges of the permanent membership including the right to veto...[and] five non-permanent seats".[57] Indeed, the AU was seizing an opportunity regarding the overdue UN reform, but the approach was completely misguided with regard to the African agency.

There are two main reasons why this demand was misguided. First, meeting these AU demands would have caused further complications within the UN system. Other UN member states would have frowned upon two permanent African seats plus another five non-permanent seats. Moreover, it is not clear how two permanent UNSC seats would have benefitted the continent while the PSC has not institutionalised permanent seats. Second, it is surprising that the AU would press for ephemeral reforms. Deservedly, the UNSC wields immense power within the UN system, but it was never going to be an easy task for a pragmatic step. Political power is superficial when considering the size of the UN system. In order to gain greater agency, African states should have instead pushed for social reforms within the UN system. For instance, there is no African language listed as an official or working language within the UN. This myopia can also be observed within the AU system where all official languages are either Western or Middle Eastern. According to a former minister of foreign affairs, the issue of introducing African languages at the AU was once raised but was met with a cold response.[58] Adding African languages to the UN would give greater weight to the African agency by promoting African identity and, by extension, endogenous African ideologies. By placing a premium on UNSC political reform showed that African states are more concerned with symbolism rather than substantive projections of agency.

African Agency Slack in the 1970s: Formation of the Africa-Arab League Partnership

The actual manifestation of Agency slack can be observed in the run up to the formation of Africa's oldest strategic partnership—the Africa-Arab League Partnership of 1976. For this account I borrow heavily from Olusola Ojo.[59]

The partnership was first proposed by both parties in the 1960s. However, there was high mutual suspicion, concerns of partnership directionality, historical wounds and hot topics around the then politics of southern Africa and the Palestinian question. However, there were three key issues relating to founding ideals, membership, and inter-organisational bureaucratic politics.

The founding mandates of the two organisations are an important starting point to discuss the origins of the partnership. The formation of the League of Arab States (LAS) was somewhat different from that of the

OAU. There are claims that Britain was the first to pontificate Arab unity, yet closer scrutiny reveals that the idea of Arab unity was prevalent in the Fertile Crescent prior to [British foreign minister] Anthony Eden's speech on May 29, 1941.[60] However, owing to different dynamics and differing interests among founding member states, the Arab League's priorities were different from those of the OAU. First, the League was formed much earlier (March 1945) than both the OAU (1963) and the UN (June 1945). While most OAU documents sought proximity to the UN Charter, this was not necessarily the case for the Arab League. Second, the Arab League was not necessarily founded on a negative self-consciousness of rejecting external influence such as characterised the OAU. While the OAU was preoccupied with decolonization and development, the Arab League was not.[61] The Pact of the League of Arab States adopted elements of (Iraqi premier) Nuri as-Said's proposals except those dealing with foreign policy coordination, defence or military issues. Moreover, there were different levels of commitment to positive self-consciousness. While pan-Africanism was at the height of its oomph and verve, there was less enthusiasm for "Arab unity" by the signing of the pact in 1945. As MacDonald put it Arab unity "...remains the sacred cow of the League: it gives little nourishment, but no one dares kill it".[62] When it came to the question of a partnership with the OAU, the Arab League was less enthusiastic about a partnership with an organisation that was more politically oriented. Initially, African states were enthusiastic about a partnership because of recent oil and petroleum fortunes made by the Arab and Gulf states. As a result of these different priorities, the Arab League minimised efforts to engage in any partnership. The different levels of enthusiasm are also attributable to the overlapping membership between the OAU and the Arab League.

At the time of brokering the partnership, eight OAU member states were already member states of the Arab League. This created problems. First, black African states were highly suspicious of African Arab states and called on them to renounce Arab League membership as a sign of commitment to African unity. The Senegalese and Sierra Leoneans directly made these calls, in fear of Arab imperialism and historical accounts of slavery, prior to and during the OAU founding conference, respectively.[63] Hence, there was a spectre of suspicion towards the Arabs by black Africans even when the organisation secretariat seemed open to a partnership. Second, Africans saw a direct competition between the OAU and what they called "militant Pan-Arabism". For instance, the Arab

League sought to block African involvement in the Algeria-Moroccan border conflict in the 1970s, and there were later public allegations that Arabs wanted to take over the organisation. All these sentiments made Africans highly suspicious of the Arabs, resulting in general reluctance to further pursue the partnership. However, the stakes quickly changed into a setting where both parties needed each other but reluctant to engage each other.

There came a time when the two organisations needed each other. On the one hand, the Arab League was increasingly preoccupied with the issue of anti-Zionism. It needed African support against Zionist expansion and militancy. In April 1970, the then LAS Secretary General, Mahmoud Riad (of Egypt), sent a letter to his OAU counterpart, Nzo Ekangaki (of Cameroon), stating that the LAS was eager to pursue a partnership. The African response was very lukewarm. They shirked because, apart from the high mistrust of "militant Pan-Arabism", they saw no other pressing need for a formal partnership. Event when the two secretary generals met in Cairo in May 1973, Ekangaki was non-committal—a slippage tactic—because the OAU thought the Arab League sought to drag them into a Middle Eastern crisis that had nothing to do with Africa.[64] However, the fortunes of African states soon changed in the aftermath of the 1973 Oil Crisis precipitated by the Arab states. In November 1973, an OAU Council of Ministers meeting instructed the secretary general to seek closer cooperation with the Arab League. The stakes were high, and neither party could afford any form of agency slack; hence, the LAS responded favourably at a meeting held in Algiers the same year and even referred to them as "sister African states".[65] Given the high stakes, the issue of dual membership worked in favour of both organisations. But the issue of dual membership showed further agential utility.

An OAU-Arab League partnership was being institutionalised by the two secretariats by February 1974. The Arabs were grateful for African support during the Israeli-Arab War of 1973 and sought to help minimise the economic impact of the oil crisis. OAU-LAS dual membership worked in favour of this effort. First, Algerian (and North African) influence helped improve cooperation. After all, the same eight ministers sat in both councils of ministers. This eased the process of negotiation and bargaining. Second, when a liaison structure was created in Cairo, Algerian diplomat, Mohamed Sahnoun—a former OAU Assistant Secretary General—who was appointed as Special Adviser on African Affairs to the League Secretary General.[66] Appointing a diplomat from Algeria meant that he understood both regions as well as had support from the dual members. Moreover, Algeria has a more pan-African foreign policy compared to other Maghreb states. Third, the Afro-Arab states helped create an "Afro-Arab Dialogue Group of Experts". In this case the dual membership made limited but laudable steps. However, the overall project would go back to the usual shirking and slippage tactics.

The enthusiasm of the secretary generals was not matched by member states. The Arabs refused to bail out African economies affected by the economic crisis, as well as refused to honour requests for financial aid to be disbursed via the African Development Bank (AfDB). Although the OAU secretary general had signed the draft agreement by 1975, member states complained that the Arab League favoured Islamic and Muslim states in their financial aid. The new OAU secretary general, William Eteki, expressed this disappointment at a joint OAU-LAS ministerial conference in Dakar, Senegal in April 1976. But Eteki was, like his predecessor, very enthusiastic about the partnership and sought to create an executive liaison office in Cairo. Once again, the OAU members states told him that he was acting "beyond his competence".[67] This was an interesting display of shirking through an empirical imbalance of power within the OAU. Finally, the partnership went into dormancy due to incessant shirking and slippage between the OAU and the Arab League. The partnership was never seriously considered until 2015.

NEGOTIATING AFRICAN AGENCY FROM WITHIN: CONFERENCES AND SUMMITRY, 1980S–1990S

What defines Africa's negotiating and bargaining position? When did it begin? What did they choose…over what?

The process of designing a new regional order began in the early 1990s. After the collapse of the Soviet Union, it was obvious that the geostrategic environment was undergoing changes. The African continent was then engulfed in many woes: interstate and intrastate conflicts, insufficient governance, institutional paralysis, political patronage and economic depreciation- to mention but few.[68] Aptly captured by one observer, Africa was "a resource-rich [continent] of poor people in which pathological substance often triumph over sanitised form: institutional recession masquerades as institution building; endless new constitutions parade as substitutes for constitutionalism; and…performance is often in direct contrast to fervent declarations of intent and achievement".[69] During that

58   T. GWATIWA

period, the OAU was unable to handle its peace and security challenges due to poor institutionalisation, flawed institutional design and sheer lack of political will among African leaders. Yet key African leaders (retired and incumbents) were not unaware of these realities.

Earlier efforts to redefine continental security were undertaken in the 1990s. In 1991 the "Kampala Movement" promulgated a range of security and governance reforms for the African continent.[70] These were codified in what is known as the *Conference on Security, Stability, Development and Cooperation in Africa* (CSSDCA). The OAU half-heartedly endorsed these reforms.[71] However, they contained genuine reforms that were aimed at introducing a new peace and security architecture. Upon scrutiny, most of the ideals reflected in the present APSA can be traced to this special declaration. Typically, it took several more conferences and negotiations, as well as catastrophic events, for the CSSDCA to translate into something meaningful.

Key forward-looking personalities became involved in this project to reify the CSSDCA into something meaningful. Following the horrors of the Rwandan genocide, the CSSDCA gained buy-in. Olusegun had been involved with the Kampala Movement after his first presidency as a dictator. Other key drivers of this project of negotiating a new regional order were President Thabo Mbeki (South Africa) and President Abdelaziz Bouteflika (Algeria).[72] When negotiations for a new order resumed in the late 1990s, these were all heads of state. Their network dated back to Mbeki's years in exile. Although this group did not trust Colonel Muammar Gaddafi, they figured they needed his money. Most Africa states initially resisted the idea of an African Union, until Gaddafi made concessions and side-payments to 32 states to accept this idea.[73] (I call this the MOB-G quartet). Hosni Mubarak of Egypt later came on board, but he was not proactive. This was a turning point in African regionalism as these five countries, currently known as "the Big Five", became the top funders of the AU Commission. Although there were various ambitions and motives in the initial move, it was later agreed that financial contributions would not result in influence.[74] However, this did not hinder the concretisation of the CSSDCA into a treaty and a security protocol.

Despite major differences about the shape and function of the Commission and its security institutions, the MOB-G quartet worked towards a tangible outcome through summitry. The Sirte Declaration of 1998 resulted in a compromise between Gaddafi's "hegemonic ambitions" and Mbeki-Obasanjo's even approach.[75] It took two years of backroom negotiation and bargaining and making "economic and financial concessions to opponents of the AU project as promoted by Col. Gaddafi and the pivotal states of Nigeria, South Africa and Algeria".[76] Obasanjo ensured that most of the components of the CSSDCA were incorporated into the new union.[77] This initially proved to be quite a challenge but following another CSSDCA conference convened in Abuja in 2000, the principles and ideals of the CSSDCA found their way into the Constitutive Act and African Peace and Security Architecture. The above-mentioned process was the collation of African regional preferences in peace and security, among others, which would be the basis of negotiating a new inter-regional framework.

The foregoing account explains the issue of political commitment as well as the institutional architecture of the AU Commission. The ability to negotiate and implement inter-regional security programmes depends on the collective diplomacy and institutions of a given regional organisation (discussed separately later); mainly because inter-regional processes begin at a regional level. Preferences between organisations are often negotiated between political principals. This means that the principals should negotiate with credibility. That credibility begins from within the region. The foregoing accounts show that the MOB-G quartet managed to steer the AHSG to a stage of actorness through credibility build overtime through transnational policy networks. The quartet, perhaps except for Gaddafi, can be traced to Mbeki's role as a key ANC negotiator when in exile.[78] He established contacts with Obasanjo (then Nigeria's military ruler from 1976 to 1979). Obasanjo also established contacts with Bouteflika while the latter was the foreign affairs minister of Algeria (1963–1979).[79] This quartet managed to steer African regional diplomacy through policy coordination and singularity of rhetoric in international affairs.

This negotiation and implementation of partnerships was a function of interstate policy dynamics among this group of states. One of the remarkable policy approaches was an agreement between Nigeria and South Africa's foreign services that they would compare notes before negotiating on behalf of the continent.[80] The idea was that "...while South Africa under Mbeki brought a sense of urgency to African diplomacy, Nigeria...brought history and diplomatic experience, as well as a sense of legitimacy to South Africa's post-apartheid role in Africa".[81] At an institutional level, Obasanjo managed to incorporate the CSSDCA into what eventually became African Peace and Security Architecture.[82] Gaddafi brought money and popularity to the whole project.[83] Essentially, this

60   T. GWATIWA

quartet steered African regional diplomacy. Obasanjo and Mbeki often worked in concert to incept numerous partnerships, including the now dormant Africa-South America Cooperation Forum (ASACOF) signed in 2006.[84] It suffices to posit that this coordination improved the agential role and capacity of the continent in international affairs.

The post MOB-G era is a contrast. African leaders in the AHSG hardly work together, thus undermining African agency. The controversy over Libya (discussed in subsequent chapters) was a result of uncoordinated interests between leaders of the leading African states. Consequently, NATO, AFRICOM and the UN were able to undermine the AU in Libya. According to a strategic advisor to the late Ethiopian Prime Minister, the debate over Gaddafi's future at the Malabo Summit lasted into the wee hours of the morning resulting in weak consensus between Meles Zenawi, Goodluck Jonathan and Jacob Zuma.[85] This poor coordination with the AHSG, the echelon of power, complicates the negotiating position of the AUC Chairperson.

In summary, we can appreciate, with the benefit of this historical trajectory, that African agency slack is rooted in a history of Africa having to contend with a heavy cloak of post-coloniality and an enduring spectre of imperialism and foreign policy jingoism from the so-called international partners.

Notes

1. Romain Esmenjaud, "The African Capacity for Immediate Response to Crisis: Conceptual Breakthrough or Anti-Imperialist Phantom?'" *African Security Review*, 23, no. 2 (2014): 172–177, https://doi.org/10.1080/10246029.2014.898589.
2. Jana Hönke and Markus-Michael Müller, "Governing (in)security in a Postcolonial World: Transnational Entanglements and the Worldliness of 'Local' practice", *Security Dialogue* 43, no. 5 (2012): 383–401.
3. Vinod Aggarwal, "Reconciling Multiple Institutions: Bargaining, Linkages and Nesting", in *Institutional Designs for a Complex World: Bargaining, Linkages and Nesting*, ed. Vinod Aggarwal (Ithaca and London: Cornell University Press, 1998); Malte Brosig, "The African Union: A Partner for Security", in *The Routledge Handbook on European Security*, eds. Sven Biscop and Richard G. Whitman (Oxon: Routledge, 2013); Malte Brosig,

3 AFRICAN AGENCY IN HISTORICAL PERSPECTIVE ...   61

Cooperative Peacekeeping in Africa (London and New York: Routledge, 2015).
4. Adrian Hewitt and Kaye Whiteman, "The Commission and Development Policy: Bureaucratic Politics in EU aid—From the Lomé Leap Forward to the Difficulties of Adapting to the Twenty-First Century", in *EU Development Cooperation: From Model to Symbol*, eds. Karin Arts and Anna Dickson (New York and Vancouver: Manchester University Press, 2004).
5. Jolyon Howorth, *Security and Defence Policy in the European Union* (New York: Palgrave Macmillan, 2007).
6. David Phinnemore, "The European Union: Establishment and Development", in *European Union Politics*, eds. Cini and Borragàn (UK: Oxford University Press, 2010), 41.
7. Howorth, *Security and Defence Policy*, 79–83, "structured cooperation", essentially means few willing and capable states can mount overseas military operations in the name of the EU.
8. Major 2005: 177, as cited in Niagalé Bagoyoko and Marie V. Gibert, "The Linkage Between Security, Governance and Development: The European Union in Africa", *The Journal of Development Studies* 45, no. 5 (2009): 789–814.
9. Bagoyoko and Gibert, "The Linkage Between Security, Governance and Development".
10. *Renforcement des Capacite's Africaines de Maintien de la Paix.*
11. *Programa de Apoio as Missões de Paz em Africa.*
12. Bagoyoko and Gibert, "The Linkage Between Security, Governance and Development", 800–801.
13. NATO, "EU-NATO Declaration on ESDP", http://www.nato.int/cps/en/natolive/official_texts_19544.htm.
14. George B.N. Ayittey, *Africa Unchained: the Blueprint for Africa's Future* (New York and Hampshire: Palgrave Macmillan, 2005). According to Ayittey, since 1961, former French colonies deposit more than 50% of their GDP revenue in the French treasury. France also controls them politically.
15. Solomon Gomez, personal interview, veteran OAU/AU worker and specialist, Addis Ababa: African Union Commission, December 2016.
16. Richard Moncrieff, "French Africa Policy: Sarkozy's Legacy, and Prospects for a Hollande Presidency", *South African Journal of International Affairs* 19, no. 3 (2012), 359–380 [360].

17. William Zartman, 1984 as cited in Terry Mays, *Africa's First Peace-keeping Operation: The OAU in Chad, 1981–1982* (Westport and London: Praeger, 2002).
18. For an extensive account of France's history in NATO, see Julian Lindley-French, *A Chronology of European Security and Defence: 1945–2007* (New York and Oxford: Oxford University Press, 2007).
19. Lieutenant Colonel Atony Gash, personal interview, United Kingdom Permanent Mission to Brussels, Brussels: June 2014.
20. Organization of African Unity, *Proceedings of the Summit Conference of Independent African States* (Addis Ababa: OAU, 1963).
21. Benedict Ijomah, "The African Military Interventions: A Prelude to Military High Command", *Journal of African Activist Association* 5, no. 2 (1974): 51–80.
22. Ijomah, "The African Military Interventions".
23. Thomas Imobighe, "An African High Command: The Search for a Feasible Strategy of Continental Defence", *African Affairs* 79, no. 315 (1980): 3241–3254.
24. Imobighe, "An African High Command".
25. Imobighe, "An African High Command".
26. Their concerns hinged on issues such as sovereignty, exorbitant costs, resource predicaments, unified training, deployment of troops, weapons standardisation, logistics, and appointment of a supreme commander.
27. Orobola Fasehun, "Nigeria and the Issue of an African High Command: Towards a Regional and/or Continental Defence System", *Afrika Spectrum* 15, no. 4 (1980): 309–317.
28. Fasehun, "Nigeria and African High Command", 55.
29. Olu S. Agbi, *The Organization of African Unity and African Diplomacy, 1963–1979* (Ibadan: Impact Publishers, 1986).
30. African Union, *Protocol Relating to the Establishment of the Peace an Security Council of the African Union* (Addis Ababa: African Union Commission), 18–20 [Article 13].
31. African Union, *Protocol Relating to the Establishment*, 21.
32. William I. Zartman, "Africa as a Subordinate State System in International Relations", *International Organization* 21, no. 3 (1967): 545–564.
33. Frank Schimmelfennig, "NATO Enlargement: A Constructivist Explanation", *Security Studies* 8, no. 2–3 (2007): 198–234.

34. Organization of African Unity, *Proceedings of the Summit Conference*.
35. See ibid.
36. Frantz Fanon, *Toward the African revolution: Political essays* (New York: Grove Press, 1964), 17–27.
37. George Shepperson, "Pan-Africanism and 'Pan-Africanism': Some Historical Notes", *Phylon* 23, no. 4 (1962): 346–358 [349].
38. Shepperson, "Pan-Africanism".
39. See Robert S. Levine, *Martin Delany, Frederick Douglass, and the Politics of Representative Identity* (Chapel Hill: The University of North Carolina Press, 1997); Tommie Shelby, "Two Conceptions of Black Nationalism: Martin Delany on the Meaning of Black Political Solidarity", *Political Theory* 31, no. 5 (2003): 664–692.
40. See Jakobi Williams, *From the Bullet to the Ballot: The Illinois Chapter of the Black Panther and Racial Coalition Politics in Chicago* (Chapel Hill: University of North Carolina Press, 2013); Kerry L. Haynie, "Containing the Rainbow: Political Consequences of Mass Racialized Incarceration", *Du Bois Review: Social Science Research on Race* 16, no. 1 (2019), 243–251.
41. OAU, Proceedings.
42. Muhammad Gassama, *From the OAU to the AU: The Odyssey of a Continental Organization* (The Gambia: Fulladu Publishers, 2013).
43. Jeffrey T. Chekel (eds.), *International Institutions and Socialization in Europe* (UK and USA: Cambridge University Press, 2007), Chapters 1 and 6.
44. Aggarwal, "Institutional Design for a Complex World".
45. African Union, "Solemn Declaration on a Common African Defence and Security Policy" (Libya: Sirte, 2004).
46. Ibid., article 25.
47. See Article IV of the *Memorandum of Understanding on Cooperation in the Area of Peace and Security Between the African Union, the Regional Economic Communities and the Coordinating Mechanisms of the Regional Standby Brigades of Eastern Africa and Northern Africa* (Addis Ababa: African Union, 2009).
48. See Samuel P. Huntington, *Political Order in Changing Societies* (New Haven and London: Yale University Press, 1968), 8–32.
49. See Paul J. DiMaggio and Walter W. Powell, "The Iron Cage Revisited: Institutional Isomporhism and Collective Rationality in

Organizational Fields", *American Sociological Review* 48, no. 2 (1983): 147–160.

50. Muhammad Gassama, *From the OAU*, 79.
51. Huntington, *Political Order*, 9.
52. Katharina P. Coleman, *International Organization and Peace Enforcement: The Politics of International Legitimacy* (Cambridge: Cambridge University Press, 2007), 116–117; Funmi Olonisakin, "Liberia", in *Dealing with Conflict in Africa: The United Nations and Regional Organizations*, ed. Jane Boulden (New York: Palgrave Macmillan, 2003), 111–126.
53. Maphoi Komanyane, personal interview, former member of (AU) Permanent Representatives Committee on Financing, Geneva: May 2013.
54. Ambassador of Benin to Ethiopia, personal interview, Addis Ababa: July 2015.
55. Tim Murithi, personal communication, former AU consultant and security expert, Geneva: June 2013.
56. Adeyeke Adebajo, "Hegemony on a Shoestring", in *Gulliver's Troubles: Nigeria's Foreign Policy After the Cold War*, eds. Adeyeke Adebajo and Abdul R. Mustapha (Pietermaritzburg: University of Kwazulu-Natal Press, 2008).
57. African Union, *Decisions, Declarations and Resolution, Fifth Ordinary Session, Sirte, Libya* (Addis Ababa: AU Commission, July 3, 2005).
58. Phandu Skelemani, personal interview, former lead SADC negotiator to the EU, and former Minister of International Affairs and Cooperation (Botswana), Gaborone, October 2017.
59. Olusola Ojo, "The Relationship Between the Organization of African Unity and the League of Arab States", *Spectrum* 16, no. 2 (1981): 131–141.
60. Robert W. MacDonald, *The League of Arab States: A Study in Dynamics of Regional Organization* (Princeton, NJ: Princeton University Press, 1965).
61. Ojo, "The Relationship Between the OAU and LAS", 133.
62. MacDonald, *The League of Arab States*, 41.
63. Osu, "The Relationship Between OAU and LAS", 134.
64. Ibid., 135.
65. Ibid., 136.
66. Ibid.

3 AFRICAN AGENCY IN HISTORICAL PERSPECTIVE ...   65

67. Ibid., 138.
68. George Ayittey, *Africa Betrayed* (London and New York: Palgrave Macmillan, 1992).
69. Extrapolating words from Adeyeke Adebajo, "Hegemony on a Shoestring", in *Gulliver's Troubles: Nigeria's Foreign Policy After the Cold War*, eds. Adeyeke Adabajo and Abdul R. Mustapha (Pietermaritzburg: University of Kwazulu-Natal Press, 2008).
70. This was a group of a few select heads of state, businessmen, scholars, and civil society. The group was led by then former head of state Olusegun Obasanjo, former Libyan Leader Muammar Gaddafi, Sudan's Omar Al-Bashir and Kenya's Arap Moi.
71. Edward Ansah Akuffo, "Human Security and Interregional Cooperation Between NATO and the African Union", *Global Change, Peace & Security* 23, no. 2 (2011): 223–237 [225–226].
72. Olusegun Obasanjo, *Conference Speech*, UNOG, Geneva, October 2013. In his own words, former President Olusegun Obasanjo said, he and Mbeki and Bouteflika had based their actions on their previous experience: he as a former dictator but then a democratically elected leader; Mbeki as a former vice-president and mediator; and Bouteflika as a former minister of foreign affairs who had gathered insight on how to ensure peace in a regional context.
73. David J. Francis, *Uniting Africa: Building Regional Peace and Security Systems* (London and New York: Routledge, 2006), 29.
74. Komanyane, personal interview, Geneva, 2013.
75. Sameul M. Makinda and Wafula F. Okumu, *The African Union: Challenges of Globalization, Security and Governance* (London and New York: Routledge, 2008), 32–33.
76. Francis, *Uniting Africa*, 29.
77. Chris Landsberg, *The Quiet Diplomacy of Liberation: International Politics and South Africa's Transition* (Johannesburg: Jacana Media, 2004), 193–196.
78. For an overview of Thabo Mbeki's pre-presidential portfolio, see Sean Jacobs and Richard Calland, "Thabo Mbeki: Myth and Context", in *Thabo Mbeki's World: the Politics and Ideology of the South African President*, eds. Sean Jacobs and Richard Calland (Pietermaritzburg: University of Natal Press, 2002), 1–24; also see John Siko, "ANC Foreign Policy Making the Mbeki Period: More Democratic or Less", *South African Journal of International Affairs* 21, no. 3 (2014): 335–349.

66   T. GWATIWA

79. Olusegun Obasanjo, *Speech at the Golden Jubilee of the OAU/AU* (Geneva: UNOG, 2014). In this unscripted speech Obasanjo stated that the transformative conferencing and summitry was involved in resulted from interacting with Mbeki and Bouteflika during the 1970s. He admits that they saw the need to transform the continent then. Curiously he did not mention their relationship with Muammar Gaddafi. (Perhaps it is for good reasons because they were ever suspicious of him).
80. Chris Landsberg, "An African 'Concert of Powers?' Nigeria and South Africa's Construction of the AU and NEPAD", in *Gulliver's Troubles: Nigeria's Foreign Policy After the Cold War*, eds. Adeyeke Adebajo and Abdul Raufu Mustapha (Pietermaritzburg: University of Kwazulu Natal Press, 2008).
81. Landsberg, "An African Concert of Powers?", 205.
82. Ansah Akuffo, "Human Security and International Cooperation".
83. Francis, *Uniting Africa*.
84. African Union, *Strengthening the Partnerships Management and Coordination Capacity of the African Union: Evaluation of Africa's Strategic Partnerships*, Draft Final Revised Report (Addis Ababa: November 2014). Section 76 of the report states that "[the] partnership has been largely initiated through the personal commitments of former President Obasanjo of Nigeria and former President Mbeki of South Africa, on the African side, and former President Lula of Brazil and late President Chavez of Venezuela...".
85. Mehari T. Maru, IGAD special adviser and former AU programme director, Addis Ababa, December 2015.

CHAPTER 4

Agential Challenges Within African Regionalism and Security

Dynamics of peace and security in Africa perplex many observers. At worst, they buffet the expectations of the foremost minds in international security. A leading duo in the domain of critical security once stated that "Africa is a pessimist's paradise".[1]

The continent's inability to building effective security systems or emulate the West, as some expect, seems equally daunting to those in the traditional security domain (i.e., realists). To that effect Randall Schweller argued that operating "...in an ideal environment for predation, 'Third World' regional powers...should provide an 'easy test' for the realist proposition that states will move quickly and resolutely to fill local power vacuums", he wondered why "regional powers such as...Nigeria, have made no attempt to gobble up their weak neighbours".[2] Such exasperation is justifiable, especially given that most students of international relations assume that the AU is modelled after the EU, and that African agents generally seek to emulate their Western or Eastern counterparts. Moreover, from a Western lens, why would a region with capable states (South Africa, Algeria, Nigeria Ethiopia, and Egypt) still be struggling to underwrite peace and security throughout the continent? Why do conflicts prevail even after the AU institutionalised up a formidable and sometimes successful framework to quell them? Why does the AU, as of the 2010s, seem unable to effectively deal with conflicts resulting in foreign powers intervening on their behalf? To address these questions, it

---

© The Author(s), under exclusive license to Springer Nature
Switzerland AG 2022
T. Gwatiwa, *The African Union and African Agency in International Politics*, https://doi.org/10.1007/978-3-030-87805-4_4

67

68   T. GWATIWA

is important to examine the institutional framework of the AU as well as the role of major member states.

It is common to come across statements implying that "the AU is a shadow of its former self". Indeed, there has been a decline in the AU's ability to deal with different forms of conflict in the continent. Similarly, its tense relationship with the United Nations Security Council (UNSC) has gained publicity. Yet, in the early years of the AU there was unquestionable optimism about the organization's ability to address conflict in the continent.[3] There were expectations that the then-emerging security regime (i.e., the African Peace and Security Architecture) would be sustainable and bring the organisation on par with its global counterparts.[4]

The optimism and the lofty expectations fuelled the scurrilous and splenetic criticism of the AU in the aftermath of the Western intervention in Libya in 2011. In fact, leading scholars questioned the role and capability of the AU and its major states in light of the 2011 debacle.[5] The AU Commission, for its part, also felt short-changed by its international partners.[6] Just before the COVID-19 pandemic, the AU failed to intervene in a political crisis in Burundi—a small state where it had previously intervened[7]—to thwart ambitions of a despot. It was COVID-19 that eventually came to the citizens' rescue. The foregoing developments raise questions about the agential position and role of the AU.

The next sections of this chapter provide a partial explain the agential challenges facing the African Union. The chapter essentially paints a picture of an organisation which agency is hampered by structural and substantive institutional factors.

Agency in Regional Security Systems: Leadership, Roles and Burden Sharing

African regional security is premised on the notion of collective security. Collective security is a legally binding agreement between states (that are not necessarily like-minded)—to not use force to resolve current or future disputes, and to act collectively against those states that break this rule.[8] Aligning with this logic, African states have relinquished part of their juridical and empirical sovereignty to the African Union and subregional organisation, with the corollary that these organisations then define the limits of the use of force.[9] Consequently, using such instruments as the Constitutive Act, the PSC Protocol and the CADSP, the AU and subregional organisations provide politico-juridical umbrella under which compliance is rewarded and dissent is punished. These rewards and punishments are however quite daunting for a relatively young region such as Africa.[10] This is exacerbated by the nascence and concomitant fragility of Africa regional security systems. More importantly, there is no discernible leadership in the continent's collective security arrangement.

Leadership is an important element of a collective security system. Typically, collective security systems rely on "...the major actors within the system accepting its legitimacy and responding together to punish those who did not".[11] For instance, until *Brexit*, European regional security systems were propelled by the twin-leadership afforded by Britain and France.[12] However, there are necessary conditions under which such leadership can thrive.

First, states in that region must be content with the territorial status quo as well as the use of force in dealing with such issues. Secondly, states must have a consensus on what aggression means and in which instances member states must act against others. Third, all member states (including those not sharing the *raison d'etre*) must comply with the main regional position and avoid supporting dissent or aggression. Finally, and most importantly, all member states and especially strong powers must commit their armed forces and resources, or cede them to others, to deal with security challenges.[13] This does not imply that this is a clear-cut formula that cannot be altered, but this is the type of regional security that has worked in various regions. This has not been necessarily the case in Africa.

ALLIANCES AND COALITIONS IN REGIONAL SECURITY

States often rely on alliances and coalitions to carry out security operations in various parts of the world. Alliances usually involve formal agreements between like-minded states for purposes of pursuing international or regional security goals, enhancing military power and coordinating deployments.[14] They usually revolve around a known or defined threat. For instance, in its early epoch, the existence of NATO revolved around the Soviet threat.[15] An alliance requires at least one or two states, especially the hegemonic power, to commit to use force when necessary; but such comes with a commitment to protect certain interests.[16] The use of alliances has not been prominent in Africa even though some scholars posit that they have manifested sporadically across the continent.[17] In empirical terms, these have not been clear or at least publicly acknowledged and encouraged as a matter of regional policy. If anything, as my research suggests, African agents are often unwilling to replicate Western practices which have caused insecurity and instability in various parts of the world. This also applies to the idea of coalitions, although Africa toyed with the idea briefly.

Africa's most famed coalition experiment is the short-lived African Capacity for Immediate Response to Crisis (ACIRC). Coalitions, which became popular after the early 1990s, are ad hoc arrangements aimed at a specific security campaign or operation.[18] They often help navigate controversies—surrounding legality and legitimacy.[19] States can also use coalitions when controversies and disagreements arise within an alliance.[20] ACIRC was an emblematic AU experimentation with the notion of coalitions.[21] The underlying notion was that it would be an arrangement through which a group of willing states can launch operations as a precursor to AU operations. However, this experiment unsettled several African states, and the AU eventually abandoned the model.

BURDEN SHARING AND ROLE PLAYING IN REGIONAL SECURITY

Burden sharing and role playing are essential elements of regional security systems. These are often assumed by prominent actors in each regional security system. Africa is a large continent, yet only a certain number of states can be expected to act on various security issues. There are two primary approaches to this. The most prominent is the "pure public goods model" within which there is the "exploitation hypothesis", which posits that larger members of the security system inadvertently bear a disproportionate share of the burden.[22] For instance, in the NATO arrangement the US usually bears most of the burden followed by major actors such as the United Kingdom, France and Germany.[23] A striking feature of this arrangement is that non-contributors cannot be excluded from the public benefits—i.e. defence and security—of these operations.[24] The second model, the joint-product model, advances the notion of "lumpy goods", which posits that a target or threshold must be achieved for any member of the group to benefit from collective effort.[25] In this case, a state is expected to contribute to the production of a lumpy good if the aggregation of the other actors does not make their donation unnecessary.[26] This means that each country makes contributions based on the total amount of materials from which it can draw as well as its aggregate security capabilities. However, role playing and burden sharing in African regional security dynamics does not necessarily align to this logic.

Politics of African Regional Security

The conventional way to understand states' approach to role playing and burden sharing in regional security is to consider the domestic determinants of their foreign and security policies. This approach often premised on the notion of "audience costs", broadly suggests that leaders who make international threats and/or commitments and back down can be punished by their domestic constituents.[27] This can apply to both democracies and autocracies, wherein leaders are beholden to the interests of various elites.[28] Yet, ideological leanings of governments, including democracies, can also vary; with conservative regimes often favouring interventionist approaches to regional security problems.[29]

In non-African contexts, evidence suggests that most democratic states participate in regional or international security issues in relation to election cycles. Kisangani and Pickering argue that democratic leaders are less likely to deploy armed forces over low-politics issues such as "humanitarian suffering" if elections are less than one year away.[30] This is not necessarily the case in African states.

African regional security cooperation manifests differently from Western-mediated expectations. The dons of international security from Hans Morgenthau[31] to Randall Schweller[32] exasperate at Africa's inability, which is essentially unwillingness, to emulate the West. The West yearns for this duplication because it is a way of defining itself in world politics.[33] However, more pointedly, African security cooperation varies from Western expectations because it is intertwined with statemaking. As Ayoob posited, "much of the activity concerned with state making is carried out under the guise of a search for security".[34] Even when African states contribute or participate in regional security, they are more concerned about their own state-making vulnerabilities which emanate from ramifications of decolonisation.[35] One-dimensional security inputs may be misconstrued for genuine regional security commitments. That is why most African states make helter-skelter inputs into African regional commitments. A state may be a commitment for a couple of years and totally disengage in a different epoch. This explains the fluctuating contributions of different African countries, such as South Africa, Nigeria, Botswana, Senegal, Angola, Egypt and others in various peace support operations.

The difficulties in commitments to regional security are also evident in the case of leading states or the so-called regional hegemons. Although some states such as South Africa, Nigeria, Algeria and Ethiopia have increasingly presented themselves as "leaders",[36] or "hegemons", they are far from being regional hegemons. Some scholars often characterise South Africa as a hegemon in Africa.[37] Others argue that it acts alongside Nigeria exercising a form of twin hegemony.[38] Most of these works ignore the standard criterion used as a test of hegemonic leadership[39] (discussed below). If such claims have credence in the economic sphere—as is often the basis of this argument—those claims are not translatable to political and security cooperation because "most decisions by AU institutions are based on consensus rather than competitive voting. Even when AU members do vote, the votes usually affirm agreements already reached informally [by consensus]", which forces "powerful African states...to treat each AU member as an equal".[40] Indeed, South Africa experimented with a realist approach to multilateral cooperation but encountered hostility from other African states, starting with its campaign for Nkosazana Dlamini-Zuma's leadership of the AU Commission,[41] and its ambitious exploits in West Africa. Nigeria has also experimented with continental leadership, but its influence remains confined to West Africa, while playing a symbolic role in other parts of Africa—especially eastern and central Africa.

From one standpoint, Africa's unwillingness—or inability—to emulate the West and other regions corrodes its agency. The gist of that argument would be that the African Union could do better if it emulated the West or East. However, it is imperative to examine the empirical dynamics of African security and examine how each element relates to its agential capacity and potential.

Empirics of African Collective Security and Implications for African Agency

The dwindling nimbus of African regional security is most conspicuous in its decreasing ability to deal with conflicts. This contrasts with the honeymoon phase in the early days when the AU launched successful missions in places such as Burundi and Comoros. However, as the region incurs dwindling prospects, it is useful to examine principles and practices that affect African agency in multilateralism.

The AU Peace and Security Council and the African Security Regime

One of the biggest challenges in African security relates to its security regime and security instruments. The notion of a regime is herein understood as "institutions possessing norms, principles, decision-rules and procedures which facilitate a convergence of expectations".[42] One of the overarching principles that developed in the post-OAU era is the intolerance for unconstitutional changes of government.[43] Moreover, the AU reshaped itself into a consolidated custodian of a new and promising security regime.[44] This ipso facto not only relates to the norms but the instrument around which these procedures, principles and decision-rules revolve—the African Union Peace and Security Council (PSC). The principles and decision-making mechanisms of the PSC significantly shape the prospects of the AU's agential situs.

The PSC's agential capacity can be understood in light of its egalitarian principles and impractical decision-making process. Part of the agential standing rests on the composition and role of members of the PSC. The council does not have permanent members (except Nigeria, explained below). This means that there is no group of states that can constantly and consistently influence the dynamics and politics of African regional security. This also means that major states such as South Africa, Nigeria, Algeria, Ethiopia and Egypt are unable to provide effective leadership. Yet, the same states actively and consistently seek to influence the same dynamics at the subregional level. This implies that the PSC enables a form of organised hypocrisy wherein the AU undercuts the empirics that unfold at the subregional level.

Moreover, the PSC operates on an egalitarian principle which places every state on the same level and does not provide room for hegemonic leadership. This means that bigger or richer do not exert any profound influence on continental politics. This does not mean that any of the big states do not wish to exert such influence, but a decision taken by states prior to 2002 inhibited any aspirants from exercising any form of hegemony. Without neither hegemonic leadership nor a concert of powers, all decisions are made based on consensus. Most decisions acted on by the PSC are usually already agreed to in the Permanent Representatives Council (PRC).[45] Due to this principle, big states that were the biggest material and financial contributors to African security have decreased their contributions since circa 2010. They have opted to increase their participation in the UN peace operations because, unlike the AU, the UN is consistent in reimbursing contingent-owned equipment (COE) contributed to global peace operations by various states.[46] However, it is the lack of hegemonic leadership in the AU which appears to dent African agency.

The limiting of hegemony in African regional security appears to be a more plausible explanation of African agential limitations. Egalitarianism in African multilateralism was instituted in between the late 1990s and early 2000s as African elites reified the transition from the OAU to the AU. There were two major rationales for institutionalising this principle. First, according to one of the AU's first consultants, it was because African states did not wish to suffer at the hands of fellow states what they had suffered from the US and European [former colonial] powers.[47] (Western jingoism in African security and politics is well documented[48]). A more robust proclamation stated that major states' financial contributions will not translate into power. The main target was the fear that Libyan leader, Muammar Gaddafi, had overt hegemonic ambitions over the rest of Africa.[49] It was even codified in AU working conditions that no employee would be allowed to represent the interests of their member states.[50] However, it was not only Libya that felt the pinch of this principle.

Nigeria and South Africa both attempted to gain permanent seats in the PSC, with differing results. Only Nigeria succeeded in its attempt. Nigeria negotiated with fellow ECOWAS states that since it bore over 70 per cent of the regional bill, it needed to permanently occupy one of the four seats designated for West Africa.[51] The idea behind this move was that Nigeria would continue to provide the hegemonic leadership that it had previously demonstrated in West Africa. Nigeria had previously overseen efficient role playing and burden sharing in the Economic

Community of West African States Monitoring Group (ECOMOG) missions and beyond.[52] That role playing and burden sharing would, ideally, be enabled by the fact that one of the three remaining seats would be occupied by the ECOWAS state chairing its troika. South Africa failed to secure the same deal from Southern African states. SADC member states quipped that all states were equal in their region.[53] Even if South Africa had secured such a deal for purposes of countering Nigeria in the PSC, it would have had difficulty exerting the same amount of control over role playing and burden sharing among SADC states. Around the same time, the SADC had taken the decision that no member state would be allowed to fund more than 20 per cent of the operational budget.[54] South Africa suffered a strategic loss to Nigeria in the PSC. However, this was something that would affect the general architecture of the AU's most powerful decision-making body in peace and security.

No Hegemonic Leadership

Whether or not African states can efficiently contribute to African peace operations is not a necessary question. Close to 12 African states are among the top contributors to UN missions. As Table 4.1 shows, no less than six states are able to provide the major requirements of AU PSOs (Peace Support Operations). These are: expert contribution, troop contributions, strategic airlift and staff officers. Several other African countries, such as Rwanda, Cameroon, Niger, Togo and Zambia are significant overall contributors to UN missions. This shows that African states can, under certain conditions, contribute to continental security. It is imperative to examine why the listed states (below) can contribute significantly to the UN and not the AU. Is it a question of money or other factors?

Lack of hegemonic leadership is a major impediment to African security. The fact that the PSC does not have a clearly defined set of major powers that can provide [hegemonic] leadership at a political and security level provides a lacuna especially in terms of political will. However, due to the limitations set by principles and decision-making at the PSC, most states are unwilling to go further than the routine of the talk-shop that the AU has become.

Inconsistent role playing and uneven burden sharing in AU operations by major African states is a key impediment. Some African states with capabilities have reduced or stopped their contributions to AU peace operations. The most notable of these missing actors are major powers

76   T. GWATIWA

Table 4.1   Capabilities of major African states according to AU/UN peace operations requirements

Country	Observers and police	UN Military Experts on Mission (UNMEM)	UN troop contributions	Staff officers	Overall army strength	Strategic airlift capacity (heavy and medium aircraft / helicopters)
South Africa	50	14	1152	21	89, 550	**Heavy (0)**, **Medium (42)**: 2 C130B Hercules, 4 C130BZ Hercules; 36 Oryx helicopters
Algeria*	–	3	–	–	280, 000	**Heavy (25)**: 3 Ilyushin-76 MD Candid, 8 Ilyushin-76 TD Candid; 14 Mi-26T2 Halo helicopters **Medium (20)**: 8 C-130H Hercules, 6 C-130H-30, 2 Lockheed L100-30s; 4 Ka-32T Helix helicopters
Nigeria	216	30	191	31	143, 000	**Heavy (0)**, **Medium (17)**: 1 C-130H Hercules, 1 C-130H-30 Hercules, 3 Aeritalia G.222; 3 AgustaWestland AW101 helicopters, 5 H215/Eurocopter AS332 Super Puma helicopters, 3 Dauphin AS365N helicopters, 1 Mi-171Sh helicopter, 1 Mi-171E helicopter

(continued)

Table 4.1 (continued)

Country	Observers and police	UN Military Experts on Mission (UNMEM)	UN troop contributions	Staff officers	Overall army strength	Strategic airlift capacity (heavy and medium aircraft / helicopters)
Egypt	754	66	2294	78	917, 500	**Heavy (21)**: 2 Ilyushin-76MF Candid; 3 CH-47C Chinook helicopters, 16 CH-47D Chinook helicopters, **Medium (101)**: 21 C-130H Hercules, 3 C-130H-30 Hercules; 2 Sikorsky AS-61 helicopters, 24 Commando helicopters, 40 Mi-8T Hip helicopters, 3 Mi-17-1V helicopters, 4 S-70 Black Hawk helicopters, 4 UH-60L Black Hawk helicopters
Ethiopia	54	94	8157	112	138, 000	**Heavy (0)**, **Medium (28)**: 3 Antonov An-12 Cubs, 2 C-130B Hercules, 2 C-130E Hercules, 2 Lockheed L-100-30s; 12 Mi-8 Hip helicopters, 1 AgustaWestland AW19 helicopter, 6 SA316 Alouette III helicopters

(continued)

78   T. GWATIWA

Table 4.1 (continued)

Country	Observers and police	UN Military Experts on Mission (UNMEM)	UN troop contributions	Staff officers	Overall army strength	Strategic airlift capacity (heavy and medium aircraft / helicopters)
Angola	-	-	-	-	107, 000	Heavy (4): 4 Ilyushin-76TD Candid; Medium (70): 6 Antonov Ant-12 Cubs; 8 Eurocopter AS565 Panther helicopters, 4 AgustaWestland AW139 helicopters, 9 SA316 Alouette III helicopters, 8 SA342M Gazelle helicopters, 27 Mi-8 Hip helicopters, 8 Mi-171Sh Terminators helicopters

Source The author's compilation is based on the UN DPKO's contribution data combined with data from the IISS's Military Balance (2002–2017). AU Data is not publicly available and not shared. Each capability is calculated on an average factor of 5.0. Data from Algeria is asterisked because its constitution does not allow it to deploy troops abroad but is a serial contributor to AU PSOs

such as South Africa, Nigeria and Egypt. There are two main reasons for this inaction.

First, there is fierce competition between major and capable states. Fierce competition is evident between South Africa and Nigeria. Adebajo and Landsberg posit that during the "the golden age of [African] diplomacy", the two states worked like a "twin hegemony" governed by a memorandum of understanding signed between their respective foreign services.[55] However, the international community's preferential treatment of South Africa irked Nigerian.[56] The author also observed this fierce competition during his fieldwork in Addis Ababa. Anti-Southern African sentiments have increased since South Africa fielded Nkosazana Dlamini-Zuma for the leadership of the position of Chairperson of the

AU Commission. This was considered a breach of an unwritten rule that big states should not vie for top post.[57] One West African ambassador stated that South Africa cannot be trusted as a lead state because it represents Western values and agendas.[58] Yet, other African states are irritated by the South Africa-Nigeria rivalry because they view it as an agency-limiting rivalry. An ambassador of a Francophone African country stated that this rivalry, and the concomitant leadership vacuum, made Francophone African states more vulnerable to France's foreign policy jingoism.[59] However, Nigeria and South Africa are not the only states with leadership capacity in the continent. Other big states such as Algeria and Egypt have a different approach to leadership in African regionalism and security (discussed in the substantive chapters). A more potent imperative is a discussion of how fierce competition affects African agency in global affairs.

There is a triangular rivalry in Africa's most capable states which has a much more debilitating effect on African regionalism. This relates to the benign competition between Nigeria, South Africa and Egypt for a permanent seat in the United Nations Security Council (UNSC). Describing that competition, Adebajo states that "cynics dismissed Nigeria as too 'anarchic', Egypt as too 'Arab' and South Africa as too 'albinocratic'".[60] Presently, Nigeria is dealing with its governmental and security challenges such as ethnopolitical schisms, corruption and the Boko Haram terrorist threat. These raises questions about the leadership credentials of Nigeria in relation to the continental roadmaps on governance and security. The characterisation of Egypt as "too Arab" can be viewed from different angles. Compared to Algeria, Senegal, Libya and others, Egypt was the least committed country during the transition from the OAU to the AU. Its approach was considered lukewarm and lackadaisical.[61] Although it is part of the Big 5—i.e. the largest contributors to the AU Commission financing—Egypt does not exhibit any worthwhile material or resources contribution to African security, rather leaning towards UN contributions.[62] This is in stark contrast to its North African regional counterpart, Algeria.

Surprisingly, Algeria is one of, if not the foremost contributor to AU security. Its political leadership and contributions (material and financial) are not accompanied by the rhetorical grand standing and pomposity of its counterparts such as Nigeria, Egypt and South Africa. It is surprising that Table 4.2 [by Williams and Boutellis] does not give due credit to Algeria's role, especially in Somalia, Sudan, Mali and CAR where

80 T. GWATIWA

Table 4.2 African Union peace support operations, 2003–2013

Mission	Duration	Size (approx. max)	Finance method	Key TCC	Main task
AU Mission in Burundi (AMIB)	2003–4	3250	TCC + donors	South Africa	Peacebuilding
AU Military Observer Mission in the Comoros (MIOC)	2004	14	TCCs	South Africa	Observation
AU Mission in Sudan (AMIS)	2004–7	c.7700	TCCs + EU + UN support packages	Nigeria, South Africa, Senegal, Ghana, Rwanda	Peacekeeping/ Civilian protection
Special Task Force Burundi	2006–9	c.750	TCC	South Africa	VIP protection
AU Mission for the Support to the Elections in the Comoros (AMISEC)	2006	1260	TCC + EU support	South Africa	Election monitor
AU Mission in Somalia (AMISOM)	2007–present	22,123	TCC + donors UN + donors	Uganda Burundi Kenya	Protection of government Counterinsurgency
AU Electoral and Security Assistance Mission to the Comoros (MAES)	2007–8	350	TCCs + EU + Arab League	South Africa Tanzania	Election support
Operation Democracy in Comoros	2008	1350 + 450 Comoros	TCCs + donors	Tanzania Sudan	Enforcement
African-led International Support Mission for Mali (AFISMA)	2013	9620	TCCs + donors + AU	Chad Nigeria	Enforcement/ stabilisation

(continued)

4 AGENTIAL CHALLENGES WITHIN AFRICAN ... 81

Table 4.2 (continued)

Mission	Duration	Size (approx. max)	Finance method	Key TCC	Main task
African-led International Support Mission to the Central African Republic (MISCA)	2013	3652	TCCs + donors + AU	DRC, Republic of Congo, Cameroon and Gabon	Stabilisation

Source Paul D. Williams and Arthur Boutellis, "Partnership Peacekeeping, Challenges in the UN-AU Relationship", *African Affairs* 113, no. 451 (2014): 254–278

Algeria contributes financial, material and human resources in substantial proportions. However, it is imperative to provide a caveat on Algerian human resource contributions necessary. The constitution of Algeria prohibits the country from deploying troops outside the country, except in expert or advisory capacity.[63] Despite these limitations, Algeria remains a leading actor in terms of role playing and burden sharing in AU peace support operations. Documents viewed by the author at the AU, circa. 2016, show that Algeria's role playing and burden sharing prominently features in leading capacity in the areas of intelligence and informational support, logistical support and strategic airlift.[64] For some time, Algeria—and recently joined by Angola and Kenya—were the only countries that consistently contributed to the AU Peace Fund while the AU heavily relied on the EU-funded Africa Peace Facility.[65] This is a unique commitment given that Algeria, Angola and Kenya do not primarily feature in intra-continental hegemonic rivalry. Meanwhile, the rivalry primarily features between Nigeria, Egypt and South Africa which's commitment to African regionalism and security has dwindled and rekindles in sporadic cases, especially high-stakes issues that seem carefully selected to augment the incessant campaigns for a non-veto permanent seat at the UNSC. This implies that politics beyond the AU security systems, have a debilitating effect on African regional agency. The continent fails to augment its politics and security systems to position it to be a united and formidable front in global politics. Yet, while these states are engaged in UN-oriented

82   T. GWATIWA

politics, they ignore their capabilities that could improve their regional agency.

The abovementioned rivalry creates a lacuna in a key element of African regional strategic citizenship—i.e. strategic airlift. Strategic airlift has been axiomatic to every AU peace operation since the earliest missions. After the successes in Burundi and the Comoros, and the ambit of African participation in peace operations widened, strategic airlift became an sine quo as most troop contributing countries did not have the capacity to transport their troops, ordnance and ammunition to these missions. Table 4.1 highlights the varying capacities in strategic airlift using heavy and medium aircraft and helicopters. Circa 2007 when the African Union Mission in Somalia (AMISOM) began, only a handful states were willing to provide strategic airlift. However, in the run up to the African Union Mission in Sudan (AMIS I), fewer countries were willing to cede their material capabilities, even though South Africa, Nigeria, Algeria, Egypt, Senegal, Botswana, Cameroon, Zimbabwe and Ghana all possess C-130s and other usable aircraft. What Table 4.1 also highlights is the varying capacities between countries possessing strategic airlift capacities. Some countries such as Angola, Egypt and Algeria have heavy airlift and helicopters while others such as South Africa and Nigeria have no useful heavy aircraft. Others possess more medium aircraft which can be used within a deployment timeframe. This highlights the importance of coordination and collaboration in African peace support operations. This implies that while smaller states were willing to contribute military, police and civilian personnel, larger states are not willing to cede their aircraft for this element of strategic citizenship. This discordance in political will between less and more capable states inadvertently corroded the agential prospects of the organisation and continent. The obstacle to this seemingly obvious factor is attributable to the issue of costs.

Peace and security missions and operations place massive costs on contributing states. Typically, a regional organisation sets terms and standards for contingency owned equipment (COE) reimbursements. Those rates are primarily aligned to those of the United Nations, which have also been used for decades within Africa. However, the AU Commission, and indeed the Peace and Security Department have no fiscal resources; and are heavily reliant on donor funding. The external funding is mostly conditional—except in a few cases of funding from the Norwegian and German (GIZ) governments. However, this non-conditional funding is mostly aimed at quick impact projects (QIPs).[66] These do not include larger projects that directly relate to COE reimbursements. Ipso facto, this leaves the AU in a serious predicament regarding these reimbursements. This caused most traditional contributors to reduce their contributions.[67] The reluctance to continue these contributions due to limited reimbursements created a vacuum in African strategic citizenship.

In order to address this predicament, African actors sought external intervention. At this point most of Africa's patrons were not willing to commit their personnel and material resources in Africa. This was especially the case regarding the US, which had just launched its new Africa command. Although this was an opportunity to promote the command, it was controversial in Africa, and the US was committed to fighting terrorism in other parts of the world. The US decided to underwrite the troop and material contributions of small and medium African states. For instance, the US funded several countries' troop and strategic airlift missions (using C-130s) for the AU Mission in Sudan.[68] Some senior security experts view this as a capacity substitution. For instance, the then dean of the Military Attachés Association (MAA) characterised AU mission planning and implementation as a travesty in comparison to the much better planned ECOMOG and SADC missions.[69] The dean attributes this to ascriptions to non-committed states which do not implement various aspects of the continental security architecture—an appeasement policy of sorts. For instance, a central African state beguiled by regional politics, internal strife and a weak military was allowed to host the logistical headquarters of the African Standby Force failed to reify the assignment. This appeasement does not necessarily exist at the subregional level: weak and unstable states are rarely ever given key roles in regional security systems. This also implies that the appeasement of various states—especially weak and unstable ones—and the inability to extrapolate subregional efforts and capabilities to the continental level negatively affects the agential prospects of the continent. This results in the current situation whereby the AU still depends on NATO and the EU for support in strategic airlift and other forms of support. Suffices to argue that African agency stands at odd, not due to lack of capacity, but due to lack of political will.

Decimated Political Will in the Era of Democratisation

There has been a decline in AU member states' political will to contribute various resources to African regional security projects. This is attributable

84 T. GWATIWA

to the accentuation of audience costs in most African states. The early 1990s saw the advent of several types of democracies which broadened the scope of accountability in many African countries. However, the element of accountability also broadened from the early 2000s, under the aegis of the African Union's Constitutive Act and the African Peer Review Mechanism (APRM).[70] Strangely, this affected the volume of states' contributions to peace support operations.

Opposition parties and groups in states such as Nigeria, Ghana, Kenya and other traditional contributors strongly opposed the deployment of troops, material and disbursement of funds in instances where the national interest was not clear. In the words of a senior AU official, "before the spread of democracy many authoritarian governments and leaders found it easy to send troops to peace missions. Now they face [formidable] opposition in their parliaments".[71] This implies that it was easier for non-democratic governments to support African security projects, hence augmenting regional agency. This not only occurred in the case of big states. Medium and small states also experienced quandaries in their contributions.

In some instances, democratic systems would frustrate states to the point where they rescind contributions previously authorised under proper democratic processes. For instance, Botswana contributed troops as well as provided a strategic airlift in the AU Mission in Sudan (AMIS II). Shortly thereafter, a senior officer (a major) of the Botswana Defence Force (BDF) was killed during deployment in Darfur. The loss of a single soldier caused widespread furore. This was surprising given that the BDF had previously lost a few soldiers during a SADC deployment in Lesotho (1998), as well as few others in previous UN deployments in Somalia and Darfur. However, there was so much furore that then President Festus Mogae promptly withdrew the BDF from AMIS II.[72] The key source of pressure was the media and civil society, which were not as active under the previous democratic government.

Authoritarian and hybrid governments are currently the largest contributors to African peace missions and AU security projects. These include states such as Rwanda, Uganda, Burundi, Ethiopia and several others. These governments do not necessarily deal with accountability issues. This does not imply that there is no opposition to their activities, but the institutional matrix and constitutional frameworks in those states do not obligate leaders to heed opposing voices. This mainly applies in the Great Lakes Region where autocratic governments in contribute troops to AU missions in Darfur (now UNAMID) as well as AMISOM and maintain their commitments even though they lose large numbers of troops.[73] They may have distinct reasons for sending troops abroad, but Museveni, Kagame and (former Burundian leader) Nkurunziza have their reasons for sending troops abroad.

The most common reason is that sending troops to AU missions helps manage politics, rivalry and dissent among senior members of the security sector. Dissenting securocrats in those three countries have often caused instability in the political sphere. Other states such as (pre-2021) Ethiopia were ruled by large coalitions which shared similar views on grand strategy and concerns about terrorism and instability in neighbouring states. Moreover, the processes of deploying troops do not require the hassle of lengthy processes, and constitutional obstacles found in democracies. In some instances, autocratic leaders had a long history of commitment to Pan-Africanism and African regional security. Ironically, the absence of democracies has been an enabler to African regional agency. However, these forms of governance have not only become unpopular but have become an aberration under various AU instruments of governance and security.

Another incentive for sending troops to such missions is the external funding from foreign powers. First, for many years the European Union paid allowances of troops deployed in AU missions in Somalia and Darfur. The allowance, then over €700, was higher than what most troops are paid in their home countries (discussed in Chapter 6). Moreover, this provided some form of budgetary support for the states struggling to pay their troops regular salaries. For this reason, the external funding cushioned the cost of maintaining a portion of these militaries. Second, the deployment also resulted in training from various states such as the US, the United Kingdom, France, Portugal and China. This also covered the cost of training under regular programmes. Moreover, the multilateral forum(s) not only broadened the number of countries offering training, but also entailed training troops in more specialties than those provided by traditional bilateral training agreements. This way various troop contributing countries reaped benefits while also promoting African agency, albeit in a smaller scale. In this manner, African agency is not necessarily a unidirectional exercise, but also entails a reciprocal process from which contributing countries benefit immensely. However, this participation in African missions by small states should be viewed in broader scope in order to determine whether it fully captures African agency.

The dominant role of externally supported small and medium African states does not augment African agency in substantial measures. First, and most importantly, the gap created by the lack of political will among major states implies that it is not that the major states cannot fully own these missions. This results in capacity substitution by external powers. External powers such as the US, the United Kingdom, France, Italy and (more recently Russia, China, and Turkey) are interested in these missions because of the rare earth minerals, petroleum and strategic resources in these areas. Thus, by absconding and leaving this role to smaller and medium states, big African states are largely responsible for undermining African agency in international affairs. Second, smaller states do not possess the diplomatic, military, material and financial capacity to enhance African agency in the same manner that major states would. The fact that they are externally supported has implications for African leadership and ownership in the security sphere. The conditions attached to foreign assistance weakens African agency in the key missions—in Darfur and Somalia (where most foreign powers have vested interests). For instance, in the case of US support, beneficiary states often lose control of the mission planning and design. The US mostly insists on influencing the architecture of peace support operations, even when they diverge to AU blueprints. Moreover, due to the limited capabilities of these small states, the provision of peace support intelligence largely aligns to US, French and UK interests in these peace missions. Most importantly, the way the external powers dictate the use of funding sometimes deviates from the mission plans of various African senior officers in the AU chain of command. However, African actors—largely dependent on foreign assistance—have little, if any, latitude to resist these conditional predicaments.

Financial Constraints

Financial contributions are a major impediment to African participation in AU peace operations. For nearly a decade, AU peace support operations were bankrolled by external parties. Exceptions were the AU Mission in Burundi (AMIB) and the AU Mission in the Comoros (AMISEC) where most African states funded their participation, with minimal external support (see Table 4.2). The decline in African states' self-funding between 2002 to 2010 deserves explanation.

African states do not necessarily lack the financial and material capacity to effectuate peace and security operations in the continent. If states were willing to fully fund the short-lived African Capacity for the Immediate Response to Crises (ACIRC) as a self-sustaining force for thirty days or more,[74] then there must be another reason for the reluctance to fully fund AU peace support operations. Granted, the majority of the ACIRC participants are financially capable in their individual and collective capacity.

ACIRC was the brainchild of South Africa—a relatively wealthy African state with unmasked hegemonic ambitions. The other volunteers were Algeria, Angola, Chad, Ethiopia, Guinea, Mauritania, Niger, Senegal, Sudan, Rwanda, Tanzania and Uganda. These not only have some of Africa's strong militaries (perhaps with the exception of Uganda and Guinea) but are key participations and financial contributors to AU peace support operations. For instance, Algeria has been a leading contributor to the Africa Peace Fund, even when most states did not contribute to the fund. From 2014, Angola has been contributing an average of $10 million to the fund.[75] Tanzania not only contributed and co-planned key AU missions such as AMIB, AMISEC and MAES (see Table 4.2), but also has an interventionist history in neighbouring states.[76] Chad emerged as a key state following the demise of Gaddafi's Libya, and has been a key contributor to the African-led Mission in Mali (AFISMA) and other security initiatives in the Sahel (see Table 4.2). Ethiopia has been a key and lead African state in Somalia and Sudan. Senegal recently led an ECOWAS operation to depose former Gambian dictator Yayah Jammeh.[77] The fact that these countries were willing to fund their own interventions as recently as 2013–2015 demonstrates capability. If that is the case, what causes the generic lacklustre participation in AU-based security project?

The main hindrance to African funding of the AU is caused by several issues. First, the AU is yet to institutionalise a credible mechanism for reimbursing states for their contingency-owned equipment (discussed earlier sections). In the current setting, various states feel that there are no benefits for participation. Different ambassadors and security experts often compare the AU process to the UN process, which they deem more reliable. Second, some states are not reluctant to contribute if there is no reliable mechanism to account for the funding disbursed to the AU peace operations. There have been several instances where millions of dollars earmarked for troops in Darfur (Sudan) and Somalia disappeared unaccounted for. In a specific case, an AU official (of Nigerian nationality) tasked with disbursing troop payments in Darfur "disappeared" with $10 million. Although this scandal did not make international headlines, it has fed into frustration among member states about accountability within the AU Commission.

Third, some AU member states are of the position that other member states and regions profit from conflict and instability. A Southern African ambassador cited her country's frustration over the double standards over the peace process in South Sudan, where their former president was, at the time, the chief mediator in the process.[78] This, and other peace support projects, caused the referent state to revise their policy position on the AU. The referent state resultantly reduced their material and financial contributions to the AU.

Fourth, some states are reluctant to make direct contributions to continental projects while they have domestic governmental and fiscal obligations. They would rather advocate external funding and support. However, domestic obligations are often a ruse. The preference for external funding is largely rooted in national political philosophies, policies and idiosyncrasies. The case of the Francophone states is most illustrative. A senior AU official explained an informational challenge in AU policymaking processes. He indicated that most staffers seconded from Francophone states habitually pass information to Paris and other European capitals before the AU can take a position on a policy issue.[79] This informational challenge is attributable to the dynamics of French neo-colonialism (described in Chapter 3) where the referent states are required to regularly pass political and strategic information to Paris. If the discussion(s) relate to Francophone states, this gives France an informational urge; with the result that France begins to mobilise financing and strategic leadership from within the EU. This does not imply that France is the only external funder benefiting from this dynamic. Other states such as Germany, China, Japan, India, the UK and others have a network of Africans with whom they exchange strategic information.

External funding and support from various states play a significant role, albeit as capacity substitution. China, the US, France, Germany, the European Union, Norway, Japan, India and emerging powers such as Turkey are the key funders of AU peace operations. These states have stylized themselves as "partners". These partners provide funding individually or collectively depending on the case. The funding may or may not entail conditionality, depending on the funder's strategic policy and politics.

Some funders are stringent on conditionality. The US has the most stringent conditions on their funding and external support. The conditions are purely designed against the funder's hard core strategic interests and very little regard for the receiver's interests (see Chapter 8). For many years the EU placed moderately to mild conditionality on its funding and support to the AU. The EU has accentuated the conditionality aspect of its support in the interest of accountability as well as "allow the AU to play a greater role in its peace and security operations". Conversely, Norway and Japan provide targeted funding for projects that are designed by both parties. These projects usually fall within the post-conflict reconstruction and development (PCRD) and human security dimensions.

Surprisingly, Germany and China have a totally different approach to funding the AU. The GIZ (German development aid) provides the AU with unconditional funding for different forms of projects, particularly quick impact projects. China also provides unconditional funding. It gives an average of $200 million to the AU Commission and does not place any conditions on the way the funding is used.

All this funding is capacity substitution. There is no evidence that African states cannot fully fund these operations. As the evidence demonstrates in the preceding sections, the major challenge lies with African states' inability to coordinate funding. Most importantly, the recent "Kagame reforms" not only demonstrated the will of African states to play a greater role, but that the previous challenges were mainly due to institutional design flaws. However, the abovementioned flaws were not a panacea. They are a step in a possibly better agential development: which might be fully realised in the next decade or more. However, more importantly, the preceding argument demonstrates that funding is closely tied to political will or lack thereof.

Mutual Suspicion

Political dynamics within the AU affect African agency in different ways. The key source of agential slackness is the lack of pragmatism among capable states. Major African states are suspicious of each other's motives and activities in their relative "spheres of influence". This is particularly the case for Nigeria—which exercises clear hegemony in West Africa; South Africa—which is struggling to exercise actual hegemony in Southern Africa; and Ethiopia—which seeks to restore its unfinished ancient or historical hegemony in the Horn of Africa.

Most of these suspicions started to accentuate after the golden age of the AU (i.e. 2000 to 2009). Nigeria and South Africa have had frictional diplomatic and strategic encounters in West Africa. For instance, when conflict erupted in Cote d'Ivoire, in 2011, South Africa sent a naval vessel—the SAS Drakensberg—to the Ivorian coast. This angered Nigeria and leading ECOWAS states, which accused South Africa of encroaching into its sphere of influence. However, the SAS Drakensburg remained docked at the coast until France fully paid its bill.[80] South Africa has also made strategic forays into central Africa, with embarrassing effects. Prior to the rebel insurgence, the Central African Republic (CAR) government had a military agreement with South Africa to train its troops.[81] Some officials argue that prior to France's launch of *Operation Sangaris*, the then CAR leader had appealed to South Africa to deploy more troops.[82] Yet, this perspective leaves out the fact that there were several high profile South Africans (linked to the ruling African National Congress) with mining interests in the CAR. Following the killing of 13 South African troops during the insurgency in the CAR, states such as France, Ethiopia and Nigeria accused South Africa of encroaching beyond its sphere of influence. This mutual suspicion also fed into the progress of some continental security projects.

Mutual suspicion between states frustrated the development of ACRIC. Nigeria largely absconded from the ACRIC project largely due to its suspicion of South Africa. In justifying its absence from ACRIC, the Nigerian foreign minister made indirect remarks to South African leadership.[83] Correspondingly, during the author's research, the then Nigerian ambassador to the AU/Ethiopia expressed deep suspicion of South Africa's activities all over the continent. The anomaly is that these attacks seem uniquely directed towards South Africa, especially since Nkosazana Dlamini-Zuma's ascension to the AU Commission premiership. This antagonism is also attributable to Nigeria and South Africa's competition for a permanent seat in the UN Security Council. On the other hand, Algeria mistrusts Egypt. This attributable to Egypt's track record in African multilateralism (see Chapter 3 on the history of OAU/AU-LAS relations). Algeria was also distrustful of Libya during Muammar Gaddafi's reign. These suspicions—often caused by a perceived strategic overreach—tend to inhibit candid debates and pragmatic approaches to African security challenges. This resultantly corrodes the mantra of

"African solutions to African problems". This lack of unity creates a lacuna that widens the gap of African agency in international politics, because the international agency ought to start at the continental level.

Due to a lack of unity on core issues among major or capable states, the AU commission continues to depend on external funding, even though more could be sourced from within the continent. As of 2014, the AU has about 12 major partners who are also key funders: China, Japan, the EU, the US, Organization of Islamic States (OIC), the Arab League and Norway, among others.[84] The main funder is the European Union which pays the stipends of troops in key peace support operations in Somalia and Sudan.[85] African states, and the AU, are manifestly comfortable with this form of funding. Different policymakers often pointed towards the satisfaction with the EU's relaxed conditions. However, as to be demonstrated in Chapter 6, the EU is not entirely comfortable with the status quo.

On the other hand, the US often provides in-kind support to some missions—especially the AU Mission in Somalia (AMISOM). A common practice in the US's support is to provide funding directly to a troop contributing country (TCC) when the need arises. This trend emerged in the early 2000s after the AU and the US strongly disagreed over how its funding should be used in AU peace operations.[86] Due to its political stringency, the US often dictates how its funding should be used. This results in a situation where the AU cannot adequately pool all the funding from partners as well as coordinate some of its activities. This directly affects the AU's agential aspirations expressed in the desire to own and lead its regional programmes and projects. This can be interpreted as the anti-agential effect of external financial support. However, there is also a much more practical effect.

Dependence on external funders has a direct effect on AU peace missions. The dependence often takes away mission design from the AU. For instance, between 2011 and 2012 the AU and ECOWAS could not intervene in Mali due to limited funding. This meant that the AU PSC could not assemble as well as authorise a peace mission. It was not until France launched Operation Serval in early 2013—which was a public humiliation of African capabilities—that the AU hastily put together the faltering African-led International Support Mission to Mali (AFISMA).[87] At the core of the decision to launch AFISMA, was a concern about African ownership and leadership. At its 358th meeting, the PSC's progress report on AFISMA reiterated the AU's position that "the appointment of the (UN) Special Representative who would lead a possible United Nations Mission be done after appropriate consultations with ECOWAS and the AU, to contribute to the African ownership of this effort and optimize the efficiency of the mission...to ensure continuity in the leadership of the mission".[88] Five months later, the vacillating AFISMA was replaced by a UN mission[89] due to limited funding and resources. The transference of the mission from the AU to the UN took away mission design and leadership from the AU. Expectedly, the resultant UN mission had African faces in some leadership positions. However, the concept of operations (CONOPS) effectively transformed into those of the UN. This effectively created a cosmetic semblance of African agency in multilateralism, but came short of full African representation.

Although the AU still struggles to fund some of its peace missions, many senior AU officials insist that the AU can fund its own operations. They also insist that overcoming financial constraints through domestic mobilisation can overcome agential challenge and help secure African ownership and leadership. However, the idea that more funding will placate AU misfortunes is simplistic. It is highly improbable that funding will significantly improve African agency without first dealing with the framing and application of coercive power within the AU and African regional security systems.

Lack of Coercive Power

Regional agency requires a proper application of coercive power. The aforementioned dynamic works well in other world regions. This coercive power is exercised by hegemons within a defined world region. The hegemonic leadership is intended to heighten agential fortunes within the given area. However, there is a lack of coercive power among African states, especially major states, because none of them possess capabilities for hegemonic leadership. Several scholars, especially in South Africa and Europe, tend to suggest that Nigeria and South Africa are hegemonic powers either in Africa or their respective sub-continental regions.[90] Although this might be a desirable notion in public discourse, it does not stand up to the test in African security.

Hegemonic leadership must be tested against five criteria. These are: a delimited region with political, economic and cultural links; willingness and preparedness to assume regional leadership; possessing material and ideational capacities to influence region; provision of collective public goods for the region and acceptance by other states in the region.[91] There is no single African country that meets at least three of those criteria, especially given the size of the continent. Moreover, neither Nigeria nor South Africa is prepared to assume regional leadership beyond their respective regional economic communities (RECs).

The foregoing must be measured against empirical capabilities, not aspirations. On the one hand, South Africa is struggling to provide effective leadership within the SADC region.[92] Thus, it is an over stretch for an aspiring hegemon to seek preponderance beyond its immediate environment. If a country does that, as South Africa has, its agential capacity as a hegemon will effectively remain hazy. On the other hand, beneath the veneer of Nigerian hegemonic leadership in West Africa lies a deep and unabated contestation with French imperialism in the region.[93] This case is even grimmer than that of South Africa. France still controls most of its former colonies as well as those ceded by Belgium. It still maintains a strong grip on the political and security affairs of those states.[94] Therefore, in light of the above, neither of the two so-called "African hegemons" exercises proper hegemony in at least half of the continent. Granted, given its superior intellectual capital, businesses and institutions South Africa possesses better material and ideational capacity than its counterparts. However, as a fledgling democracy it also has immense challenges that relate to its foreign policy consistency. For instance, former President Jacob Zuma prioritised domestic policy challenges and repealed his predecessor (President Thabo Mbeki)'s continental projects.[95] Apart from the foreign policy inconsistency, South Africa and Nigeria or other states cannot readily secure acceptance from fellow states. Most African states prefer hegemonic leadership from outside the continent.

Major African states such as Nigeria, Algeria, Egypt, South Africa and Ethiopia, should be characterised as middle powers (in African security). There are two major reasons why this should be, but it is important to preface those by explaining a middle power. A middle power is a capable state, neither weak nor powerful, that pursues its foreign and security policy with carefulness not to upset major powers, while also seeking an element of self-help.[96] It spends more time leaning on soft issues such political issues, and when dealing with security issues it pays attention to the manoeuvres of major powers.[97]

Nigeria, despite its anti-imperial rhetoric, has often had to react to French interventionism in West Africa. For instance, ECOWAS, led by Nigeria and Chad, launched AFISMA months after France's unilateral

94 T. GWATIWA

Operation Sérval.[98] Moreover, even though South Africa lost its troops in the CAR, it could not assist the weak *Force Multinational d'Afrique Centrale* (FOMAC) to launch the MICOPAX soon enough before France could launch Operation Sangaris. Both Nigeria and South Africa cannot gain control of any of the so-called Francophone states because France has military bases of varying strengths in all those states.[99] Finally, recent events show that Nigeria and South Africa cannot collectively curtail imperial and jingoistic policies of foreign powers. In a typical case of Western jingoism, which some described as "skilful" diplomacy,[100] France worked with the US and UK to undermine African preferences within the UN Security Council. The trio skilfully isolated Nigeria, South Africa and their sympathisers (Russia, China, and Brazil) in order to legitimise a military intervention in Libya.[101] All the above cases show that the influence and coercive power of Nigeria and South Africa are grossly limited. This implies that African security, and by extension issues of role playing and burden sharing, will remain in limbo for the foreseeable future.

Summarily, this chapter demonstrates that Africa is in a difficult agential position due to factors and dynamics emanating from within the continent. First, the dynamics of the AU Peace and Security Council and its security regime are wanting. It is not primarily that the AU regionalism project is a work in progress, but because the foundations are flawed. If the foundations are flawed, it is highly improbable that any accompanying efforts will result in better fortunes for African agency within and beyond the continent. Second, the lack of hegemonic leadership also creates a vacuum in the continent's ability to own and lead its projects of regionalization. Third, the decimated political will due to frustration with democratic processes also has a negative effect on African agency. Fourth, and related to the third, financial constraints place a heavy toll on AU capacity to exercise agency. Fifth, even if funding was available, the mutual suspicion among capable African states creates challenges that only add to the continent's agential woes. Finally, the continent lacks coercive power. Without coercive power from within the continent, there is limited agency. From the above, it appears that the primary challenges to African agency in, or relating to, the AU is mainly political and procedural.

NOTES

1. Barry Buzan and Ole Waever, *Regions and Powers: The Structure of International Security* (Cambridge: Cambridge University Press, 2003), 219.
2. Randall Schweller (2002: 2–4), cited in Andrew Hurrell, "Regional Powers and the Global System From a Historical Perspective", in eds. Daniel Flemes and Detlef Nolte, *Regional Leadership in the Global System: Ideas, Interests and Strategies of Regional Powers* (London and New York: Routledge, 2010), 15–30, 22.
3. Paul D. Williams, "From Non-Intervention to Non-Indifference: The Origins and Development of the African Union's Security Culture", *African Affairs* 106, no. 423 (2007): 253–279.
4. Ulf Engel and James Gomes Porto, eds., *Africa's New Peace and Security Architecture: Promoting Norms, Institutionalizing Solutions* (London and New York: Routledge, 2010).
5. Alex de Waal, "African Roles in the Libyan Conflict of 2011", *International Affairs* 89, no. 2 (2013): 365–379.
6. African Union, "Report of the Chairperson of the Commission on the Situation in Libya and the Efforts of the African Union for a Political Solution to the Libyan Crisis", PSC/AHG/3(CCXCI), 26 August 2011.
7. Festus Aboagye, "The African Mission in Burundi: Lessons Learned from the First African Union Peacekeeping Operation", *Peacekeeping* (2004), https://www.issafrica.org/uploads/CT2_2004%20PG9-15.PDF.
8. Gary Wilson, *The United Nations and Collective Security* (London and New York: Routledge, 2014), 5–8.
9. Ibid., 8–12.
10. Alex Vines, "A Decade of APSA", *International Affairs* 89, no. 1 (2013): 89–109.
11. Daniel S. Papp, *Contemporary International Relations: Frameworks for Understanding*, 6th ed. (London: Pearson, 2001), 153.
12. Howorth, *Security and Defence Policy*.
13. Brian Frederking, *The United States and the Security Council: Collective Security Since the Cold War* (London and New York: Routledge, 2007).

14. Glen H. Snyder, *Alliance Politics* (Ithaca and London: Cornell University Press, 2007).
15. Stephen M. Walt, *The Origins of Alliances* (Ithaca and London: Cornell University Press, 1987).
16. Snyder, *Alliance Politics*, 169–172.
17. Gilbert M. Khadiagala and Terrence Lyons, *African Foreign Policies: Power and Process* (Boulder: Lynne Rienner, 2001).
18. Patricia Weitsman, *Waging War: Alliances, Coalitions, and Institutions of Interstate Violence* (Stanford: Stanford University Press, 2014), 26–27.
19. Weitsman, *Waging War.*
20. Christian Anrig, *Allied Air Power Over Libya* (London and New York, 2015).
21. AU Peace and Security Council, *Report of the Chairperson of the Commission on the Operationalisation of the Rapid Deployment Capability of the African Standby Force and the Establishment of an 'African Capacity for Immediate Response to Crises'* (Addis Ababa, Ethiopia: African Union, April 30, 2013).
22. Mancur Olson and Richard Zeckhauser, "An Economic Theory of Alliance", *Review of Economics and Statistics* 48 (1966): 266–279.
23. See Anrig, *Allied Air Power.*
24. Todd Sandler and Hirofumi Shimizu, "NATO Burden Sharing 1999–2010: An Altered Alliance", *Foreign Policy Analysis* 6 (2012): 1–18.
25. Fred Thompson, "Lumpy Goods and Cheap Riders: An Application of the Theory of Public Goods to International Alliances", *Journal of Public Policy* 7, no. 4 (1987): 431–449 [p. 433–437].
26. Andrew Bennet, Joseph Lepgold and Danny Unger, "Burden Sharing in the Persian Gulf War", *International Organization* 48, no. 1 (1994): 39–75.
27. James D. Fearon, "Domestic Political Audiences and the Escalation of International Disputes", *American Political Science Review* 88, no. 3 (1994): 577–592.
28. Jessica L. Weeks, "Autocratic Audience Costs: Regime Type and Signalling Resolve", *International Organization* 62, no. 1 (2008): 35–64.

29. Jürgen Schuster and Herbert Maier, "The Rift: Explaining Europe's Divergent Iraq Policies in the Run-Up of the American-Led War on Iraq", *Foreign Policy Analysis* 2 (2006): 223–244.
30. Emizet F. Kisangani and Jeffrey Pickering, "Diverting with Benevolent Military Force: Reducing Risks and Rising above Strategic Behaviour", *International Studies Quarterly* 52 (2007): 277–299.
31. Hans Morgenthau (1985: 369) claimed that before World War I, Africa was "a politically empty space".
32. Hurrell, "Regional Powers".
33. Achille Mbembe, *On the Postcolony* (Berkeley and London: University of California Press, 2006), Valentin-Yves Mudimbe, *The Invention of Africa: Gnosis, Philosophy and the Order of Knowledge* (Bloomington: Indiana University Press, 1988).
34. Mohammed Ayoob, "Defining Security: A Subaltern Realist Perspective", in *Critical Security Studies: Concepts and Cases*, eds. Michael C. Williams (Minneapolis: University of Minnesota Press, 1997), 121–146 [132].
35. Amitav Acharya, "The Periphery as the Core: The Third World and Security Studies", in *Critical Security Studies: Concepts and Cases*, eds. Michael C. Williams (Minneapolis: University of Minnesota Press, 1997), 299–327.
36. Mikael Eriksson and Linnéa Gelot, eds., *The African Union in Light of the Arab Revolts: An Appraisal of the Foreign Policy and Security Objectives of South Africa, Ethiopia and Algeria*, Nordic Africa Institute Discussion Paper 76, 2013.
37. Alden and Soko, "South Africa's Economic Relations"; Alden and Schoeman, "South Africa's Symbolic Hegemony"; Karen Smith, "South Africa and India as Regional Leaders: Gaining Acceptance and Legitimacy Through the Use of Soft Power", in *South-South Cooperation: Africa on the Centre Stage*, eds. Renu Modi (Basingstoke: Palgrave Macmillan, 2011), 68–83.
38. Adekeye Adebajo and Chris Landsberg, "South Africa and Nigeria", in *Gulliver's Troubles: Nigeria's Foreign Policy After the Cold War*, eds. Adeyeke Adebajo and Abdul Raufu Mustapha (Pietermaritzburg: University of Kwazulu Natal Press, 2008).
39. For a five-point criterion of a hegemon see Daniel Flemes and Detlef Nolte, "Introduction", in *Regional Leadership in the Global System: Ideas, Interests and Strategies of Regional Powers*,

eds. Daniel Flemes and Detlef Nolte, 15–30 (London and New York: Routledge, 2010), 6–7.

40. Thomas Kwasi Tieku, "South Africa and the African Union", in *The African Union in Light of the Arab Revolts: An Appraisal of Foreign Policy and Security Objectives of South Africa, Ethiopia and Algeria*, eds. Mikael Eriksson and Linnéa Geloteds. Mikael Eriksson and Linnéa Gelot, Nordic Africa Institute Discussion Paper 76 (2013), 13.

41. Mehari Taddele Maru, "Rethinking and Reforming the African Union Commission Elections", *African Security Review* 21, no. 4 (2012): 64–78.

42. Stephen Krasner, *International Regimes* (Ithaca, New York: Cornell University Press, 1983).

43. Williams, "From Non-Intervention to Non-Indifference".

44. Engel and Porto, *Africa's New Peace and Security Architecture*.

45. See Tieku, "South Africa and the African Union"; also see Heidi Hardt, *Time to React; The Efficiency of International Organizations in Crisis Response* (Oxford and New York: Oxford University Press, 2014) *Time to React*, 45.

46. Iyah Onuk, personal interview, AU Peace and Security Department, Addis Ababa, June 2014.

47. Ademola Abbas, personal interview, former AU peace and security consultant, Addis Ababa, July 2015.

48. Rene Lemarchand, "The CIA in Africa: How Central? How Intelligent?" *The Journal of Modern African Studies* 14, no. 3 (1976): 401–426; Elizabeth Schmidt, *Foreign Intervention in Africa: From the Cold War to the Present* (Cambridge: Cambridge University Press, 2013); Larry Devlin, *Chief of Station, Congo: A Memoir of 1960–67* (New York: Public Affairs, 2007); Akwasi B. Assensoh and Yvette M. Alex-Assensoh, *African Military History and Politics: Coups and Ideological Incursions* (New York: Palgrave, 2001).

49. Maphoi Komanyane, personal interview, former Member of the Permanent Representatives Committee for AU financing, Geneva: May 2014.

50. Tieku, "South Africa and the African Union".

51. Jide M. Okeke, personal interview, AU Peace Support Operations Division, Addis Ababa: July 2014.

52. Kathrina P. Coleman, *International Organization and Peace Enforcement: The Politics of International Legitimacy* (Cambridge: Cambridge University Press, 2007).
53. Tim Murithi, telephone interview, May 2013.
54. Tomaz Salomao, personal interview, former Executive Secretary of the SADC Secretariat, Johannesburg, January 2016.
55. Adebajo and Landsberg, "South Africa and Nigeria"; also see Chris Landsberg, "Nigeria-South Africa Tensions Leave African Leadership Gap", *World Politics Review* (2012), https://www.worldpoliticsreview.com/articles/11857/nigeria-south-africa-tensions-leave-african-leadership-gap.
56. Landsberg, "An African 'Concert'".
57. Maru, "Rethinking and Reforming".
58. African Ambassador to the AU, personal interview, Addis Ababa, July 2015.
59. Francophone [African] Ambassador to the AU, personal interview, Addis Ababa, August 2015.
60. Adekeye Adebajo, "Hegemony on a Shoestring", in *Gulliver's Troubles: Nigeria's Foreign Policy After the Cold War*, eds. Adeyeke Adebajo and Abdul Raufu Mustapha (Pietermaritzburg: University of Kwazulu Natal Press, 2008).
61. Adeyeke Adebajo and Abdul Raufu Mustapha, *Gulliver's Troubles: Nigeria's Foreign Policy After the Cold War* (Pietermaritzburg: University of Kwazulu Natal Press, 2008).
62. Cairo International Center for Conflict Resolution, Peacekeeping and Peacebuilding, "Egypt and Peacekeeping", http://www.cairopeacekeeping.org/en/egypt-and-peacekeeping; also see United Nations Peacekeeping, "Egypt", https://peacekeeping.un.org/en/egypt.
63. Political Officer, personal interview, Algerian Embassy to Ethiopia, Addis Ababa, July 2014.
64. I was based at the AU Commission as a researcher from July to September 2015. During this time I was allowed to view some documents at the AU Peace Support Operations Division (PSOD) but was prohibited from making copies or publicly citing those documents.
65. Iyah Onuk, personal interview, AU Peace and Security Department, Addis Ababa, June 2014; In 2018, an unprecedented number of African states contributed to the AU Peace Fund in

order to reduce dependency on the EU-funded APF. For a statement of the AU Commission Deputy Chairperson, see African Union, "Financial Reforms".

66. Gerhard Mai, personal interview, head of peace and security, GIZ, Addis Ababa: August 2015; Christian Ghare, personal interview, Second Secretary, Royal Norwegian Embassy in Ethiopia, Addis Ababa: August 2015.

67. Onuk, personal interview, June 2014.

68. Colonel William C. Wyatt, personal interview, November 2014.

69. Brigadier General Emmanuel Teteh, personal interview, Senior Military Advisor to the Ghanaian Embassy in Ethiopia, and Dean of the Military Attachés Association (MAA), August 2015.

70. African Union, "African Peer Review Mechanism (APRM)", 2003, https://au.int/en/organs/aprm.

71. Okeke, personal interview, July 2014.

72. For a comprehensive account of the saga, see Morula Morula, "Botswana to Maintain its Presence in Darfur", *Sunday Standard*, 28 March 2008, http://www.sundaystandard.info/botswana-maintain-its-presence-darfur; Morula Morula, "No Decision Made on Enlarging Botswana Contingent in Darfur", 25 November 2007, http://www.sundaystandard.info/no-decision-made-enlarging-botswana-contingent-darfur; Gideon Nkala, "Killer of Botswana Soldier on Trial at ICC", 23 October 2009, http://www.mmegi.bw/index.php?sid=1&aid=172&dir=2009/October/Friday23/.

73. David Bax, "True Cost of World's Most Dangerous Peacekeeping Mission Shockingly High", *The East African*, 25 January 2018, http://www.theeastafrican.co.ke/oped/comment/World-most-dangerous-peacekeeping-mission/434750-4278124-114vow4z/index.html.

74. AU Peace and Security Council, "Report of the Chairperson".

75. Onuk, personal interview, June 2014.

76. See Réne Lemarchand, "Foreign Policy Making in the Great Lakes Region", in *African Foreign Policies: Power & Process*, eds. Gilbert M. Khadiagala and Terrence Lyons (Boulder: Lynne Rienner, 1976), 87–106.

77. Paul D. Williams, "New African Model of Coercion? Assessing the ECOWAS Mission in the Gambia", IPI Global Observatory, 16 March 2017, https://theglobalobservatory.org/2017/

03/ecowas-gambia-barrow-jammeh-african-union/; unidentified author, "Gambia Crisis: Senegal Sends in Troops to Back Elected Leader", *BBC News*, 19 January, 2017, https://www.bbc.com/news/world-africa-38682184.

78. Interview, Ambassador of Botswana to Ethiopia, Addis Ababa, June 2014.
79. Interview, AU officer, Addis Ababa, December 2015.
80. Colum Lynch, "On Ivory Coast Diplomacy, South Africa Goes Its Own Way", *Foreign Policy*, 23 February 2011, https://foreignpolicy.com/2011/02/23/on-ivory-coast-diplomacy-south-africa-goes-its-own-way/; Unidentified author, "ECOWAS Miffed at SA Navy Ship to Ivory Coast", *News24*, 8 February 2011, https://www.news24.com/SouthAfrica/News/Ecowas-miffed-at-SA-warship-in-Ivory-Coast-20110208.
81. Interview, Alfredo Tjiurimo Hengari, South African Institute for International Affairs, Johannesburg, January 2016.
82. Ibid.
83. Jason Warner, "Complements or Competitors? The African Standby Force, the African Capacity for Immediate Response to Crises, and the Future of Rapid Reaction Forces in Africa", *African Security* 8 (2015): 56–73 [p. 64].
84. African Union, "Strengthening the Partnerships".
85. Iyah Onuk, interview.
86. Interview, Linda A. Darkwa, AU PSOD Consultant and Researcher, Geneva, November 2013.
87. Unidentified author, "Dancing Nigerian Troops Prepare to Deploy in Mali", *BBC News*, January 2013.
88. AU Peace and Security Council, *Progress Report of the Chairperson of the Commission on the African-led International Support Mission in Mali at the Peace and Security Council 358th Meeting*, Addis Ababa: AU Commission, March 7, 2013; https://au.int/fr/node/25051.
89. United Nations, "Mission multidimensionnelle intégré des Nations Unies pour la stabilisation au Mali (MINUSMA)", www.un.org/.
90. See Alden and Soko, "South Africa's Economic Relations"; Alden and Schoeman, "South Africa's Symbolic Hegemony"; Smith, "South Africa and India".
91. Flemes and Nolte, "Introduction", 6–7.

102   T. GWATIWA

92. Interview [telephone], Tim Murithi, former AU Peace and Security Consultant, Cape Town, May 2013.
93. William Zartman 1984, cited in Terry M. Mays, *Africa's First Peacekeeping Operation: The OAU in Chad, 1981–1982* (Westport and London: Praeger, 2002), 26–27.
94. Schmidt, *Foreign Intervention*.
95. Interview, senior official, South African Department of Defence, July 2016.
96. Carsten Holbraad, *Middle Powers in International Politics* (UK: Macmillan, 1984); Joshua B. Spero, *Bridging the European Divide: Middle Power Politics and Regional Security* (Maryland, USA: Rowman and Littlefield, 2004); Jonathan H. Ping, *Middle Power Statecraft: Indonesia, Malaysia and the Asia Pacific* (England: Ashgate, 2005).
97. Arthur Andrew, *The Rise and Fall of a Middle Power: Canadian Diplomacy from King to Mulroney* (Ontario: James Lorimer, 1993), 23–42.
98. Stockholm International Peace Research Institute, *SIPRI Yearbook 2015: Armaments, Disarmament and International Security* (Oxford: Oxford University Press, 2015), 231.
99. Zartman (1984); Elizabeth Schmidt, *Foreign Intervention in Africa*.
100. Rebecca Adler-Nissen and Vincent Pouliot, "Power in Practice: Negotiating the International Intervention in Libya", *European Journal of International Relations* 20, no. 4 (2014): 889–911.
101. Ibid., 902–904.

CHAPTER 5

African Agency in the Early Design of African Security Institutions

It has become clear in the preceding chapters that African agency is not a novelty in African regionalism and multilateralism. If anything, as implied in Zartman's early treatise, African agency was the foundation of African multilateralism.[1] Yet, the potency of African agency predates the colonial period such that even the colonial institution made use of it.[2] In the post-OAU period, African agency was more salient and was unabashedly included in policy documents or the rhetoric of African political and technocratic elites.

African agency was most salient in the inception and institutionalization of the African Peace and Security Architecture (APSA). This is one of the biggest and most important projects of the African Union. Ordinarily, most press reports exhibit an APSA primarily developed through the patronage of international partners. However, this only obscures the role of African actors in the conception of the underlying ideas, the design of those institutions and their role subsequent to the advent of international partnerships. One of the ways to unearth this agency is to trace the role of African actors in a process that is currently ascribed to international partners.

The African Peace and Security Architecture is an important threshold for understanding African agency. In order to understand the origins of agency slack—both shirking and slippage—it is important to consider the processes and levels of institutionalisation of each component of APSA.

© The Author(s), under exclusive license to Springer Nature Switzerland AG 2022

T. Gwatiwa, *The African Union and African Agency in International Politics*, https://doi.org/10.1007/978-3-030-87805-4_5

103

APSA consists of the Peace and Security Council, the Continental Early Warning Systems (CEWS), the Africa Peace Facility (APF), the Panel of the Wise and the African Standby Force (ASF).[3]

THE INSTITUTIONALIZATION OF THE PEACE AND SECURITY COUNCIL

The AU's Peace and Security Council (PSC) is emblematic of African agency. It is the most institutionalised of the APSA institutions. It was also the first to be fully institutionalised. Empirically, it is one of (if not the) most effective organs of the AU Commission. Interestingly, the PSC was mainly developed without partner support. It was at a later stage that China offered to provide it with an annual grant of nearly $200 million. However, its genesis evinces the role of African actors.

The PSC is a successor to the Central Organ of the Mechanism for Conflict Prevention, Management and Resolution (or simply the Central Organ). The Central Organ was established in 1993, before the age of partnerships. This was the OAU's key decision-making body on peace and security issues. Made up of nine, and later 14 member states, the organ operated at summit, ministerial and ambassador levels.[4] This was slightly different from the current PSC, which operates at the ambassadorial level.

When the idea of an African Union was finalized, it did not include a PSC. Nigeria strongly lobbied for the creation of the PSC,[5] largely because it resembled one of the then structures of ECOWAS (now reformed to resemble recent AU reforms). The lobbying resulted in the institutional transformation of the Central Organ into the Peace and Security Council. Correspondingly, the organ had to be reconstituted to conform to the then overall institutional design that was underway. The main difference between the old and new institution is that the decisions of the 15 member states elected by the AU Executive Council are binding. It is advised by the Permanent Representatives' Committee (PRC), which is a group of African ambassadors.

Essentially, the agential transformation entailed the role of a self-pontificated regional hegemon, which—at the time—was coordinating its continental institutional inputs with another self-pontificated hegemon in the southern part of the continent. This effectively improved the fortunes of regionalisation. These developments also entailed the accentuation of the authority of the new institution, from a merely recommendatory body to one issuing binding decisions. These were better agential developments. African states, in this case, also ensured that the new institution worked closely with the PRC so as to preserve the notion of "consensus" which is sacrosanct in modern African regionalism. This tripartite treatment of agency, and the insulation of this institution from international partners, placed the PSC in a better position.

THE INSTITUTIONALIZATION OF THE PAN-AFRICAN NETWORK OF THE PANEL OF THE WISE

A similar case of African agency is evident in the case of the Pan-African Network of the Panel of the Wise (PANWISE). The PANWISE was basically a revival of the OAU's Commission on Mediation, Conciliation and Arbitration, which was created on July 21, 1964. However, the commission immediately became dormant. Under Article 19 of the OAU Charter, it was supposed to be responsible for the settlement of disputes between OAU member states. In 1993, the mediation commission was replaced by the Mechanism for Conflict Prevention, Management and Resolution (commonly referred to as The Mechanism).[6]

The mediation commission resurfaced under the APSA. Under article 11 of the PSC Protocol, a new "Panel of the Wise" would advise the PSC on issues dealing with mediation and preventive diplomacy. Apparently the idea of a Panel of the Wise was borrowed from ECOWAS' Council of Elders where the "wisdom of seniors" is perceived to be of value.[7] This implies that a subregional initiative revitalised a dormant continental institution. However, the Panel did not become operational until 2007. The Panel was to be built with assistance from the UN Mediation Unit,[8] but this never happened. As it shall evince itself in Chapter 7, the key mediation personnel at the UN and the AU had strongly divergent perspectives and preferences on how to approach mediation.[9] This created a gridlock; and as a result, the African Union built the PANWISE on its own using resources from within the continent. The new approach involved collating the Panel with subregional mediation structures and creating new ones where they did not exist.[10] This process mainly involved the AU's collaboration with African institutions such as the African Centre for the Constructive Resolution of Disputes (ACCORD), based in Durban, South Africa.[11] Former President Thabo Mbeki, of South Africa, and other retired heads of state (especially from Algeria, Nigeria and Ghana) played a critical role in the development of the PANWISE. This was

106   T. GWATIWA

the second security institution to be brought to completion without partnerships' input.

The key role of African political elites, as well as majority funding inputs from African states, and subregional organisations played a key role in the full institutionalization of the PANWISE. Key funding from African states, especially Algeria, insulated the institution from external influence. This ensured that African actors, particularly those at the AU— as a result of their major disagreements with their UN counterparts—were able to retain their preferences in institutional design. This resulted in ample agenda and priority setting by African actors.

CONTINENTAL EARLY WARNING SYSTEMS

Much like the preceding institutions under discussion, the Continental Early Warning Systems (CEWS) also evinces ample African inputs in the formation of African security institutions. It also follows a similar trajectory of African agency.

The CEWS is a successor to the OAU's Centre for Conflict Management (CCM) which was formed in 1994. The function of the CCM was to collect, analyse and disseminate early warning data on current and potential conflicts in Africa. It also served to support the then organization's political, civilian and military missions.[12] It is not clear how much was achieved by the CCM since there is not much record of the institution. However, its earlier design influenced the preference for open-source information to current early warning systems. The CEWS outright rejected support offers of the UN's intelligence-based approach to early warning systems, as well as the EU's intelligence-based early warning systems.[13] Instead, they chose to work with the EU's Joint Research Centre (in Italy) to develop an analytic software which collates information from all sub-continental early warning systems.[14] However, the SADC region already had a strong intelligence-based early warning system. Yet, the AU did not deviate from this strong preference. As a result the AU made an exception to the SADC approach because the latter had already augmented its institutional approach to early warning systems.

This demonstrates the role and capacity of African actors in managing deviating preferences from within and outside the continent. The varying approaches in the most effective sub-continental organizations did not strongly influence the AU as was the case with the PSC, even though the regional approaches preceded the AU institution. Moreover, the AU also managed to resist the overtly possible influence of the UN and EU in institutional design, even though these two were providing some external support (i.e. funding in the case of the EU). The reason the AU was able to resist this was because open-source approaches were already augmented and effectively used by non-state actors in the most conflict-prone regions of Africa: central Africa, the Horn of Africa and West Africa. Due to this pre-existing efficacy, the AU was able to advocate a more open-source approach, which involves less politics than an intelligence-based approach. This somewhat insulated the institutionalization process from member states from either the AU or its partners. Furthermore, by choosing the least politicized institution within the EU for collaboration, the AU also insulated this project from unnecessary influence.

The African Standby Force

The African Standby Force (ASF) is a unique case in this discussion. It has been one of the most difficult projects to institutionalize under APSA. It not only entails heavy commitments but also involves the politics of security cooperation discussed in Chapter 4.

As an idea, the ASF dates back to the formation of the OAU in the 1960s. The debate started with the idea of a Joint Africa High Command (JAHC), resulting in the OAU Defence Commission with a supervisory role,[15] possibly a precursor to the Peace Support Operations Division (PSOD). In 1978, the Frontline States (forerunner to SADC) revived the idea of a continental army with more powers.[16] The current idea of a continental force took shape in the Cairo Declaration of 1993 when it was "agreed to develop an African capacity to participate in peace support operations at the continental and sub-regional level", and finalised following the recommendation of the African Chiefs of Defence Staff (ACDS) in Harare in 1997.[17]

For various reasons, the ASF is the institution most preferred by partners. Part of the reason is that the individual state armies are strongly tied to Paris, London and Washington.[18] Furthermore, the idea of a rapid deployment capability was influenced by NATO.[19] Given the hybridity of most peace operations, it was agreed that the Force should not be too dissimilar to the UN force composition. Thus, the UNOAU influenced the doctrine, legal instruments, roadmaps and the multidimensionality of the Force.[20] The other reason why the partners converged on the ASF is

108   T. GWATIWA

because it lacked the proper concepts of strategic airlift and airlift, which were provided by NATO[21] and US AFRICOM,[22] respectively. Unlike the other APSA institutions, the ASF has a central role in most deployments that involve international partners. Logically, participation is an investment in the shadow of the future. Influencing its institutionalisation creates room for adaptability should there be need for future standalone or multilateral co-deployments. Thus, the institutionalisation of the ASF was the most prolonged, contested and complicated.

The abovementioned evince a key challenge in the role of African actors in institutionalization their security institutions. It is important to note that while defence chiefs and their counterparts from the intelligence and police sectors might be keen to create institutions that ensure peace and stability in the continent, their political counterparts do not share those views. Only a select number of states, especially those with the strongest militaries and intelligence services, seem to support the idea. During the author's research residency at the AU Commission (July–September 2014), it emerged that small and medium states were not fully supportive of the ASF, largely due to fear of the ASF's politicised use subsequent to its operationalization in 2015. These fears were stocked by the short-lived African Capacity for Immediate Response to Crises (ACRIC), which some states such as Nigeria characterized as an interventionist force. ACRIC was eventually "folded" into the ASF. Another impediment was the slothfulness with which it was institutionalized; often giving international partners opportunities to become more involved. For instance, in one eerie development, the AU was tempted to make the ASF a "multidimensional force" in the similitude of the UN forces. This was surprising in two respects. First, the AU was already struggling to operationalize a solely military institution. It was unlikely that the AU would operationalize a multidimensional standby force. Second, the idea of emulating the UN in what was also a relatively new idea within that organization was overly ambitious. When the forgoing submissions were raised with AU officials, they insisted that the "multidimensional" idea was an African idea (proposed to the UN) based on experiences from peacekeeping operations on the continent. That notwithstanding, the idea of instituting a critical component of the APSA using what was then a new and experimental practice from a partner organization was an overstretch. Aside from the "African" origins of the idea, its impracticality in an underfunded organization evinced a simplification of the AU's agential efforts.

The AU Peace Fund

The idea of the AU Peace Fund is not clear, but it is also the brain child of the African Union. However, what is ostensibly clear is that it is heavily underfunded because African member states were, until 2014, not willing to contribute to it. Since its inception in the early 2000s, Algeria was the sole contributor to the Peace Fund. By 2014, Angola and Kenya were two new contributors, annually disbursing $10 million and $1 million, respectively. However, these African contributions are voluntary, and come short of the overall AU budget for peace operations.

African peace support operations are still supported through donor funding. They are primarily supported through the European Development Fund (EDF), under the auspices of the EU's Africa Peace Facility (APF). It is the only peace and security institution at the AU Commission, which is fully supported by external patrons. However, the idea is that the APF will be rolled back once the AU has its own money.[23]

Currently, African financing of peace operations relies on financial contributions from China, Saudi Arabia, Japan, Norway and others. As of January 2015, thirty-five years since the Lagos Plan of Action, the AHSG promulgated the "Declaration on Self-Reliance"; wherein 75 per cent of the overall Commission funding would come from within the continent. It cautiously stated that "self-reliance is not self-isolation, but a commitment to base the development of our continent primarily on own resources, and to mobilise resources within our continent for development".[24] No sooner than a month after the aforementioned promulgation did most African states begin to complain about this new formula.

The forgoing highlights a key impediment to African agency. Funding, or lack thereof, is a major challenge to APSA and African security in general. African states' unwillingness—not inability—to play a bigger role in funding peace operations corrodes their agential role in institution building. Their absence in this dimension cedes preference formation and reification to partners.

110   T. GWATIWA

Agency Without Leadership: An Experiment in Strategic Citizenship

In the preceding chapter, there was a discussion on the role of hegemonic leadership and its link to agency. However, regional agency does not solely rest on the role of hegemons or aspirants. Regional security requires collective efforts. In a continent where unilateralism is almost anathema, collective effort is the most preferred approach to institution building and norm suasion. This is what, for the purposes of this discussion, shall be termed "strategic citizenship".

Strategic citizenship herein refers to how states fulfil the role of membership within a defined regional organisation. This is an extrapolation of Eckstein's treatment of the notion of civic reciprocity between an individual and their geopolitical cleavage in citizenship. It entails compliance with rules and roles, or dissent through self-exclusion from such obligations of membership.[25] Correspondingly, similar [civic] roles and obligations on membership is required to institutionalise regional security. In a strategic context, these obligations come in the form of role playing and burden sharing. Therein states can provide different forms of leadership, collaboration or participation depending on the nature of the project. However, leadership often seems to be the most prominent element when it comes to agency, partly because it ensures sustainability.

There are no established leaders in African strategic citizenship. The claims of South Africa as a regional hegemon[26] or an aspirant[27] are highly contestable. The idea of Nigeria and South Africa as representing twin hegemony is equally contestable.[28] The existing evidence presented hereunder suggests that South Africa, Nigeria and others (Algeria, Egypt, Ethiopia and others) are simply middle powers with limited reach. The following paragraphs will provide a response to Hurrel's exasperation as to why "Third World regional powers" do not easily exploit their neighbours[29] or why strategic citizenship is not an easy feat in Africa. This can be understood from historical, ideational and empirical realities.

Historically, the idea of hegemonic leadership in strategic citizenship was mute. From the onset, most states often conceived security within limited geographical location, usually the subregional level. Even [apartheid] South Africa, which was born out of imperialism, did not have ambitions beyond Southern Africa. Its furthest military intervention was in Angola, which threatened the South West African (Namibian) territory which was under South African trusteeship. Other nations such

5 AFRICAN AGENCY IN THE EARLY DESIGN ... 111

as Algeria, Libya, Ghana and Nigeria supported anti-colonial or anti-apartheid movements in the south only as a part of fulfilling the objectives of the OAU.

Nigeria's case of continental ambitions is a bit different. In 1970, Bolaji Akinyemi—who would later be Nigeria's foreign affairs minister—coined the term "Pax-Nigeriana" to indicate Nigeria's aspirations for continental leadership. This Pax-Nigeriana informed three military interventions in Chad between 1979 and 1982.[30] To be sure, Nigeria was the largest economy in the 1970s. However, apart from the military interventions, this "constructive" hegemony only manifested through a leading role in Africa's collective diplomacy. Empirical hegemony was not possible beyond West Africa. During that time, Nigeria had no match in terms of strategic ambitions. There were never any strategic indications that Nigeria sought influence in other parts of Africa. However, it provided other forms of strategic guidance, such as the financial and political support of the liberation movements in Africa, particularly the African National Congress (ANC) which subsequently became partner-cum-competitor in African strategic citizenship. Therefore, between the 1960 and late 1990s, the idea of continental hegemony was not a preoccupation of many states including.

The idea of regional leadership emerged as an ideational aspect of post-apartheid South Africa. Post-apartheid South Africa created the expectation that it would act as some form of intermediary between Africa and the Global North. Indeed, several big African states acquiesced to this idea given the standing that South Africa was gradually given in the Commonwealth, the G20 and [subsequently, much later] the BRICS. Initially, South Africa worked closely with Nigeria on issues ranging from security to development.[31] This strategic condominium would later unravel, with costs to African regional agency.

The competition for leadership in African strategic citizenship openly manifested itself during the contest for a permanent non-veto seat in the UN Security Council. The *Ezuwlini Consensus* demanded "full representation of Africa in the Security Council... [with] no less than two permanent seats with all prerogatives and privileges of the permanent membership including the right to veto...[and] five non-permanent seats".[32] Nigeria and Egypt also fought for this candidacy. Although South Africa was not an initially strong contender, it enjoyed the same level of support as Nigeria from within the continent and beyond, endorsed by American statesmen and diplomats such as Henry Kissinger,

Gwendolyn Mikell and Princeton Lyman.[33] Adebajo observed that the three states "entered a Byzantine contest...Cynics dismissed Nigeria as too 'anarchic', Egypt as too 'Arab' and South Africa as too 'albino-cratic'".[34] This case reveals the source of polarised leadership in African strategic citizenship.

A further impediment to African strategic citizenship was the neutralization of hegemonic leadership within African multilateralism. The AU, unlike the EU and the UN, does not accommodate hegemonic leadership by a handful of member states. The Constitutive Act and the PSC Protocol state that voting and decision-making is guided by the principle of consensus. In cases "where consensus cannot be reached, the Peace and Security Council shall adopt its decisions on procedural matters by a simple majority, while decisions on all other matters shall be made by a two-thirds majority vote of its Members voting".[35] However, in practice all PSC decisions are reached by consensus, following extensive discussions at the level of the PRC.[36]

According to one of the drafters of the Constitutive Act and the PSC Protocol, this process was deliberately put in place to avoid a replication of power and domination found in the UN Security Council or the European Union.[37] The idea was that no AU member state should subject fellow member states to the imperial oppression that African states have suffered at the hands of the West (and East). Although Nigeria has a "permanent" seat in the PSC, due to a West African agreement regarding its four seats, it does not give Nigeria a strategic leverage on continent-wide issues as Nigeria remains focused on the subregional level.[38] That is why some African regional security experts often say "there are no permanent powers in Africa".[39] With such a framework, member states are always keen to escape the influence of aspiring regional hegemons, especially South Africa, by referring security issues to the African Union where the impact of bigger states can be neutralised or diluted.

The foregoing shows the role of role playing by various member states. The role playing by different states is possible, but is shaped by various institutional bottlenecks which mostly hinder institutional and regional agency. This does not imply that member states are not aware of the costs of these bottlenecks, but they consider them more bearable than creating an environment in which a preoccupation with African agency in international politics creates bigger challenges to interstate and security cooperation in Africa. However, this agential challenge manifests better in the area of burden sharing.

There is lack of effort in burden sharing in the area of continent security projects and programmes. The biggest need in peace support burden sharing is strategic airlift. It is currently provided by international partners, especially the North Atlantic Treaty Organization (NATO). The number of states that used to make such contributions has decreased. South Africa, Nigeria and other capable states have reduced their contributions in this regard. Yet, the nine key African countries with strategic airlift capacity (Nigeria, South Africa, Botswana, Algeria, Egypt, Cameroon, etc.) are unwilling to cede contingent-owned equipment (COE) to the AU because there are no clear reimbursement procedures like in the UN system.[40]

There are only two states that provide strategic airlift to various missions without compensation—Algeria and Angola. Angola is fairly a newcomer in African strategic citizenship. It is currently playing its strategic role in both SADC and ECCAS, through troop contributions, expert deployment and missions funding. Algeria has funded and staffed the portfolio of the Commissioner of Peace and Security since 2002 and provides strategic airlift in Somalia, Sudan and Chad.[41] Troop contribution to missions is prohibited by the Algerian constitution and thus only contributes to observers, planners and pilots. Top troop contributing countries (TCCs) include Rwanda, Burundi and Uganda for various reasons. There is no pattern whereby a certain country is always a leading country in a majority of PSO deployments. These deployments differ according to regions as well as the stakes in each mission. The limited and uneven contributions to burden sharing undermine the sustainability which is necessary for accentuating regional agency.

The foregoing case implies that there is a challenge regarding leadership in regional [African] strategic citizenship. Continent-wide leadership among states is uncertain. The two claimants to African leadership, Nigeria and South Africa, are mainly operating in a state of strategic pareidolia. These two states command some form of leadership at the subregional level: Nigeria in West Africa and South Africa in Southern Africa. Others such as Algeria, Ethiopia, Chad and Egypt are limited by the constitutions, internal fragility, instability and strategic ambivalence. The limited influence of these brings its own agential challenges. On the one hand, these states are aware of their limitations as well as the varying capabilities among them. This then creates a form of resentment, mistrust and outright competition. On the other, outside powers such as the US, the UK and others wish to deal with a single state to represent Africa.[42] These external wishes, and the attempt to impose them on African states,

114   T. GWATIWA

have caused a wider rift between African states, particularly Nigeria and South Africa. This has played itself out at the level of the UN which is the highest level of world politics (discussed earlier).

International Partners' and APSA Institutions: Navigating Agency in the Mission Space

The role of the AU's international partners in African security provides a clear trajectory and architecture of the agency slack in the partnerships. The interaction between the AU and its international partners around the institutionalisation of APSA explains the various outcomes in the partnerships, but more importantly explains why the AU has resorted to different forms of agency slack. It is important to highlight the indispensability of APSA to regional agency. It is one of the major projects and programmes which the AU and its member states guard jealously. The following sections explain the dynamics of each partnership under study. The explanation will also proffer a threshold for a much deeper discussion of the type of agency slack found in any of the partnerships.

EU Support Towards APSA Institutions

The partnership with the EU has a unique place in African multilateralism. The partnership is the second oldest of OAU/AU partnerships, but the most voluminous in terms of technical and non-technical exchanges. In the subsections below is a descriptive analysis of how the EU contributes to the development of APSA, a key project to African agency.

The PSC and the COPS
The PSC has a strong relationship with its EU counterpart. There are two types of contributions towards the PSC. The first contribution is in the form of capacity building of the PSC secretariat. This involved a form of visiting fellowships and in-house training at the EU Commission.[43] Capacity building has diminished or rather outlived its usefulness. It was not useful because the secretariat existed as the Central Organ for a longer period since the 1990s until it was translated into the PSC in 2002. It has been superseded by a second contribution, namely inter-collegial meeting.

There is a highly institutionalised annual meeting of the collegial bodies. The EU COPS and the AU PSC (both made up of permanent representatives) hold annual meetings in order to address divergent views on a peace and security approach.[44] This covers, among other things, how the partners build institutions as well as how to collaborate in the mission spaces across Africa. The chairpersons of the two bodies also hold informal meetings twice a year to coordinate interests and preferences. The meeting is so useful that it has been suggested that comity should be extended to New York to avoid what led to Libyan intervention in 2011. This high institutionalisation of interactivity is crucial to improving the type of equality that is necessary to accommodate the agency of a relatively materially weaker partner.

The institutionalisation of this component of the partnership has shaped views on peace and security. According to various respondents, frequent interaction between the two bodies has enabled them to move away from a traditional (military) towards a non-traditional (comprehensive) approach to security. The partners eventually agreed to a human security approach in the partnership.[45] It is imperative to note that human security already existed in the founding AU peace and security policy documents.[46] Thus, the realisation that peace and security crises are attributable to political issues moved the AU, as the central organization, from a subaltern position of engaging in ephemeral security projects that do not deal with the root causes of conflict.

THE AFRICAN STANDBY FORCE AND PEACE SUPPORT OPERATIONS

The Gambari Report notes that the idea of an African Standby Force should not be treated as an aspirational idea, but a work already in process. The current AU or hybrid peace support deployments in Somalia and Sudan, the report highlights, should be treated as existing elements (and perhaps experiments) of the ASF. This implies that the current PSOs are ongoing tests of the ASF. Thus, partners' contributions to key PSOs are an indirect contribution to the operationalisation of the ASF.

The EU is one of the main contributors of the AU's PSOs. It contributes in several ways. In the broadest sense, the EU has bankrolled the ASF project from concept development to testing exercises (including the AMANI II exercise) as well as the actual PSOs. The Europeans significantly contributed to the development of key ASF doctrines and concepts such as the logistics and strategic airlift concepts.[47] In the words of a top PSOD official, "the European Union is a pillar in the Africa Peace and Security Architecture".[48] The EU also trains or assists AU troops in some of the missions. However, the EU prefers short engagements which give room for the AU to take over the missions. This trajectory began with Operation Artemis in the DRC in 2003. As of 2007, the EU Military Staff (EUMS) prefer capacity building and programme planning which is equally managed by both parties even though the Africans failed to institutionalise the AU Military Staff Committee (a EUMSC counterpart).

The EU also funds the ASF by paying the salaries of troops serving in the mission spaces. Key troop contributing countries such as Rwanda, Uganda, Ethiopia and Burundi do not have enough resources to sustain their troops in Darfur and Somalia. It is to that end that the EU pays each troop a monthly salary of €700 (was €1200 until November 2015). This funding is managed and disbursed through the Africa Peace Facility.

This is indicative of a bigger and more powerful organisation providing and widening the latitude of a materially weaker organisation, in order to accommodate its agency.

The Africa Peace Facility and the AU Peace Fund

The Africa Peace Facility (APF) is an EU-funded and managed institution which was set up on request from African heads of states. The idea was for Europe to fund the AU peace and security project until the latter can fully operationalise the AU Peace Fund (African states are unwilling to finance the Peace Fund). The APF finances a broad set of peace and security components.

The APF finances close to 90 per cent of peace and security employees in the AU Commission. This comprises employees at the AU HQ and the mission spaces. Ideally the Peace and Security Directorate should consist of "about 400 personnel at the AU Headquarters...and about 80 officers elsewhere (in every mission)".[49] This means that the APF helps fund both uniformed and civilian personnel. It also finances the meetings and conferences that may involve other partners.

However, the EU and AU have an uneasy relationship regarding financial disbursements through the APF. The AU perceives the EU's insistence on accountability as unreasonable coercion. The EU demands for accountability coincided with increased diversification of funds from top African nations and a few Scandinavian donors. For example, the Joint Financial Arrangements which currently finance mission spaces are funded by the EU, Denmark and several African countries whose fractional contribution amounted to $13 million out of a budget of $41 million in 2014.[50]

With time, the EU preferred to engage directly with the Regional Economic Communities (RECs) and RMs to ensure accountability. This meant that it had to decide what could be part of the security projects. AU officials perceive this as a "balkanization of African security".[51] The EU tried to direct attention from the AU, but the RECs stood in solidarity with the continental body.[52] However, there are those within the AU who support the EU's demand for accountability because there are concerns about maladministration of funds within the AU Commission.

According to the new approach, the EU requires the AU to coordinate with its RECs before it can disburse funding through the APF. This means that the EU delegations to the RECs need to vet project funding requests.[53] This means that projects within the partnership take longer than they used to. Most interestingly, the new arrangement requires that the AU returns all the unused funds. For example, the AU had to return 2/3 of the €40 million allocated under the 10th EDF funding for May 2011 to December 31, 2014. The prolongation of the funding element as well as returning of money is yet to be strongly contested to a degree that they affect the other aspects of the partnership.

THE EARLY WARNING SYSTEMS AND THE PANWISE

The EU appears to be cognizant on when to reduce its involvement in AU security project. It did not make significant contributions to the CEWS and the PANWISE during their operationalisation. Indeed, the EU was a main partner on the CEWS project when the partnership started. As explained earlier in the chapter, the CEWS coordinated with the EU Joint Research Centre (JRC) to assist in the design of the system that could be used for continental surveillance. In this case, the EU permitted the AU to decide on the nature of its continental early warning system instead of imposing their system even though the EU funded the entire project. This does not mean that the EU did not try to influence the AU towards an EU-like approach. They did. However, the AU rejected the idea of an intelligence-based early warning system similar to the EU Situation Room.[54] The EU then acceded to the idea of an AU-led approach which would only involve the EU JRC (based in Italy).

The EU does not have a strong relationship with the PANWISE. To a certain extent, the Panel of the Wise benefits from the general funding made available to APSA institutions. However, they are not strongly involved because from 2006 it was agreed that the UN would assume a leading role in the operationalisation of the Panel of the Wise. Therefore, the UN recruited the first coordinator of the Panel of the Wise and paid her salary for the first three years. The UN also provided an expert to work with the Panel of the Wise secretariat.[55] The EU purposely avoided being fully involved in duplication given that the UN has better capacity and experience in mediation and preventive diplomacy.

The evidence in this section suggests that the EU accommodated African ownership and development. There are several reasons for this (explored in the next chapter). The issue of African agency is not necessarily new in this partnership. It has been negotiated and contested between the early 1970s (around the signing of the Lomé Agreement) and the early 2000s (around the signing of the Cotonou Agreement). The EU had a reason to accommodate African agency both at the political and technical level. The most powerful of EU member states have vested strategic interests in Africa. At the time of renegotiating the Lomé Agreement, in the late 1990s, not only was the nature of world politics changing but African elites were strongly opposed to what they considered "Eurocentricism".[56] Thus African agency featured as a bargaining chip in the renegotiation. The successful use of African agency into this partnership set the tone for subsequent partnerships.

UN Support to the APSA

The United Nations, as a platform of global politics and international cooperation, has an inseparable relationship with the AU. First, the UN is legally and politically more cogent than the AU. However, as argued in Chapter 7, the AU has several competencies over the UN in some areas. Yet, the UN is generally respected for technical expertise from which regional organisations can benefit. Moreover, all AU member states are also UN member states; hence, the dual membership is often understood as mutually reinforcing.

UN Support to the ASF: AU PST to the UNOSOA

United Nations contributions to the African Standby Force mostly occurred at the outset of the AU project. UN contributions were predominantly noticeable during the first phase of the force operationalisation.[57] The UN mainly provided expert support for the design of the ASF legal and policy frameworks. These were jointly produced as part of Roadmaps 1 and 2 which dealt with frameworks and the multidimensionality of the force, respectively.[58] There was a shared view, between the AU and UN, that the ASF should not be too different from the UN peacekeeping forces for the sake of mission transferability.[59] However, UN contributions to the ASF were punctuated by a number of operational irregularities.

The earliest efforts to support the ASF project were poorly coordinated. The aim was to support the operationalisation of the ASF at the strategic (headquarters) and operational (mission) levels.[60] In the early phase of the partnership, the UN deployed two teams to help the AU operationalise the ASF. These were the AU Peacekeeping Support Team (AU PST) from the DPKO and mission planners from the Department of Field Services.[61] These units could not coordinate between themselves, but directly reported to their respective unit offices in New York. The resulting slow pace and poor coordination negatively affected the AU. The overall pace of operationalising the ASF slowed down. However, the redeeming factor was that there were other committed partners on board.

UNSC Relationship with the Peace and Security Council

The United Nations Security Council (UNSC) has an uneasy relationship with the AU PSC. It would be an overstatement to argue that the UNSC made any significant contributions to the operationalisation of the PSC secretariat. Indeed, there are indications that the UN contributed to the early training of the PSC secretariat. However, this was short-lived for two reasons. First, the PSC evolved from the Central Organ of the Mechanism for Conflict Prevention, Management and Resolution (or simply the Central Organ).[62] The Central Organ operated consistently without external support since its inception in 1993, and therefore needed very little external support. Part of that capacity building was offered by the EU. More importantly, and second, China provides an unconditional grant to the AUC on an annual basis.[63] Given this scenario, UN support mainly entails its traditional sphere of competence: mission authorisation and transference, thus limiting its own agency.

The UNSC contributions to the PSC are diminished by their perennial tensions over the principles applicable to peace enforcement. The two councils contend over the best approach to peace operations in Africa. The AU uniquely conducts peace support operations (PSOs) while the UN still conducts their traditional peacekeeping operations (PKOs). The former creates conditions for peace, while the latter seeks to keep peace after a ceasefire.[64] In terms of operational congeniality, the AU prefers the principle of subsidiarity wherein it would be the first to deploy and set the agenda while the UN prefers the principle of complementarity wherein it would have an upper hand across the mission timeline. To the AU, subsidiarity and PSOs reflect a form of agency because it entails African ownership, agenda setting and leadership. Complementarity and PKOs, on the other hand, involve lots of external actors whose contributions and influence obscures the role and preferences of African actors.

UN Support to the Continental Early Warning Systems

The UN has not made any significant contributions to the development of the CEWS. This owes to two reasons. First, the UN was primarily focused on the PANWISE. Support to the PANWISE was considered a priority and flagship project within the partnership. As a matter of fact, the PANWISE support project was earmarked prior to the signing of the AU-UN agreement in 2006. This was because the AU requested such support on the PANWISE. There was also a large focus on the ASF. As a result, UN involvement came much later. Second, the AU had made it clear that it prefers an open-source type of early warning systems, which is different from that of the UN Situation Room. However, there have been changes lately.

At the time of completion of the field work in 2017, the AU was in negotiations with the UN over its early warning systems. The idea was to combine existing early warning capability [at the AU] with the UN's "horizon scanning" and crisis watch systems.[65] However, there is a clear intent to avoid the UN Situation Room which already has a fluctuating relationship with the AU Situation Room. There is a clear attempt to only engage the UN in a state of full operational capability to retain agency in the design of the institutions.

UN Support to the APF: The Parallel Funding

The UN does not make direct contributions to the Africa Peace Fund, but has its own modes of funding. There are three main channels of funding to the APSA. The first type of UN funding to the APSA comes from the United Nations Development Programme (UNDP). The UNDP funding to the Peace and Security Department and APSA, which is also the most voluminous, predates the AU–UN partnership agreement (of 2006). The UNDP funding mainly goes to capacity building of the PSD as well as its programmes in the field. This mode of funding is preferable and the UN is considered a "dependable partner".[66] The second type of funding comes from the UN Trust Fund. This trust fund is free from the control of UN member states, especially the permanent members of the UNSC. It has often been used to fund the UN support to AMISOM. The third type of funding is derived from UN-assessed contributions. This type funding is used sparingly because its use is often contested by the permanent five, notably the US (and France). However, these three categories of funding do not make a large fraction of overall funding to APSA.

Despite the different types of UN funding to APSA, UN financial support to the AU forms only a fraction because it competes with the EU and a host of bilateral funding programmes. This broad fiscal spectrum enables the AU to avoid any heavy influence from the UN. Indeed, the EU remains the largest and often most preferable substitute for the AU Peace Fund because the AU and EU have agreed that "the Africa Peace Facility will be rolled back once the AU has its own funding".[67] It seems that the AU chooses to avoid contested funding (such as above) and move towards more recent bilateral funding programmes which are considered impact oriented and without conditionality—i.e. Norway, China and Germany.

Failed UN Support to PANWISE

The UN and the AU failed to conjointly operationalise the Panel of the Wise. The original arrangement was to professionalise mediation by setting up structures for professional mediation.[68] This idea had been mooted four years before the signing of the partnership (i.e. in 2002) and would thus serve as litmus test of the agreement. Following the signing of the agreement, the UN offered a consultant to help set up and augment the AU's mediation and prevention diplomacy unit known as Panel of the Wise. The UN provided a single expert to work with the Panel during their mandate in the Central African Republic during the 2007 unrest.[69] However, the support programme disintegrated within the first three years.

The project failed due to issues of agency and preferences. The AU was not satisfied by the UN approach.[70] As a result, the coordinator of the Panel of the Wise opted for a different approach that does not involve the UN. It is not clear whether this was the sole prerogative of the coordinator. It is imperative to note that the original Panel of the Wise involved former heads of state that had fought for African independence and agency over the years—former President(s) Ben Bella (of Algeria), Kenneth Kaunda (Zambia) and others. Moreover, prominent statesmen such as Thabo Mbeki and Alpha Konare also led ad hoc mediation teams which would often act in parallel or alongside the UN. There is reason to suspect the foregoing's influence because the coordinator turned towards indigenous resources to operationalise the Panel of the Wise.

The coordinator and indeed the Panel abandoned the UN support to reinvent the institutional design of PANEL. They collated all pre-existing and new mediation structures of mediation and preventive diplomacy. RECs such as ECOWAS and SADC already had thriving structures. The outcome was the Pan-African Network of PANWISE. This new design was a result of concerted efforts between the PANWISE secretariat, SADC, ECOWAS, ACCORD (a South African research think tank) and several African NGOs working in multi-track diplomacy and peacebuilding, with auxiliary funding from the Finnish government.[71] Surprisingly, the UN seems unaware of the progress made by the AU and still believes that the PANEL has not reached full operational capability.

NATO Support to APSA

SUPPORT TO THE ASF: BETWEEN HQ AND THE MISSION SPACE

The largest amount of NATO support to APSA is mainly in the African Standby Force. This takes two forms. This comprises support to the operations planning and control at the AU headquarters and the mission space.

NATO provides capacity building to the Peace Support Operations Division (PSOD) of the AU. It has seconded officers to provide capacity in the areas of strategic airlift, sealift, intelligence and communications, and logistic support.[72] There are questions within the AU whether such support has a trickledown effect or is mere capacity substitution.[73] This partnership has no action plans or reviews to measure the amount of skills and knowledge transfer. Without action plans and reviews the partnership deliverables are not measured. This implies that it is difficult to determine the extent to which NATO affects African agency. However, the focus should not squarely be on NATO's role, but also that of the AU. The most obvious omission in case of the AU-NATO partnership is a general lack of reflection on lessons learned or deep reviews from within the PSOD, even though the department has ample civilian personnel.

In the mission space, NATO's contribution is mainly in strategic airlift. NATO is filling a gap left by capable African states. There are about nine African states capable of providing strategic airlift.[74] However, there are concerns about reimbursements for using COE in AU missions. For example, South Africa was not refunded for its deployment in the AU Mission in Burundi.[75] Nigeria also airlifted its own troops into Darfur during the early part of AUMID. However, major African states stopped volunteering their equipment and resources for AU peace missions due to a lack of a clear reimbursement for COE.[76] The reliability of NATO's strategic airlift makes it an important contributor to the ASF.

NATO also makes significant contributions in the field of intelligence and communication. The AU has no clear policy on peacekeeping intelligence. NATO intelligence shared with the AU is intelligence shared by individual member states such as the US and France.[77] For that reason, such intelligence is often used politically. For example, in 2014 NATO dangled pertinent intelligence about Al-Shabaab to the Ethiopian government when it was reluctant to continue hosting the NATO SMLT, and granting the team diplomatic status. Communication and intelligence remain a key challenge to AU PSOs, although Algeria has made efforts to fill that gap through secondment of officers to the PSOD and the then ACRIC arrangement.

NATO also trains some of the regional brigades of the African Standby Force. This element came at a later stage. This arrangement began with informal agreements with individual TCCs and subregional organisations, especially ECOWAS. However, the significance of this training remains in question as AU staffers prioritise training arrangements from the EU and US AFRICOM.[78]

Explaining Lack of Support to the PSC, CEWS, PANWISE, APF

NATO does not have a relationship with the PSC. The NATO equivalent of the PSC would be the North Atlantic Council (NAC). However, these two do not have a relationship due to the way the partnership was framed. The partnership was negotiated in such a way that it was not expected to involve political engagement. In fact, during (former Commissioner of Peace and Security) Djinnit's visit to the NAC, the latter shied away from a stronger relationship with the AU. As a result, the NAC does not have regular dialogue with the PSC. The dialogue is restricted to the Department of Peace and Security, and not the PSC.

NATO also does not have a relationship with the CEWS, although NATO possesses advanced capacity and capabilities in early warning systems. Its Airborne Warning and Control Systems, which consists of a fleet of Boeing E-3As, is used to provide surveillance cover for missions—notably used in Libya in 2011 (NATO, n.d.). Although it is intelligence-based surveillance, it has been used for international sporting events such as Olympics and World Cup tournaments. However, the AU has avoided engaging NATO because it used intelligence-based early warning systems.[79] Conversely, NATO insists that it can only provide such resources if the AU requests them.[80]

NATO does not contribute to the PANWISE and the AU Peace Fund for the same reasons. The main reason is that NATO does not have corresponding structures and expertise in these fields. NATO's diplomacy is public diplomacy which borders on public relations (NATO 2014). Even the recent creation of the Comprehensive Crisis and Operations Management Centre (CCOMC) is a far cry from the preventive diplomatic tool it is purported to be.[81] If anything, it is very different from its AU counterpart. NATO also does not provide funding as a form of support. Moreover, according to then head of the NATO SMLT, the AU has not looked to NATO as a possible funder. Whether or not the PANWISE will develop a relationship with the NATO CCOMC is open to debate, but the idea of funding from NATO seems highly unlikely.

In essence, the contribution of NATO to APSA is limited. There are no plans to expand the scope of engagement (explained). The NATO intervention in Libya further compounded this partnership.

US AFRICOM Support to the AU and APSA

SUPPORT TO THE AFRICAN STANDBY FORCE

The largest contribution of US AFRICOM is towards the ASF. The Command trains troops for the ASF. These are troops from top troop contributing counties such as Rwanda, Uganda and Burundi. These are countries which have a history of close relations with the US.

AFRICOM also provides resources in strategic airlift. US helps airlift troops from TCCs using its C17 aircrafts. However, the US AFRICOM is only filling a gap left by member states which have capacity. Between 2004 and 2007, most African states airlifted most of their troops to various AU peace support operations. For instance, South Africa airlifted most of its more than 1000 troops during its lead role in the AU mission in Burundi (AUMIB) between 2004 and 2006.[82] Nigeria also airlifted its troops to the AU mission in Darfur.[83] Botswana also used to airlift troops to Darfur on request from the Americans.[84] AFRICOM continues airlift support to smaller states without their own strategic airlift resources.

The training of troops (for the ASF) has not graduated from its bilateral characteristics. The US AFRICOM still provided training based on the ACOTA template. The ACOTA programme was specifically designed to increase the peacekeeping capacity and capability of African states (US State Department, n.d.). Since AFRICOM is a state security "organisation", it inadvertently continues some of its bilateral security programmes. However, its unwillingness to realign ACOTA with the AU's training guidelines strained the partnership. The disagreements resulted in AFRICOM increasing its support to the 25 participants of ACOTA. These recipients thereafter participate in various peacekeeping missions.

The contributions of the US AFRICOM are limited to the ASF for two reasons. First, it has to do with the nature of AFRICOM. Despite attempts to create an amalgamated command, it remains largely militaristic. The civilian component of the State Department in AFRICOM is not salient. To that end, AFRICOM has not developed a strong relationship with other APSA institutions whose functions are similar to those found within the State Department. In 2012, AFRICOM officials consulted various APSA institutions on possible cooperation. According to the CEWS coordinator's personal account, the subsequent report only mentioned some of the CEWS in the preamble. Second, as a corollary of the nature of AFRICOM, some gatekeepers and top-decision-makers (outside of the PSOD) do not prioritise a partnership with AFRICOM. There is recalcitrance towards AFRICOM because it is a military. This is reinforced by the lack of political support for AFRICOM at the highest level. Third, some programme coordinators prefer to insulate the programmes from international partnership due to an uneasy past relationship with partners. For example, the coordinator of the Panel of the Wise prefers an endogenous process of building the institutions. The endogenous process is seen as protecting African agency and building on pre-existing structures and approaches.

SUPPORT TO THE AU PEACE FUND

The US does not provide direct support to the AU Peace Fund. The US does provide direct funding towards APSA. However, this funding has changed in form over time.

In the early phase of the US–Africa collaboration the US provided direct financial support to the AU. However, this funding was heavily contested. The US insisted on dictating the manner in which the funding was to be used, even when it undermined AU principles. For example, the US could dictate that certain AU member states should not benefit from its funding.[85] The AU was dissatisfied with this approach but there was little they could do without local funding.

In the second phase, AFRICOM reduced and eventually changed the form of funding it provides to the AU. Instead of funding, it resorted to material contributions. For example, as a founding member of AFRICOM attested, instead of providing funding AFRICOM installs structures or training equipment wherever needed in African peace support operations.

EXPLAINING LACK OF SUPPORT
TO CEWS, PANWISE AND PSC

AFRICOM does not have a collaborative relationship with the CEWS. It uses intelligence for its early warning activities. Of the three APSA units without a link to AFRICOM, the area of early is the only area in which the US AFRICOM repeatedly showed interest. In the first instance, circa 2010, AFRICOM was conducting a wide consultative study on how it could collaborate with various APSA institutions. CEWS only featured in the abstract of the final copy of the study.

AFRICOM showed interest in early warning and communications systems during the second testing exercise of the African Standby Force (i.e. AMANI AFRICA II). They proposed to install equipment at various RECs to facilitate the interoperability of the ASF. However, the AU eventually refused because such support was on condition that only the AFRICOM would maintain and service the equipment. The first instance was, according to sources, not appealing because it would be intelligence-based. The second instance was rejected on grounds that there would be no conjoined design and operation.

AFRICOM also does not have a relationship with PANWISE. The State Department, which constitutes part of AFRICOM, has expertise in preventive diplomacy and mediation through the Bureau of Conflict and Stabilisation Operations.[86] The US is already a key player in the peace negotiation processes in Sudan.[87] However, the US is yet to develop a collaborative relationship with the PANWISE. This is owed to two factors. First, there is little evidence to the effect that AFRICOM has incorporated mediation expertise in its organisational structures. Such expertise remains outside the scope of AFRICOM. Second, the PANWISE is seemingly intent on fully operationalising its institutional capacity using indigenous expertise. It is beyond the scope of this study to postulate whether the two will collaborate in the foreseeable future; but it is possible for the two to have a collaborative relationship if there are converging interests.

Finally, AFRICOM does not have a strong relationship with the PSC. At present there are no corresponding structures for engagement. AFRICOM does not even have a structure resembling the North Atlantic Council. Perfunctorily, it appears that the four-star general and civilian ambassadors heading AFRICOM are best suited to collaborate with the PSC. However, the echelons of AFRICOM seem diffusely institutionalised, lacking internal organisational synergy. On the one hand, real power within the partnership lies with US president and the Secretary of State (especially the latter) who do not even have a strong relationship with the AHSG. On the other, AFRICOM remains largely militaristic in nature.[88] The only existing current links are lowly institutionalised "exchanges" between the PSC and AFRICOM, especially over the conflict in the Horn of Africa.[89] This engagement is not only selective but is not malleable to accommodate resource directionality and preference coordination, because it translates a plethora of pre-partnership issues (discussed later).

128   T. GWATIWA

AFRICOM also does not provide any form of capacity building to the PSC like other partners. The US is generically poised to provide such capacity. However, the idea and possibility of AFRICOM providing such support to the PSC seems far-fetched because the PSC is relatively more institutionalised than the AFRICOM Secretariat; and more experienced than the US in African regional security.[90] I observed that Department of Defence (DOD) officials and their counterparts at State Department have different views about Africa: the former have a conservative hard-liner approach, while the latter have a malleable and diplomatic approach. This primarily owes to the Command's institutional nascence. In that arrangement, the DOD historically boasts operational dominance in US Africa policy, with the State Department playing second fiddle or pursuing parallel projects. Therefore, in the current structure and operations of AFRICOM, the State Department seems to be embedded in an overall DOD agenda. This curtails a potentially strong collaborative relationship between the US Africa Command and the PSC.

Partners' Support and the Situs of African Agency

The idea and practice of building or improving African security institution through international support is not value free. It has benefits as well as costs. It is imperative to highlight that it is not that Africans cannot build political and security institution. The problem is that Africans do not seem heavily invested in the building of these institutions. This is partly caused by African states' preoccupation with their respective state-making and nation-building projects which are relatively newer than those found elsewhere in the Global South. States seem more concerned with domestic and subregional processes than those at the continental level. African states have limited resources, and can only do much. Although there is periodic excitement with continental projects, several hiccups at the national and subregional level often force states. These hiccups can incite states to adopt shirking and slippage techniques which are discussed in the next chapters.

The foregoing descriptive analysis provides an explanatory threshold of the shirking and slippage explained in the next three chapters. The next chapters explain in detail why a particular partnership exhibits agency slack, but the overview of partnership support proffers a generic explanation of each partnership's uniqueness. The descriptive narrative in this chapter explains why a certain partner would or not provide certain types of support. In most cases, partners support the AU based on their competency. However, in some cases the partner may not provide a particular type of support. That would depend on the specificities of the partnership (see each of the subsequent chapters and case study). However, it is important to highlight the AU's power and freedom to choose which partner to engage on a specific aspect of the APSA project.

The power and freedom to secure certain types and degrees of engagement is dependent on three major factors. The first determinant is the extent to which the OAU/AU had already institutionalised a particular institution even though it might have been dormant by the late 1990s and early 2000s. A primary example is the inception of the Central Organ, which translated into the PSC, and The Mechanism, which transformed into the PANWISE. The second determinant is the extent to which a larger number of African states, as per the required workload, is willing to assume the onus of augmenting that project. In the case of the PSC, there were more states (big and small) willing to protect the sanctity of the PSC as a key decision-making institution in the APSA. Moreover, this institution is more political than the rest: involves the role of ambassadors who often have direct access to their respective heads of state and government. In the case of The Mechanism and PANWISE, which does not require massive resources and perennial involvement likes other counterparts, a number of capable states—South Africa, Algeria, Nigeria and others—assumed the responsibility and played the part. The zenith was when the AU PSD decided to reconcile these structures, with their more established subregional counterparts—into a continental network. Third, the freedom to choose is determined by the other party's willingness to concede more agency to the AU. The subsequent chapters will explain why this varies a lot for different institutions in each partnership. They provide a more detailed account of what actually transpires within the partnership. The third factor seems more potent than the others.

NOTES

1. William I. Zartman, "Africa as a Subordinate State System in International Relations", *International Organization* 21, no. 3 (1967): 545–564.
2. Mahmood Mamdani, "Historicizing Power and Responses to Power: Indirect Rule and Its Reform", *Social Research* 66, no. 3 (1999): 859–886.

3. See the African Union, *Constitutive Act*, (Addis Ababa: AU Commission, 2000); African Union, *Protocol Relating to the Establishment of the Peace and Security Council of the African Union* (Addis Ababa: AU Commission, 2002).

4. Alhaji Sarjoh Bah, Elizabeth Choge-Nyangoro, Solomon Dersso, Brenda Mofya and Timothy Murithi, eds., *The Africa Peace and Security Architecture: A Handbook* (Addis Ababa: Friedrich-Ebert-Stiftung, 2014), 29.

5. Ulf Engel and Joào Gomes Porto eds, *Africa's New Peace and Security Architecture: Promoting Norms, Institutionalizing Solutions* (London and New York: Routledge, 2013).

6. Bah et al., *The Peace and Security Architecture*, 34.

7. Tim Murithi and Charles Mwaura, "The Panel of the Wise", in *Africa's New Peace and Security Architecture: Promoting Norms, Institutionalizing Solutions*, eds., Ulf Engel and James Gomes Porto (London and New York: Routledge, 2010).

8. Ibid.

9. Astrid Evrensel, personal interview, Head of Mediation, UN Office to the AU, Addis Ababa: November 2015; Yvette Ngandu, personal interview, Coordinator of the Pan-African Panel of the Wise, Addis Ababa: June 2014.

10. Ngandu, personal communication, June 2014.

11. Natacha Kunama, telephone interview, Mediation Expert, African Centre for the Construction Resolution of Disputes, October 2014.

12. Bah et al., *The Peace and Security Architecture*, 33.

13. Charles Mwaura, personal interview, Coordinator of (AU) Continental Early Warning Systems, Addis Ababa: July 2014.

14. Ibid.

15. Benedict Ijomah, "The African Military Interventions: A Prelude to Military High Command", *Journal of African Activist Association* 5, no. 2 (1974): 51–80.

16. Olu S. Agbi, *The Organization of African Unity and African Diplomacy, 1963–1979* (Ibadan: Impact Publishers, 1986).

17. AU Peace and Security Department, *Criteria for Operationalization of the African Standby Force*, Final Draft (Addis Ababa: African Union Commission, July 2015), 2.

18. See section on the enduring colonial and imperial legacies.

19. Colonel Mamadu Mbaye, personal interview, Coordinator of the African Standby Force, AU Peace and Security Department, Addis Ababa: June 2014. .
20. Benjamin Namanya, personal interview, Head of the Police Component, UN Office to the AU, Addis Ababa: June 2014.
21. Captain Tongulac Hakan, personal interviewcommunication, Head of the NATO Senior Military Liaison Team, Addis Ababa: June 2014.
22. Commissioner Sayibu Gariba, personal interview, Coordinator of the Police Element, African Standby Force, Addis Ababa: August 2015.
23. Iyah Onuk, personal interview communication, AU Department of Peace and Security, Addis Ababa: June 2014.
24. African Union, "Declaration of Self-Reliance".
25. Harry Eckstein, *Regarding Politics: Essays on Political Theory, Stability, and Change* (Berkeley and Oxford: University of California Press, 1992) Chapter 10.
26. Chris Alden and Mills Soko, "South Africa's Economic Relations with Africa: Hegemony and Its Discontents", *Journal of Modern African Studies* 43, no. 3 (2005): 367–392.
27. Karen Smith, "South Africa and India as Regional Leaders: Gaining Acceptance and Legitimacy Through the Use of Soft Power", in *South-South Cooperation: Africa on the Centre Stage*, eds. Renu Modi (Basingstoke: Palgrave Macmillan, 2011), 68–83.
28. Adekeye Adebajo and Chris Landsberg, "Nigeria and South Africa as Regional Hegemons", in *Gulliver's Troubles: Nigeria's Foreign Policy After the Cold War*, eds. Adeyeke Adebajo and Abdul Raufu Mustapha (Pietermaritzburg: University of Kwazulu Natal Press, 2008).
29. Andrew Hurrell, "Regional Powers and the Global System From a Historical Perspective", in *Regional Leadership in the Global System: Ideas, Interests and Strategies of Regional Powers*, eds. Daniel Flemes and Detlef Nolte (London and New York: Routledge, 2010), 15–30, 22.
30. Adekeye Adebajo, "Hegemony on a Shoestring", in *Gulliver's Troubles: Nigeria's Foreign Policy After the Cold War*, eds. Adeyeke Adebajo and Abdul Raufu Mustapha (Pietermaritzburg: University of Kwazulu Natal Press, 2008).
31. Landsberg, "An African Concert of Powers".

32. AU Executive Council, *The Common African Position on the Proposed Reform of the United Nations: the Ezulwini Consensus*, Ext/EX.CL/2 (VII) (Addis Ababa: African Union, 2005), Article 2.

33. Landsberg, "An African Concert", 205.

34. Adeyeke Adebajo and Abdul Raufu Mustapha, eds., *Gulliver's Troubles: Nigeria's Foreign Policy After the Cold War* (Pietermaritzburg: University of Kwazulu Natal Press, 2008).

35. African Union, *Protocol Relating to the Establishment of the Peace and Security Council of the African Union* (Addis Ababa: AU Commission, 2004), 13, [article 13].

36. Batlokwa Makong, personal interview, member of the Permanent Representatives Commitee's Committee on Multilateralism, Addis, July 2015; Punkie Molefe, personal interview, Ambassador of Botswana to Ethiopia, member of the Permanent Representatives Committee, Addis Ababa: July 2015; Naim Akibou, personal interview, Benin's Ambassador to Ethiopia, Addis Ababa: August 2015.

37. Ademola Abbas, personal interview, former AU peace and secuity consultant, Addis Ababa: July 2014.

38. Ambassador Usman Baraya, personal interview, Nigeria's Ambassador to Ethiopia, Addis Ababa: August 2015.

39. Mehari T. Maru, personal interview, former AU programme director and international security consultant, Addis Ababa: December 2015.

40. Ambassador Musa Aphane, personal interview, Head of the Multilateral Desk, Department of International Relations and Cooperation, Pretoria: February 2013.

41. Political officer, personal interview, Algerian Embassy to Ethiopia, Addis Ababa: July 2014.

42. See Khadija Bah, "Africa's G4 Network", in *Networks of Influence? Developing Countries in a Networked Global Order*, eds. Leonardo Martinez-Diaz and Ngaire Woods (Oxford and New York: Oxford University Press, 2009), 147–170.

43. Jose Fernando Costa-Pereira, personal interview, EEAS, Brussels: June 2013.

44. Carmen Csernelhazi, personal interview, Political officer, EU Delegation to the AU, Addis Ababa: November 2014; Costa-Pereira, personal interview, June 2013.

45. Ibid.
46. Abbas, personal interview, November 2014.
47. Colonel Michael Nuyens, telephone interview, EU Military Staff, Brussels/Geneva: October 2015.
48. Jide M. Okeke, personal interview, Senior Civilian Officer, AU Peace Support Operations Division, Addis Ababa: June 2014.
49. Onuk, personal interview, June 2014.
50. see AU Program Budget, 2014.
51. Okeke, personal interview, June 2014.
52. Tomaz Salomao, personal interview, former Executive Secretary of SADC Secretariat, Johannesburg: January 2016.
53. Onuk, personal interview, June 2014.
54. Charles Mwaura, personal interview, Coordinator of (AU) Continental Early Warning Systems, Addis Ababa: July 2014.
55. Yvette Ngandu, personal interview, Coordinator of the Pan-African Panel of the Wise, Addis Ababa: June 2014.
56. Organization of African Unity, *Technical Report No.1 Prepared for African Negotiators by OAU Advisory Panel of Experts on ACP-EU Negotiations* (Addis Ababa: OAU, February 1999).
57. Note that the operationalisation of the ASF involved two phases. These phases were in the form of exercises. The phase was a combination of conceptualisation and a mapping exercise (MAPEX). It is known as AMANI AFRICA I. This took place in Addis Ababa in 2010. The second phase was an actual military exercise. The initial exercise was an experimental exercise using the East African Standby Brigade in an exercise dubbed Operation Njewa. The final exercise for the entire ASF was conducted in South Africa in 2015. It is known as AMANI AFRICA II.
58. Namanya, personal interview, June 2014.
59. The experiences in Sudan, Somalia and elsewhere had shown that most African missions would end as UN missions. The idea of multidimensionality was encouraged by the AHSG because their view was that the original design of the ASF was too militaristic. The final design of the ASF is 70 per cent military complemented by a remainder percentage which comprises police and civilian elements.
60. Once again it is imperative to note the idea of the ASF as per the Gambari Report of 2011. It was decided that the ASF should not

134 T. GWATIWA

be viewed as an aspirational force, but one to be built based on the existing troop deployments in AU peace support operations.
61. Abdel-Kader Harieche, personal interview, Head of Politics, UN Office to the AU, Addis Ababa: November 2014.
62. African Union, 2014c.
63. Onuk, personal interview, June 2014.
64. Okeke, personal interview, June 2014.
65. Mwaura, personal interview, July 2014.
66. Onuk, personal interview, June 2014.
67. Ibid.
68. Fiona Lortan, personal interview, Coordinator of the AU-UN Partnership, Addis Ababa: July 2015.
69. Murithi, personal interview, October 2013.
70. Surprisingly, the two ladies leading these efforts from the AU and UN seemed to have an uneasy relationship. Moreover, I observed that the UN expected the AU to blindly endorse its model. I also observed or rather inferred from the interview that the UN also expected to "lead" the project. This was ironic given the element of African ownership and leadership underpinning the partnerships. Generally, the UN seems unreceptive of that notion.
71. Ngandu, personal interview, June 2014.
72. Hakan, personal interview, June 2014.
73. Okeke, personal interview, June 2014.
74. Aphane, personal interview, February 2013; Teteh, personal interview, July 2015.
75. See Aboagye, "African Mission".
76. Onuk, personal interview, June 2014.
77. Lieutenant Colonel (rtd.) William Haag, personal interview, former Lead Planner for NATO Missions to the AU, Lisbon: 2014.
78. Mbaye, personal interview, June 2014.
79. Mwaura, personal interview, July 2014.
80. Colonel Vincent Alexandre, personal interview, Head of NATO Military Partnerships Branch, Naples: November 2014.
81. NATO, "New Integrated NATO Center Support the Alliance with Improved Approach to Emerging Security Challenges and Crisis", May 4, 2012, http://www.nato.int/cps/en/natolive/news_86912.htm; also see Steven A. Zyck and Robert Muggah. "Preventive Diplomacy and Conflict Prevention: Obstacles and Opportunities", *Stability: International Journal of Security and*

Development 1, no. 1 (2012): 68–75, http://www.stabilityjournal. org/articles/10.5334/sta.ac/#r11.
82. Colonel (rtd) Festus Aboagye, personal interview, Executive Director of he African Peace Support Trainers' Association, Nairobi: April 2016.
83. Abbas, personal interview, November 2014.
84. Wyatt, personal interview, November 2014.
85. Linda Akua Darkwa, personal interview, AU Peace and Security Department consultant, Geneva: June 2013.
86. United States Department of State, n.d.
87. Boitshoko Mokgatlhe, personal interview, Head of AU Liaison Team to Khartoum AU Peace and Security Department, Addis Ababa: November 2014.
88. David Wiley, "Militarizing Africa and African Studies and the U.S. Africanist Response", *African Studies Review* 55, no. 2 (2012): 147–161.
89. Ambassador Reuben Brigety, telephone interview, former US Amabassador to the AU, July 2016.
90. Sandra Oder, personal interview, Civilian Officer, Peace and Security Department, Addis Ababa: December 2015.

CHAPTER 6

The Africa–EU Partnership and African Agency: Model or Pareidolia?

Academic and policy discussions of African agency tend to tout the Africa–EU strategic partnership as a model for inter-regional cooperation. Indeed, the longevity of this inter-regional partnership can neither be overstated nor understated. However, it is important to subject this partnership to rigorous analysis because, unlike any other, this partnership has the benefit of the confidence of the press and think tanks compared to the rest. A perfunctory review of this partnership will reveal that many issues lie below a veneer of a seemingly rosy partnership between Africa and the EU. Therefore, it is imperative to examine the extent to which this partnership is indeed a model or simply a pareidolia.

Origins of the Partnership

The origins of this partnership can be placed at two critical junctures in Africa–Europe history. The earliest shadow of European influence over the design of African institutions was the fact that the OAU Charter was drafted, as mentioned in a previous chapter, by a retired Irish general.[1] This can be explained by the fact that most African political leaders were educated in Europe and the US. Thus, Western influence cast an ominous shadow over African institutional design.

From another perspective, this partnership has roots in an inter-regional economic relationship. That aside, imperial powers' economic

© The Author(s), under exclusive license to Springer Nature Switzerland AG 2022
T. Gwatiwa, *The African Union and African Agency in International Politics*, https://doi.org/10.1007/978-3-030-87805-4_6

137

138   T. GWATIWA

interests in Africa defined processes of decolonisation. Those economic factors influenced negotiations of early European treaties.[2] The current partnership between Africa and Europe is also driven by economic interests of former colonisers as well as imperial states. The peace and security element is just a part of broader (economic) strategic partnership (i.e. the Cotonou Agreement of 2003) that succeeded the Lomé Agreement of 1974 which was prodigiously economic.

The inclusion of the peace and security component in the Cotonou Agreement derives from a perceived security–development nexus. Article 11 of the agreement states that "the Parties [sic] acknowledge that without development and poverty reduction there will be no sustainable peace and security, and that without peace and security there can be no sustainable development".[3] To Europe, this is important because it needs more economic resources from Africa. To Africa, this means that they will not bear the burden of stabilising the continent alone. The goal of stabilising the continent was already captured in the CSSDCA, the Constitutive Act, as well as the PSC Protocol all of which highlight the need for a multifaceted and perhaps isomorphic approach to political and economic challenges in the continent. The most defining of these approaches is the security-development nexus doctrine, which purports that security and political stability should ideally precede economic development. As a corollary, the partnership is currently skewed towards peace and security with the hope of creating necessary conditions for investments and development.

DIPLOMACY AND ENGAGEMENT: FROM LOMÉ TO COTONOU

During the renegotiation of the Lomé Agreement in the late 1990s, the African group demanded more room for African agency. OAU negotiators strongly emphasised the need for principles of ownership and equality on the part of Africans. The African experience under the Lome Agreement compelled Africans to seek an end to European unilateralism in the relationship. An archival report prepared for negotiators states that:

> [The] ACP should guard against an EU blue-print of these essential elements and should not accept conditionalities or directives regarding the *pace or nature of reforms*...Such an approach should respect the overriding principles of ownership and sovereignty.[4]

The above suggests that the Africa group sought an end to a partnership whereby it is on the receiving end. It sought greater levels of ownership and partnership management.

The partners eventually agreed on ownership and equality for different reasons. For Africa, it was an opportunity for continuity of institutional design and building which started in the 1960s. There was also a desire to insulate this process from Western interference in ACP regional affairs. African and European political leaders eventually agreed on an equal partnership at the first Africa–EU Summit held in Cairo in 2000.[5] For Europeans, this framework relieved them from the burden of underwriting African problems.[6] Both sides walked away with relief: Africans with an "agenda and priority setting" onus and Europeans with a "blood and treasure" framework.[7]

This bargaining chip worked for a larger part of the partnership lifespan. The AU was able to revive and assume full control of the Central Organ which translated into the PSC. The Africa Group also successfully requested what eventually became the Africa Peace Facility (APF) during the AU Summit held in Maputo in 2004. Interestingly, the APF has not been a controversial institution and is expected to be rolled back to make way for the Africa Peace Fund when African states increase their monetary contributions.

The principle of ownership was captured in key partnership documents. This is captured in Article 11 of the Cotonou Agreement, which states that "[the] Parties shall pursue an active, comprehensive and integrated policy of peace building and conflict prevention and resolution, and human security, and shall address situations of fragility...This policy shall be based on the principle of ownership..." (European Commission 2000). This was also captured in Article 18 of the [subsequent] Joint Africa–EU Strategy which stated that "EU support to Africa has been and continues to be guided by the principle of African ownership".[8] This means three things. First, it assured the AU that it would efficiently manage its preferences. Second, it placed the EU in a mentorship position. Third, a coded principle ensured a shadow of the future for both parties.

Support Towards APSA Institutions and Latitude for More African Action

The EU partnership is the only partnership that makes resource contribution to a majority of the APSA institutions.

The PSC has a strong relationship with its EU counterpart. There are two types of contributions towards the PSC. The first contribution is in the form of capacity building of the PSC secretariat. This involves a form of visiting fellowships and in-house training at the EU Commission.[9] Capacity building has diminished or rather outlived its usefulness. It was not useful because the secretariat existed as the Central Organ for a longer period from the 1990s until it was translated into the PSC in 2002. It has been superseded by a second contribution, namely an inter-collegial meeting.

There is a highly institutionalised annual meeting of the collegial bodies. The EU COPS and the AU PSC (both made up of permanent representatives) hold annual meetings in order to address divergent views on the peace and security approach.[10] This covers, among other things, how the partners build institutions as well as how to collaborate in the mission spaces across Africa. The chairpersons of the two bodies also hold informal meetings twice a year to coordinate interests and preferences. The meeting is so useful that it has been suggested that comity should be extended to New York to avoid what led to Libyan intervention in 2011.

The institutionalisation of this component of the partnership has shaped views on peace and security. According to various respondents in a study conducted, frequent interaction between the two bodies has enabled them to move away from a traditional (military) towards a non-traditional (comprehensive) approach to security. They eventually agreed to a human security approach in the partnership.[11] It is imperative to note that human security already existed in founding AU peace and security policy documents.[12] Thus, there was no exceptional ingenuity, it was simply a realisation that peace and security crises are attributable to political causes.

The African Standby Force and Peace Support Operations

As the Gambari Report notes, the idea of an African Standby Force (ASF) should not be treated as an aspirational idea. The current deployments are in key AU peace support operations (PSOs) such as Somalia and Sudan. What is at issue as of now is testing the readiness of the ASF. With that caveat in place, I highlight that this entwines PSOs and the ASF.

The EU is one of the main contributors of the African Union's PSOs. It contributes in several ways. The EU also bankrolled everything from concept development to exercises and the actual missions of the ASF. The Europeans significantly contributed to the development of key ASF doctrines and concepts such as the logistics and strategic airlift concepts.[13] In the words of a top PSOD official, "the European Union is a pillar in the Africa Peace and Security Architecture".[14] The EU also trains or assists AU troops in some of the missions. However, the EU prefers short engagements which give room for the AU to take over the missions. This trajectory began with Operation Artemis in the DRC in 2003. As of 2007, the EU Military Staff (EU MS) prefer capacity building and programme planning which is equally managed by both parties even though the Africans failed to institutionalise the AU Military Staff Committee (an EUMSC counterpart).

The EU also funds the ASF by paying the salaries of troops serving in the mission spaces. Key troop contributing countries such as Rwanda, Uganda, Ethiopia and Burundi do not have enough resources to sustain their troops in Darfur and Somalia. It is to that end that the EU pays each troop a monthly salary of €700 (was €1200 until November 2015). This funding is managed and disbursed through the Africa Peace Facility.

The Africa Peace Facility and the AU Peace Fund

The Africa Peace Facility (APF) is an EU-funded and managed institution which was set up on request from African heads of states. The idea was for Europe to fund the AU peace and security project until the latter can fully operationalise the Africa Peace Fund (African states are unwilling to finance the Peace Fund). The APF finances a broad set of peace and security components.

The APF finances close to 90 per cent of peace and security employees. This comprises of employees at the AU HQ and the mission spaces.

142   T. GWATIWA

Ideally the Peace and Security Directorate should consist of "about 400 personnel at the AU Headquarters...and about 80 officers elsewhere (in every mission)".[15] This means that the APF helps fund both uniformed and civilian personnel. It also finances the meetings and conferences that may involve other partners.

However, the EU and AU have an uneasy relationship regarding financial disbursements through the APF. The AU perceives the EU's insistence on accountability as unreasonable coercion. EU demands for accountability coincided with increased diversification of funds from top African nations and a few Scandinavian donors. For example, the Joint Financial Arrangements (JFAs) which currently finance mission spaces, are funded by the EU, Denmark and a number of African countries whose fractional contribution amounts to $13 million out of a budget of $41 million in 2014.[16]

With time, the EU preferred to engage directly with the RECs and RMs to ensure accountability. This meant that it had to decide what could be part of the security projects. AU officials perceive this as a "balkanization of African security".[17] The EU tried to direct attention from the AU, but the RECs stood in solidarity with the continental body.[18] However, there are those within the AU who support the EU's demand for accountability because there are concerns about maladministration of funds within the AU Commission.

According to the new approach, the EU requires the AU to coordinate with its RECs before it can disburse funding through the APF. This means that the EU delegations to the RECs need to vet project funding requests.[19] This means that projects within the partnership take longer than they used to. Most interestingly, the new arrangement requires that the AU returns all the unused funds. For example, the AU had to return 2/3 of the €40 million allocated under the 10th EDF funding from May 2011 to December 31, 2014. The prolongation of the funding element as well as returning of money are yet to be strongly contested to a degree that they affect the other aspects of the partnership.

The EU did not make significant contributions to the Continental Early Warnings Systems (CEWS) and the Panel of the Wise (PANWISE). The EU is the main partner on this project because the partnership started in 2006. The CEWS coordinates with the EU Joint Research Centre. The EU JRC largely assisted in the design of the system that is used for continental surveillance. The EU generally provides funding for the entire project. However, the AU has relatively more control over the early warning systems project. The AU rejected the idea of an intelligence-based early warning system in the similitude of the EU Situation Room.[20] The EU then ceded the collaboration to the EU JRC which is located in Italy, far away from the headquarters. From close examination this project runs a bit parallel to the larger set of activities coordinated from Brussels. This has enabled the AU and EU JRC to develop a relatively manageable inter-collegial amity.

The EU does not have a strong relationship with the PANWISE. To a certain extent the Panel of the Wise benefits from the general funding made available to APSA institutions. However, they are not strongly involved because from 2006 it was agreed that the UN would have a lead role in the operationalisation of the PANWISE. Thus, the UN recruited the first coordinator of the PANWISE and paid her salary for the first three years. The UN also provided an expert to work with the PANWISE secretariat.[21] The EU deliberately avoided duplication given that the UN has better capacity and experience in the field of mediation and preventive diplomacy.

PREFERENCE COORDINATION BETWEEN AFRICA AND EUROPE

The level of preference of coordination within this partnership stands out as relatively better. The links between the various organisational components help coordinate preferences. The highest level of preference coordination is the summits, which are meetings between heads of state. During the era of Mbeki, Qaddafi, Bouteflika and Obasanjo, the heads of states were key negotiators for African interests. This quartet comprised the chief proponents of the idea of African ownership (i.e. agency) through the notion of "African solutions to African problems". This notion was primarily to gain buy-in in a world where African or Global South preferences were under constant challenge in global politics. This worked because on several occasions Mbeki and Obasanjo lamented "imperialism" or "global apartheid" whenever Europe undermined their preferences.[22]

While the heads of state were the main defenders of the preferences, their implementation was ensured by ministers and *securocrats*.[23] Once the heads of states have agreed on the terms of the partnership, ministers and senior security officials and experts have meetings to create roadmaps. The EU, unlike most partnerships, is uniquely characterised by the use of action plans to ensure that there is minimal [if no] deviation from an agreed framework. This does not imply that there are no imperfections. However, it is imperative to underscore the fact that there is a highly institutionalised system of preference coordination in the partnership.

The epic failure in this regard was the preference coordination during the Western intervention in Libya in 2011. The AU strongly opposed the UN-sanctioned NATO intervention. It proposed a "Government of National Unity"—a typical mediation model in modern African history. Ironically, it turned to the EU for funding. Since all but three members of NATO are also EU member states, they rejected the idea of funding such a programme from the APF or the European Defence Community.[24] The EU typically argued that they could not prevent a UN-sanctioned operation. However, the main troop contributors to the Libyan intervention are also top funders of the European Defence Community. Nevertheless, this did not significantly affect AU–EU relations as the public rage was directed against NATO and the US.

On Palpable Agential Outcomes

History has played a critical role in the realisation of AU agency in this partnership. The two parties engaged each other for nearly three decades before they reached what presently appears to be an emblematic agency-accommodating partnership. This 30-year period (1974–2003) involved intense engagement during which the African group fought for this notion of agency. It particularly contended against European unilateralism. By the time the EU fully committed itself to the entire APSA project, the two parties had fully addressed their preferences over how the external support to APSA projects should be carried out. This suggests that a partnership goes through a rough and often acrimonious interactive process before it can accommodate the preferences of a fledging counterpart. This implies that agency could be contestable in a newer partnership where there are more cognitive barriers. However, this linkage also seems contingent upon other factors.

Mimicry plays a critical role in producing African agency. This can be understood in the context of the extent to which mimicry (evinced by institutional replication) catalysed the partnership. After decades of multifaceted influence, most African security institutions resemble their European counterparts. Suffice it to argue, perhaps counter-intuitively and ironically, that "Africa is Europeanized". In fact, there was an African consensual position that the AU, as well as much of the APSA, should be modelled after the EU.

This elicits a caveat on the EU's accommodation of African agency. If African institutions are essentially European, what is the cost of accommodating African agency? It is also apparent to an armchair analyst that the mantra of "African solutions to African problems" is a face-saving façade for sub-Europeanism. This is because the causes of most African (security) problems are traceable to European colonial and postcolonial policies. Further, this implies that agency is easier to cede if there is a comfortable degree of mimicry or intricate institutional ties. This suggests that if APSA were to be a shadow of European security institutions, implementation would be easier. However, this also suggests that such African agency would be under threat when the mimicry unwinds.

The type of agreement (documentation) governing this partnership played an important role in its outcomes. Agreements differ in wording, length and complementarity. The agreement governing this partnership is somewhat the most specific and probably the lengthiest of the AU partnerships. It is clear on the principles governing the partnerships as well as the modalities of the implementation of APSA. It is also explicit regarding the resource delivery and use. It also has periodic action plans, usually set for a period of three years. There are also several addendums that provide further clarity on the division of labour in the implementation of APSA projects as well as the informal structures that are meant to complement their formal counterparts. This implies that [positive] agential outcomes are dependent on the wording, specificity, frilliness and pragmatism of the agreement governing the partnership.

Institutionalisation of this partnership has widened the latitude of African agency in this partnership. This institutionalisation can either be in the formation of new intercessory institutions or the restructuring of existing ones. The EU and AU sponsored the creation of liaison offices to facilitate dialogue and coordination within the partnership. For instance, there is an EU Delegation to the AU. This delegation comprises various experts including one for peace and security, with expertise on each of the APSA institutions—the ASF, the CEWS, the Panel (although not useful to the AU) and the APF. There is also an AU Permanent Mission to Brussels (EU). These two liaison offices facilitate diplomatic dialogue and engagement between the two commissions. These liaisons played an important role in monitoring resource disbursement as well as facilitating dialogue and compromise whenever the partners had divergent preferences. The

146   T. GWATIWA

informal structures for dialogue and implementation at various levels are owed to these liaisons. To facilitate engagement and the delivery on various APSA projects (including other issue-areas), the EU established liaison offices to all RECs/RMs. Furthermore, it sponsored the creation of AU liaison offices to the RECs as well as the RECs liaison offices to the AU. This catalysed the two partners' dialogue and engagement on APSA projects. The impact of liaison structures in both institutions shows they tended to widen the latitude for the exercise of the African agency.

Is This an Epitome of African Agency in International Partnerships?

Expectedly, there are signs of strain in the partnership. This is mainly evident around the issue of funding. By 2013 there was a notion of a "JAES fatigue" (Joint Africa–EU Strategy fatigue) among European policymakers. The notion suggested that the partnership had lost momentum. However, that notion did not seem to suggest that the EU had finally reached its limit to accommodate African agency, or such as state to incite the AU to resort to agency slack.

Perceptions within the two organisations suggest that there are more gains than losses in the partnership. It suggests that the abovementioned "strain" is a natural institutional process and does not portend a potential paralysis of the partnership. For instance, the then head of the Pan-African Desk at the European External Action Service (EEAS) argued that the partnership was moving in the right direction.[25] Similarly, AU officials considered this partnership the most efficient in terms of outcomes of building APSA institutions.[26] These views were pronounced against a background of a strong institutional framework within which the two partners could effectively address their differences. This implies that institutional framework bulwarked the partnership against this mild recession and saved it from the compromising of African agency.

It would be grim to argue that this partnership was or could ever be on the verge of agency slack identifiable in other partnerships. To the contrary, the "JAES Fatigue" does not have a significant impact on the notional and empirically sacrosanct idea of African leadership and ownership (i.e. agency). Various respondents often highlighted the integral role of the deep institutionalisation of this partnership. As corollary, the reader is led to assume that the idea of "fatigue" was oblivious to the temporality of this strain on the partnership. For instance, this strain did not lead to replacement of the EU as a major partner of the AU. If anything, the partnership enabled the parties to address these differences better than any other partnership by virtue of deep networks across the two continents.

Temporal strains in a partnership should be considered an innately constitutive part of the AU's partnerships. If two parties with different interests and goals collaborate, they should be expected to hold divergent perspectives occasionally.[27] This is due to the cognitive barriers between two organisations situated in two different geographies, with different (also inter-relating) histories and sociologies. These cognitive barriers exist within this partnership for two entwined reasons. There is a new generation of senior EU commissioners, and they rarely visit the AU Commission for dialogue (and vice-versa), and thus have a poor grasp of African issues.[28] This is likely to change depending on the shifting cycles of partnerships or political processes suggested by Galtung.

Parties to this partnership possess the capacity to circumvent agency slack. The threat of recession into "fatigue" or dysfunction would be apparent in partnership with monitoring structures such as this one. The EU did not permit the risk of recession especially with regard to the ASF. When the initial cooperation between the EU MS and the AU Military Staff Committee (AU MSC) failed, the two parties replaced that comity with an ad hoc team to operationalise the ASF. This team involved four officials seconded by Senegal, Italy, Cameroon, Germany, France, Britain, Ghana and Nigeria. Surprisingly, this arrangement yielded quicker and better results.[29] Even when the AU brought more partners on board, namely NATO, UN, US AFRICOM, the EU quickly transcended to another element of the ASF by providing capacity for the logistics component instead of insisting to retain its position.[30] This implies that one of the partners can save a partnership from receding into agency slack when threatened by competition, by finding a niche in the scope of projects within the partnerships.

SOFT COERCION, POWER AND FORUM SHOPPING: TEETERING ON THE VERGE OF AGENCY SLACK?

The risk of polarisation and agency slack from either party is ever present. Causes of such polarisation are many and varied. To be sure, the process is fungible and will always be defined by what the AU wants at a particular time. If the AU demands what the agency-respecting partner feels is insurmountable, what should be the other party's response? Parties tend

148   T. GWATIWA

to resort to soft coercion, power projection and forum shopping, albeit with varying degrees of subtlety.

This partnership gradually became bumpy over the issue of funding. There were signs that the AU is not happy with its financial support—which is predominantly from the EU. The EU finds itself in a difficult context because even though it supports AU security programmes, it is accountable to its regional and bilateral constituents. As a result, the EU's demand for accountability is mostly misconstrued for soft coercion. This image is also ever lingering due to the colonial legacy of the EU's lead nations such as France, Britain, Brussels, Spain and Italy. The AU began seeking alternative forms of funding. Between 2012 and 2013 the Chairperson of the AU Commission, Dr. Nkosazana Dlamini-Zuma, concluded a six-year effort to persuade China to play a greater role in African peace and security.[31] In one case, Dlamini-Zuma barred partners from attending some meetings in which partners have observer status.[32] Do these manoeuvres suggest that African agency in partnership is under threat?

The EU is reluctant to use the forum shopping opportunities provided by states overlapping membership of various organisations. Most European countries are members of the EU, NATO, UN and OSCE. Typically, the EU–NATO duality and strategic agreement of 2003 should be a source of concern. The EU and NATO are aware of the advantages of this overlap. However, the two organisations choose to keep their partnerships separate when dealing with the AU.[33] As a result, there is variance in the gains and losses made by both organisations. This implies that the propensity to avoid forum shopping tends to save a partnership from agency slack or complete disintegration.

On the other hand, the EU's potential for forum shopping is inhibited by two actors within the European continent. These two actors have slightly different policies to those of the EU, despite one being a member. These cause the EU to proceed without compromising the partnership. The *Deutsche Gesellschaft Für Internationale Zusammenarbeit* (GIZ), i.e. the German Development Cooperation Agency, is the AU's most celebrated financier because it does not have conditionality.[34] GIZ provides its own funding mainly because it differs with France's approach to the continent (a co-main funder of the EU).[35] Norwegian funding also has a different design, i.e. quick impact projects, and goals which earned the state a strategic agreement during a moratorium on the partnerships.[36] The foregoing suggests that these are alternatives to the

EU funding. These place restraints on the EU's capacity to forum shop or flex its coercive capacity. This implies alternative actors providing the same resources as a more powerful actor place restraint on the latter, and thus [inadvertently] saving a partnership from receding into a state of impotence.

Similar counter-actions arise from within the African continent. In fact, the growing recalcitrance of the EU funding has prompted a review of African contributions to regionalism and security. Regional contributions to the AU peace and security budget only constitute 6 per cent of the entire budget.[37] Apart from the annual $325 million contributed by the Big 5 to the AU Commission, a select number of countries contribute directly to the AU Peace Fund: Angola contributes $10 million, Kenya contributes $1 million, while Algeria contributes an undisclosed amount. These are recent initiatives that are meant to balance European dominance and growing conditionality in support to APSA projects. This limits the EU's ability to be more coercive than it already is. It also inadvertently saves the partnership from dysfunction, especially that the AU is aware that its balancing capacity is limited.

Despite the above, shirking or slippage cannot be inferred from any of the various elements of support. The contestation only exists around funding. The other aspects of support to APSA remain intact and productive. If anything, this anomaly in funding implies the partnership, particularly due to its institutionalisation, is able to accommodate African agency. If the overall partnership is generally progressive and delivers the agreed outputs in other areas of the APSA, then it suggests that African agency is thriving. This aligns with Galtung's application of the Hegelian triad to how processes go through an imperfect cycle of thesis, anti-thesis and synthesis.[38] These temporal and spatial strains should not be viewed as a threat to African agency. If anything, this partnership has shown such resilience to protect African agency, because the interests of the two parties are closely linked. It is against this background that there has been little evidence of the AU engaging in any shirking or slippage.

NOTES

1. Organization of African Unity, *Technical Report No.1 Prepared for African Negotiators by OAU Advisory Panel of Experts on ACP-EU Negotiations* (Addis Ababa: OAU, February 1999).

2. Adrian Hewitt and Kaye Whiteman, "The Commission and Development Policy: Bureaucratic Politics in EU Aid—From the Lomé Leap Forward to the Difficulties of Adapting to the Twenty-First Century", in *EU Development Cooperation: From Model to Symbol*, eds. Karin Arts and Anna Dickson (New York and Vancouver: Manchester University Press, 2004), 133–134.
3. European Commission, *Cotonou Agreement* (Brussels: European Commission, 2000), 22.
4. Organization of African Unity, *Technical Report*, 8.
5. Europafrica.net, n.d., Joint Africa-EU Strategy, http://www.europarl.europa.eu/meetdocs/2009_2014/documents/dpap/dv/jeas_action_plan_/jeas_action_plan_en.pdf.
6. Colonel (rtd) Festus Aboagye, personal interview communication, Executive Director of he African Peace Support Trainers' Association, Nairobi: April 2016.
7. see Alhaji M.S. Bah, "West Africa: From a Security Complex to a Security Community", *African Security Review* 14, no. 2, (2005): 77–83.
8. Council of European Union, "The Africa–EU Strategic Partnership: A Joint Africa-EU Strategy" (Lisbon: 2007), 6.
9. Jose Fernando Costa-Pereira, personal interview communication, EEAS, Brussels: June 2013.
10. Carmen Csernelhazi, personal interview communication, Political officer, EU Delegation to the AU, Addis Ababa: November 2014.
11. Ibid.
12. Abbas, personal interview, November 2014.
13. Colonel Michael Nuyens, telephone interview personal communication, EU Military Staff, Brussels/Geneva: October 2015.
14. Jide M. Okeke, personal interview, Senior Civilian Officer, AU Peace Support Operations Division, Addis Ababa: communication, June 2014.
15. Okeke, personal interview, June 2014.
16. see African Union, "AU Program Budget", 2014.
17. Okeke, personal interview, June 2014.
18. Tomaz Salomao, personal interview communication, former Executive Secretary of SADC Secretariat, Johannesburg: January 2016.
19. Onuk, personal interview, June 2014.

20. Charles Mwaura, personal interview communication, Coordinator of (AU) Continental Early Warning Systems, Addis Ababa: July 2014.
21. Yvette Ngandu, personal interview communication, Coordinator of the Pan-African Panel of the Wise, Addis Ababa: June 2014.
22. see Sean Jacobs and Richard Calland, "Thabo Mbeki: Myth and Context", in *Thabo Mbeki's World: the Politics and Ideology of the South African President*, eds. Sean Jacobs and Richard Calland (Pietermaritzburg: University of Natal Press, 2002), 1–24.
23. "Securocrat" is a term popularly used in South African security studies or military history to refer to high ranking officers who were very close to senior policymakers.
24. Sandra Oder, personal interview communication, Civilian Officer, Peace and Security Department, Addis Ababa: December 2015.
25. Costa-Pereira, personal interview, June 2013.
26. Alhaji M.S. Bah, personal interview, Head of AU Delegation to SADC, Gaborone: January 2013.
27. see Johan Galtung, *Essays in Peace Research* (Copenhagen: Ejlers, 1980); Richard Higgot, "Alternative Models of Regional Cooperation? The Limits of Regional Institutionalisation in East Asia," in *European Union and New Regionalism: Regional Actors and Global Governance in a Post-Hegemonic Era* (2nd edition), ed. Mario Telo (England: Ashgate, 2013), 71–106.
28. Csernelhazi, personal interview, November 2014.
29. Lieutenant Colonel Arcieri, personal interview, EU Military Staff, Brussels: February 2014.
30. Nuyens, personal interview, May 2015.
31. Ministry of Foreign Affairs, "Le Keqiang Meets with Nkosazana Dlamini Zuma of the African Union", https://www.mfa.gov.cn/zflt/eng/zt/1_1/t1153417.htm.
32. E.A. Tafa, personal interview, Political Officer, Botswana Embassy to Ethiopia, Addis Ababa: June 2014.
33. Csernelhazi, personal interview, November 2014; Hakan, personal interview, June 2014.
34. Onuk, personal interview, June 2014.
35. Gerard Mai, personal interview, Head of peace and security, GIZ, Addis Ababa: August 2015.
36. Christian Gare, personal interview, Norwegian Royal Embassy to Ethiopia, Addis Ababa: August 2015.

37. Onuk, personal interview, June 2014.
38. Johan Galtung, *Methodology and Ideology* (Copenhagen: Ejlers, 1977).

CHAPTER 7

Shirking in AU Partnerships: The UN and NATO

INTRODUCTION

The African Union's approach to international partnerships also demonstrates "agency slack". This refers to an independent action that is undesirable to contracting parties. According to Hawkins et al., this takes two forms: "shirking" which is when an agent minimises the effort it exerts or "slippage" when an agent shifts policy away from a preferred outcome to its own preferences.[1] Partnerships with NATO and the UN exhibit different motives and techniques of shirking. This variation in shirking relates to the political and technical salience or expediency of the partnerships.

THE AU–UN PARTNERSHIP

The AU exercises a shirking technique that is uniquely identifiable to this partnership. The AU has a complicated relationship with the UN. The two organisations have been in the press regarding their strong differences over their approach to peace operations. The AU prefers subsidiarity while the UN prefers complementarity.[2] Subsidiarity protects African agency and ownership. It gives the AU more latitude to determine the design and operations of peace support operations. The UN prefers a contrary process of complementarity which ossifies its influence and agency within

© The Author(s), under exclusive license to Springer Nature Switzerland AG 2022
T. Gwatiwa, *The African Union and African Agency in International Politics*, https://doi.org/10.1007/978-3-030-87805-4_7

153

154   T. GWATIWA

the partnership. With complementarity, the UN retains its seniority and leadership in aspects of the partnership.

The AU exercises shirking in several ways. The most common way is limiting UN activity in the design of APSA institutions. Whenever the AU differs with the UN, it finds a willing partner in the EU, NATO and key member states. This mostly applies to the design and operationalisation of the African Standby Force, the Panel of the Wise, the APF and the Continental Early Warning Systems. To understand the causes and modes of shirking, it is imperative to trace everything from the origins of the partnership.

Origins of the Partnership

The initial agreement between the AU and UN was signed on the 11th of November 2006. It was signed by the then AU Chairperson, Alpha Konare, and UN SG, Kofi Anan. This was a ten-year capacity building agreement (TYCBA). Article 6 of the UN–AU agreement highlighted institution building by stating the following:

> In the context of the evolving framework, we agree to give special emphasis to enhancing the AU's capacities in the following areas:
>
> 1. institution building, human resources development and financial management
> 2. peace and security
> 3. human rights ....[3]

The TYCBA was based on a cluster system. The cluster system was a mechanism for operationalising eight clusters. During that time (2006–2009), delegations perambulated between Addis Ababa and New York to address various issues. Under this Ten-Year Capacity Building Plan for the AU (or "TYCBP-AU" as it was known), it was agreed that the UN was to co-share clusters of peace and security, and eight other clusters that include trade and agriculture. The first three years were to be dedicated to the peace and security cluster. Under the peace and security cluster, there were the partners would focus on the following: (a) operationalise the African Peace and Security Architecture, (b) human rights, (c) transitional justice, and (d) humanitarian emergencies. The operationalisation of these clusters, especially peace and security, also comprised Regional Coordination Mechanisms.

From the onset, there were intentions to upgrade the TYCBP-AU to a strategic partnership. It was also agreed that, like the Africa–EU partnership, this would be an AU-led partnership agreement. This was easier to agree to at the echelons for two reasons. First, the two signatories of the agreement had developed an understanding through transnational policy networks. Alpha Konare had served as the president of Mali prior to becoming the Chairperson of the AU Commission. Kofi Annan had previously served UN Assistant Secretary General for Peacekeeping Operations between 1993 and 1996. The Rwandan genocide took place under his watch. It was easier for both to relate to a Chapter 8 arrangement. Second, it is always easier to sign agreements at a high level if there are no outstanding issues between organisations. At that time, the two organisations had no history of strong affinity.

Engagement and Contention

The primary motivation for this partnership is that the AU exists under the legal aegis of the UN, which is the main guarantor of global security. The other motivation is that AU member states are UN members, who are paying assessed contributions.[4] There is also a view that the AU can learn from some experienced UN staff.[5] The UN also provides a comparatively less politicised international forum for engagement on global security issues. If this be the case, the argument goes; it should be much easier for the AU and its member states to contest for African agency in international politics.

However, AU and African agency is most contested in the UN's most powerful organ—the United Nations Security Council (UNSC). The UNSC and the AU Peace and Security Council have tense relations. They are competing for seniority, leadership and authority over peace operations in Africa.[6] The two organisations have separate as well joint operations in Sudan, Somalia, the Central African Republic, Mali and Libya. Since 2002, the two councils have been meeting periodically for dialogue over peace operations in Africa. Surprisingly, the meeting is a source of tension. Since 2014, the PSC has consistently protested that the periodic UNSC-PSC meeting was not a meeting of equals: i.e., the UNSC does not treat the PSC as an equal. The UNSC posits that this is an informal meeting without a binding effect on how they should conduct peace operations. As a corollary, the PSC tends to play victim, and the meetings have not resulted in any useful discussions that can improve the nature and impact of their separate and joint missions. The AU, realizing its subaltern state and accompanying predicaments, does not cease to highlight the agential standing of the meeting. This is an evasion tactic which minimises the chances of being smothered by the seniority of the UNSC. By maintaining the status quo, the AU can continue deciding on the nature and scope of their peace support operations—except that they eventually depend on UN funding and technical support.

Ironically, the abovementioned is a contrast of an inter-departmental meeting that the (AU) Peace and Security Department periodically holds with the Department of Peacekeeping Operations (UN DPKO). This meeting takes place at an operational level, following on issues agreed by the two councils and the AUC Chairperson and UN Secretary General. The offices of the UNSC and AUC Chairperson are largely on good terms, even though there has been a drop in cordiality and efficacy since the tenures of Kofi Annan and Alpha Konare. This inter-departmental meeting, which consists of experts at a field level, gives the AU room to manoeuvre the politics at the inter-council level. In other words, this provides room for agency slack on the part of the AU.

The AU and UN have a fuzzy trajectory of preference coordination. This partnership exhibits poor preference coordination.

The problem of preference coordination between Africa and the UN dates back to the 1960s. The differences largely relate to the use of force. In the 1960s, the then Congolese Prime Minister, Patrice Lumumba, and the UN Secretary General, Dag Hammarskjöld, differed over the interpretation of the UN Charter on use of force in the UN Operation in the Congo.[7] The reluctance to use force let the country descend into chaos which resulted in Lumumba's assassination of which one scholar said "UN willed it and the US permitted it".[8] This difference has persisted until now. On the one hand, the AU prefers a hardliner approach to conflict resolution which often results in short-term missions, while the UN prefers a softer and prolonged approach. Why are there divergent approaches? The answer lies in the historicity of conflict resolution between the UN and African subregional organisations.

History shows that the UN approach to conflict resolution has failed in Africa. Both the Economic Community of West African States (ECOWAS) and the Southern African Development Community (SADC) preferred a hard approach to conflict resolution, which informed the actual nature of what came to be known as "peace support operations".

However, while ECOWAS preferred UN-sanctioned missions, SADC preferred launching its own interventions.

Compared to SADC, ECOWAS has patience for UN lethargy. In 1990, it took the UNSC two years to authorise ECOMOG deployment in Liberia[9] In 1997, it took the UN four months to authorise ECOMOG deployment in Sierra Leone, only to replace ECOMOG with a large and pompous mission that quickly disintegrated once launched.[10] The SADC has a culture of independent deployments, which often occur without UN authorisation. In August 1998, the SADC deployed its first intervention mission ever in the DRC. Operation Sovereign Legitimacy was without UN authorisation. In September 1998, the SADC deployed another intervention in Lesotho...dubbed Operation BOLEAS [i.e. Botswana, Lesotho, and South Africa].[11] This mission was also without UN authorisation. These transregional contradictions have played into how the AU coordinates its preferences with the UN. Within the AU organization, different regions still exhibit different appetites for engagement with the UN. The following example is illustrative of those dynamics.

The politics of agency and preference coordination re-emerged in the formation of the so-called UN Force Intervention Brigade (UNFIB). The UNFIB is essentially an SADC Brigade in UN coating. Between 2011 and 2012, DRC President Joseph Kabila threatened to expel the UN Stabilization Mission in the DRC (MONUSCO).[12] In January 2013, the SADC Troika authorised an SADC Brigade [comprising battalions from South Africa, Malawi and Tanzania] to intervene in DRC.[13] AU insisted on authorising the mission before the UN Secretary General (Ban Ki Moon) said the same thing at an AU ordinary summit weeks later. The wrangle between UN, AU and SADC resulted in the appendage of the SADC Brigade to MONUSCO—a costly and largely ineffective mission.[14] This was a matter of protection of interests in the DRC for P5 who are already manifestly failing MONUSCO.[15] This boils down to an overarching difference in preferences.

The AU prefers subsidiarity while the UN prefers complementarity.[16] Subsidiarity protects African agency and ownership. This implies that the AU has more latitude to determine the design and operations of the ASF in various peace support operations. Ideally this would give the African group, despite AU-REC differences, to authorise and deploy missions—which would be a further operationalisation of the ASF. The UN prefers a contrary process of complementarity which ossifies its influence and agency within the partnership.[17] Complementarity retains its seniority and

158   T. GWATIWA

leadership in all elements from planning to implementation. The two partners still spar over this element as evinced by several AUC Chairpersons' reports complaining about the occlusion of African agency.

Nested Causes of Shirking

There are a set of causes that are not attributable to the organisational structure of an international institution. I have closely examined a set of causes which slip down to the level of member states. It is useful to consider these to be a set of intricate causal mechanisms which are inescapable even though international organisations are often considered to assume a life of their own once created by member states.

Preference coordination between the partners is closely related to agential outcomes. The shirking in this partnership is attributable to poor preference coordination. This occurs at two levels. At a strategic level, within the Security Council, there is a pattern whereby the P3 (France, Britain, and USA) project interests without P2 protestation.[18] For example, the US vetoed the use of UN-assessed contributions to support the African Union Mission in Somalia (AMISOM) only for it to compensate that with its own bilateral support to the AU.[19] The replacement is exclusionist and undermines the inclusive mandate of AMISOM.[20] At an operational level, i.e. in the mission space, the P3 and other actors typically do the opposite of what they pledge to at the diplomatic level. For example, on average the AU's Special Representative to Somalia (who is also political head of AMISOM) spends 40 per cent of his time managing partners' interests.[21] Member states often undermine the work of the AU or their organisations which are in partnership with the AU. This implies that even though organisational partnerships may have a partially productive collaborative relationship, the selfish choices and behaviour of member states portend to undermine it.

The foregoing is mainly attributable to a political economy of peace operations. The AU–UN partnership has a uniquely lucrative political economy. This political economy covers the areas of logistics, procurement, business and private security. Although the UN Support Office to AMISOM had a little operational efficacy in Somalia, it manages logistics and procurement business valued at nearly $800 million per annum, which is mainly awarded to developed countries such as Canada, Japan and France.[22] Despite AU protestation, this system remains in place and accounts for the recalcitrance of many UN member states, which is undermining the agential goals of the partnership.

There is also a controversial subject of arms and ammunition flow within Somalia. Between 2012 and 2013, the AU held discussion around the increasing sophistication of rebel and terrorist groups around the continent. It was suspected that most partners and/or member states supply resources to terrorists and rebels.[23] Thereafter PSC called on "all member states and the larger international community to cease immediately any further support for extremist elements or those who seek to block progress by violent means...".[24] The partners are not in a position to address this issue candidly, mainly because the partnership agreement places no such obligations on UN member states.

The emergence of a plum market for private military and security companies (PMSCs) within the conflict sphere also contributes to the tensions between the AU and UN. These PMSCs are primarily from the Global North. The UN is an avid contractor of PMSCs from Asia, North America and Europe.[25] Surprisingly, the UN system encourages the use of private security within AU member states. For example, following an attack on the UN compound in Mogadishu, a UNSC resolution called for protection of UN Staff. The resultant UN Guard Unit was made up of three Ugandan military battalions.[26] This not only expands the political economy of peace enforcement but compounds the AU's ability to develop an effective policy for the private security industry. The AU and its member states have been struggling with incepting and consolidating an oversight mechanism for PMSC regulations. Thus, the UN's accommodation and encouragement of PMSCs' utility in a relatively conflict-ridden continent portends further problems for African actors.

The foregoing issues imply that the size and lucrativeness of the political economy of peace support missions keep the partnership in a state of shirking between the AU and the UN. This is more so if the partnership agreement does not articulate the obligations of member states under the partnership.

Shirking in an Indispensable Partnership

This partnership exhibits several implications for shirking. This partnership is emblematic of shirking when considering levels of engagement, interaction, resource directionality and interest coordination, all of which measure at a mediocre level. Why would the AU retain participating in a partnership that seems contrary to its interests? Evidently, the AU has chosen to minimise its actions in the partnership—shirking—instead of departing from the agreement. There are several factors to consider.

The approaches to problem solving in conflict resolution have caused some differences between the AU and the UN. It is not the method of intervention that is contested, it is the approach. The UN subscribes to the doctrine of peacekeeping operations (PKOs) while the AU deploys peace support operations (PSOs). The UN, which is the larger and more powerful partner, is reluctant to find common ground between the two approaches. This has resulted in delays and alterations of APSA project designs and implementation. This is because the AU often chooses to minimise its engagement of the UN around select contentious issues. As much as AU security approaches derive from UN templates, the AU occasionally limits engagement by turning to other partners when the UN is not willing to forgo some of its preferences in the design of APSA institutions. This does not only apply to APSA institutions. This also applies to other common peace-related projects, with various UN agencies such as the UNDP, UNESCO and others. It is important to draw a line between UNSC based engagements and those in other agencies which are less political. However, the contentiousness of projects outside the UNSC rubric cannot be underplaid, yet they are not as common. This sparse distribution of politics and, by extension, agential outcomes also owes to the type of agreement between the two organisations.

The type of agreement between the AU and UN has a bearing on the outcomes of the partnership. The initial AU–UN partnership agreement (of 2006) was relatively abstract. This was because the two parties did not engage in strong dialogue prior to the signing the agreement. The agreement also had no action plans or addendum to specify the terms of engagement, resource directionality to various AU institutions, funding, as well as modalities of preference coordination between the two organization. It was not until the finalisation of the second agreement (in 2014)—which was a result of contentious relations—that these issues were nearly addressed. Moreover, the assumption that the UN would solely provide capacity building support to the AU without learning anything from the AU was a misplaced calculation, especially given that the AU Commission, as a secretariat had some form of experience from the OAU era. Moreover, by the time the agreement was signed the AU had already launched a couple of successful peace operations. In terms of asserting its agency, the AU on the other hand was in the process of asserting its role in international politics regardless of the partners' experience and comparative advantage. For instance, by 2006, the AU had already negotiated a new partnership with the EU based on African ownership and equality.[27] While the Africa–EU negotiations started in 1998 and sought to renew a partnership, the AU–UN relationship did not have the benefit of a similar historical trajectory. As a result, the relationship has been tense on various levels including the creation of liaison and implementation capacity.

If there was one salient instance of shirking, it manifested through the institutionalisation of this AU–UN partnership. The two parties agreed on the creation of a UN Office to the AU (UNOAU) in Addis Ababa as a way of institutionalising the partnership. Ironically, there were contestations on the form and function of the office—not between the partners per se, but within the UN system. This emerged from competing interests between the various UN organs and specialised agency already engaged in African projects. As indicated earlier, this problem was not new. In the days of the AU Peace Support Team, different UN liaison units at the AU Commission could not effectively work together. The AU capitalised on this self-repeating angular anomaly, and used it as an excuse to engage other partner organisations. The AU did not totally disengage from the UN, but somewhat "gave them room" to work on the modalities of institutionalising this new liaison entity.

The process of setting up the UNOAU was akin to setting up a new organisation. The office needed to expand from a few officers to a new office with 22 expert planners and an annual budget of $10 million.[28] The mandate of the UNOAU implied transition from a light to a heavy UN presence.[29] With time, the UN organization grappled with the question of whether the UNOAU was an entity of the UN Economic Commission for Africa (UNECA) or a separate entity. This was an intra-organizational process that excluded the AU.[30]

The most contested issue, within the UN system, was the authority of the head of the UNOAU. By virtue of being an Assistant Secretary General, and not an Under-Secretary General, the office had an uneasy relationship with the UN Economic Commission for Africa (UNECA) which also had a collaborative relationship with the AU. Resolving this issue took time and often complicated the UN's ability to deliver APSA outputs which were prior funded through UNECA or other UN agencies based at the UNECA compound.[31] Thereafter there was a strong debate about the structure of the UNOAU. UN staffers felt the structure of the UNOAU did not reflect the mandate.[32]

This also took some time to resolve. Finally, there were debates as to whether this was to be; a temporary or permanent liaison office. In fact, the permanency of the UNOAU was only introduced a few years after the creation of the office. (30) These structural changes, which had little to do with resource outputs, still affected the viability of the partnership. Yet there were some technocrats, particularly from the African Union and AU member states, who questioned the then timely relevance of the UN as a primary partner. Thus, the delays lent by the UN system was a welcome development on their part. The foregoing issues retarded UN inputs into the APSA project. Given the competitiveness of the partnership milieu, other international partners were willing and available to fill the gap created by the process of creating the UNOAU. This worked in the AU's favour primarily because various agencies of the UN did not have the same view or approach to [African] peace and security—especially the UNSC, the DPKO, the Department of Field Services. In fact the AU often found it easier to accommodate the less intrusive and more compatible doctrines of the UNDP and UNESCO (which's activities are more tangential to UNSC politics). These developments generally provided an opportunity for shirking. This should not be confused as a strategy, but a tactical gain that was a result of an opportunity created by the UN system's self-corroding tendencies.

Teetering on the Brink of Full African Agency?

The question that arises is whether this partnership ever came close to graduating from agency slack. To determine that, it is instructive to closely examined the implications of another set of attributable causes of the shirking in this partnership.

Institutional learning plays a part in partnership outcomes, and by extension on African agency. The shirking in this partnership is partly attributable to a slow process of institutional learning. According to a UNOAU policy officer, it took long for the UN to abandon a top-down (condescending) approach in the partnership, as well as abandon "capacity substitution" in favour of capacity building.[33] This is owed to two factors: the partnership agreement lacked detail and the operational support in the field was mostly left to chance; and oftentimes different UN programmes and agencies (assigned to the AU) have very different approaches to peace and security.

The slow process of learning was a result of the role played by the UN in the early phase of the partnerships. The AU Peace Support Team was proactive in the early stages of developing the African Standby Force (ASF). The AU basically relied on the UN's doctrinal and policy instruments because the ASF sought to adopt a multidimensional form as found in most UN peacekeeping operations. Moreover, there was need to work closely with the UN because most AU missions would, customarily, eventually be transferred to the UN.[34] Thus the AU allowed the UN to replicate its legal and policy frameworks. The UN was also given the lead in AMANI AFRICA I's table-top and field exercises largely due to the appreciation of the inevitable transition from AU to joint missions. Meanwhile, the UN ignored the experience gained by the burgeoning ASF in peace operations in Sudan and Somalia. The failure, and in some instances outright refusal, to incorporate AU experiences in a conjoined manner strained partners' relations. There was a perception that the UN was not willing to learn from the AU or at least allow AU preferences and experience supercede UN modalities into cojoined project. Thus, the partnership remained in a state shirking because the senior partner was unwilling to accommodate the experiences of the lesser. This was a missed opportunities for better cooperation based on agential equity.

Flexibility in resource directionality also had a bearing on partnership and agential outcomes. The collaboration in Somalia is a case in point, where UN provides support to the AU Mission in Somalia (AMISOM). The purpose of AMISOM was, and still is, to support the Transitional Federal Institutions of Somalia.[35] It appears that the real pressure to deploy troops came from the US prior to early AU assessment of the Somali security crisis in 2006. In 2009, the UNSC authorised the mission and created the UN Support Office to AMISOM [UNSOA]. Perfunctorily, it appears that this was a complementary process, especially given the then short time-gamut of AMISOM and the intent to transfer it to the UN. However, this arrangement became the source of operational shirking.

The cause was the incongruence of strategic priorities between the AU and the UN. AMISOM followed the model of the AU Mission in Burundi (AMIB), which was essentially a stabilisation mission that included protecting the transitional government and key infrastructure, security sector training and reform, disarmament, demobilisation and reintegration, as well as support humanitarian operations.[36] UNSC Resolution 1863 had a different priority which effectively diminished African agency: stating the need to jettison transition to a peacekeeping operation, establishing a trust fund for AMISOM, transfer of assets from UN Mission in Ethiopia and Eritrea and a request for "AMISOM forces to be incorporated into a United Nations Peacekeeping Operation". This model did not work in the case of AMISOM because the AU and the UN had different views. This was because the AU had incorporated its institutional learning in previous peace support missions, while the UN stuck to its old doctrine. Even after a series of negotiations the UN was not willing to adopt a flexible approach to this somewhat different approach to peacemaking. The lack of flexibility impeded collaboration and thus locked the partnership in a state of shirking.

The accommodation of Africa preferences agency also played an important role in partnership outcomes. This issue was, and is still, more pronounced in this partnership than any other, especially at an operational level. The report of the AU–UN Panel on Modalities for Support to AU Peacekeeping Operations (also known as the Prodi Report) revealed a yawning gap between the two parties' approach to peace and security. The AU pointed the following preferences to the panel: (a) the need for [AU] capacity to handle own affairs, (b) a partnership based on subsidiarity not complementarity,[37] (c) predictable funding because AU member states were already paying dues to the UN and (d) respect from the UN because the AU was doing the job of the UN. This was an articulation of a desire for more African agency within the partnership.

Correspondinly, the final Prodi Report recommended a reformed partnership with better accommodation African agency. It recommended regular and intensive interactions between the UN Secretariat and AU Commission, the AU commissioners and [UN] Under-Secretary Generals, the UNSC and the [AU] PSC; as well as a focus more on capacity building and using UN-assessed contributions to finance AU operations.[38] The UNSC secretariat did not take kindly to these recommendations, which they viewed as an affront to the seniority of the UN. The UNSC heavily modified the earlier version of the Prodi Report.[39] The Prodi Report was subsequently released by the UN General Assembly. The real sentiments of the UNSC, DPKO, Field Support Services and Political Affairs were included in the UN Secretary General's Report on Support to UNSC Authorised AU Missions.[40] These two reports have had no positive impact on the form and progress of the partnership. The partnership remained in a state of shirking with contestation over the situs of African agency. This was primarily caused by the fact that the larger and senior partner, i.e. the UN, had a managerial prerogative over the partnership.

By failing to incorporate African preferences, institutional learning and flexibility within the partnership, the partnership missed an opportunity to move towards an emblematic agential status. It is imperative to digress and emphasize that shirking does not imply that there was no delivery of projects. It means that projects were not delivered timely and in the agreed form. Thus, the failure to accommodate African agency, preferences, institutional learning and flexibility retained the highly contested status quo. It is not implausible to submit that the accommodation of African agency, efficacy of institutional learning and flexibility (plus other structural congruencies) would have led to similar outcomes to those exhibited in the Africa–EU partnership.

THE AU–NATO PARTNERSHIP

Origins of Contentions in the AU–NATO Partnership

The origins of NATO's relations with Africa are unclear. There is a somewhat speculative view that NATO first operated in Africa in the 1970s. Some scholars link NATO to Operation Shaba II. This was a Western-sponsored unilateral intervention in the Shaba Province of Zaire in 1978, primarily sponsored by France and Belgium.[41] This operation was undertaken at the behest of the then president of Zaire, Joseph Mobutu.[42] Even though the idea of NATO involvement seems inferential and political, it was not refuted by senior NATO officials during a recent AU–NATO high-level symposium (in 2014). However, the controversies and uncertainties surrounding earlier relations do not undermine the fact that the post-millennial partnership is different.

The post-millennial partnership originated from a policy network between Africa and Europe. The partnership was a result of direct dialogue between the then Chairperson of the AU Commission, Alpha Konare and the then NATO Secretary General, Jaap de Hoof Scheffer. The partnership agreement was signed between May 17th and 26th during Konare's official visit to the NATO headquarters in Brussels. The partnership was initially limited to strategic airlift support to AU peace support operations. The AU was experiencing a serious strategic airlift deficit in its mission in Darfur.

The scope of the partnership began to expand with the increase of interaction between the parties. For example, on June 22nd Konare made further requests for logistical planning and the North Atlantic Council (NAC) approved the request the same day. In 2006, Hoop Scheffer made an official visit to the AU Commission where he and the then AU Commissioner for Peace and Security, Said Djinnit, agreed to expand the role of NATO to building the African Standby Force. In 2007, the then NATO Deputy Secretary General, Maurits Jochems, led a high-level delegation to the AU Commission to brief the PSC on the envisioned partnership. The partnership thus expanded to mission planning, logistical planning, communication and intelligence and other elements related to AU peace support operations.

Lackadaisical Diplomacy and Engagement: A Symptom of Shirking

The initial engagement was premised on capacity building. This partnership espoused the same principles as its other counterparts—African leadership and ownership.[43] The lead officers at the Joint Combatant Command (at Lisbon) were advised to let Africa lead (and not impose) in a process that was perceived to enable the AU to be a capable security provider.[44] This meant that they could only act based on requests from the AU headquarters in Addis Ababa. There was a locational shift in the partnership as well.

From the initial negotiations between 2005 and 2007, the partnership management was moved away from the NATO headquarters. From 2007, the NATO command in Lisbon was responsible for the partnership. A mid-level component of NATO was responsible for the partnership. This implied that the perimeters of engagement were sealed because the command has no political mandate to (re)negotiate the form and function of the partnership. The command in Lisbon sporadically reported to the NATO Supreme Headquarters Allied Powers Europe about the general progress of the partnership.[45]

NATO has a liaison team which is the first point of contact between the partners. The NATO Senior Military Liaison Office/Team (SMLO/T) was created by a Strategic Military Mission Order (SMMO) in 2005. At this point there was a single liaison officer. Following a successful collaboration in Darfur, the office was upgraded to a team which was comprised of a brigadier general (Andrew Defawe), two lieutenant colonels (Carsten Petersen and Ed Mead) and a sergeant major (Pascal Wijkman).[46] The SMLT is now led by a captain (which is four ranks lower than the initial form) due to issues related to the diplomatic status of this office.

The SMLO serves two main functions. The head of the SMLO is responsible for screening AU requests. S/he has the prerogative to refer or decline requests from the [AU] Peace Support Operations Division (PSOD).[47] This team is responsible for immediate dialogue with the AU. Anything that requires higher authority is referred to the responsible command (which has since moved from Lisbon to Naples, Italy). The SMLT also comprises officers embedded in the PSOD (discussed later). Of all the members of the SMLT, only the head has a negotiating mandate. However, this mandate is not substantial. The role of the team leader is to police the perimeters of the agreement. S/he and their counterpart in Naples have no negotiating mandate which is reserved for the senior members of the NATO secretariat in Brussels.

Direct negotiations between NATO and the AU began under difficult circumstances in 2012. The partnership was at the risk of collapse following the NATO intervention in Libya in 2011. During this period there was a strong feeling within the AU not to renew the partnership. NATO was in panic mode and thus sought to negotiate a broader strategic partnership.[48] Negotiations were handicapped by a hiatus of non-engagement between the negotiating teams—the senior members of NATO secretariat and the Peace and Security Department. During the conference, and apparently during negotiations, the NATO team kept referring to shared values and interests—an irony considering Operation Unified Protector. However, the idea of African leadership and an equality in the partnership was a deal breaker during the actual negotiations.[49] That such an issue was a deal breaker evinced its centrality to African partnerships.

A Continuum of Diverging Preferences and Linked Interests

The subject of preferences and interests is taken for granted in this partnership. During the AU–NATO there was a common phrase about existing linked interests and preferences between the two organisations. This is contestable in theory and practice. Logically, there can be no linked interests in a partnership that was not negotiated vigorously. There was a hiatus in high level or political engagement between 2005 and 2012. The empirical record of the partnership also speaks to the contrary. Key members of NATO, which are also in the UNSC, circumvented AU structures in creating the NATO intervention in Libya. It was the P3 that proposed a no-fly zone in Libya in 2011. The US persuaded the Arab League to submit UNSC Resolutions 1970 and 1973 on February 26th and March 17th.[50] This undermined the agency of the Africa Group or African states within the UNSC. Moreover, the assigning of NATO to enforce a no-fly zone, appeared to be a smokescreen for a premeditated operation. While African states debated the upcoming NATO intervention, the US AFRICOM launched Operation Odyssey Dawn four days prior to NATO's Operation Unified Protector.[51] Furthermore, channels of communication were shut during this time. The AU chairperson tried, unsuccessfully, to address the NAC. The AU tried to negotiate and bargain for its interests but was undermined in a perfect scheme of forum shopping by the same set of like-minded states using the UNSC, NATO and AFRICOM.

Why was there such poor coordination of interests between the two parties? This can be traced to a failure to collate overlapping structures and interests. The AU and NATO have different interests in the region. NATO has stronger strategic interests in North Africa than sub-Saharan Africa. According to the then Head of the NATO Military Partnerships Branch, the NATO Mediterranean Dialogue (MD) was premised on the idea that the Mediterranean region was Europe's immediate neighbourhood posing greater threats to Europe. There was never any attempt to collate the AU–NATO partnership with NATO MD[52] This potentially isolated the AU from North African affairs from a NATO standpoint.

On the other hand, the AU was never able to form a strong position about its preferences in the North African region. Informal discussions during the fieldwork suggested that although the North African Regional Coordination was the least institutionalised of Regional Mechanisms, it was not a top priority for political stabilisation within the AU. There was contentment with the higher level of infrastructural development in the area, and focus was shifted to much poorer regions of Africa. Moreover, North African states showed stronger interest in the Organization of Islamic Cooperation (OIC) and the Arab League.

Sources of Shirking in the AU–NATO Partnership

The AU exercises a different sort of shirking in its partnership with NATO. The AU is aware that NATO is a strategic partner willing to offer goods that even member states are unwilling to provide. The most salient form of shirking involves AU maintaining a low level and short-term partnership with NATO even though the latter has sought to upgrade from an operational to a strategic partnership since 2012. Among other things, the AU (with the tacit help of Ethiopia as the host nation) declined to grant diplomatic status to its liaison office. Moreover, it has also refused to broaden the scope of the deliverables within the partnership. By doing this, the AU actively minimises the status of the partnership and, hence, limits the options of NATO within the continent. Thus, it is important to understand how and why the AU engages in shirking.

To identify sources of shirking it is imperative to examine the levels of engagement, interaction of parties, resource directionality and interest coordination within this partnership. It is also useful to realise from the onset that the sources or causes of shirking in this partnership are different from those in the AU–NATO partnership.

Shirking is partly attributable to historical factors. The two parties do not have a long history of engagement. NATO is relatively a newcomer to the continent. The purported role of NATO in Africa in the 1970s is speculative. The two organisations have a short, if not thin, history of engagement. There was no convergence of purpose and interests prior to the signing of the agreement in 2005. Moreover, the OAU was not a capable security provider—or at least one to be taken seriously—while NATO assumed a defensive posture within the Cold War. As a result, the two organisations never engaged each other. Without a history of engagement, an observer cannot expect NATO to fully understand and duly support APSA project. If anything, Africans developed a sceptical view of NATO which was ossified by the NATO intervention in Libya in 2011, which is widely viewed as an undermining of the overall APSA project. The foregoing submission suggests that a short history of engagement is a contributing factor in this shirking.

Cognitive [regional security] frameworks or security approach plays a big role in the agential outcomes found in this partnership. How can the two organisations, with a short history of engagement, be expected to see eye to eye on APSA? The two organisations emanate from two distinct histories and security cultures. NATO is historically a defensive security

170   T. GWATIWA

organisation. It was designed and equipped to deal with the communist threat from the Soviet Union. This influenced its security doctrine for about half a century. The AU, and indeed inferable from APSA, is premised on the idea of comprehensive security. At the beginning of the AU–NATO partnership, the then NATO Secretary General was promoting a paradigm shift in NATO's security approach.[53] However, the rhetoric did not match resource directionality and use in the partnership as NATO, given its strong capacity and unique cognitive framework and tradition, failed to encourage African agency as it had pledged at the beginning of the partnership. Moreover, simple omissions such as definitions at the beginning of the partnership eventually boomeranged. A senior NATO official confirmed the lack of dialogue around such issues because they "do not deal with definitions in [their] field"[54]—even though these help clarify policies. The combined effect of cognitive regionalism, power and agency had an eroding effect on the partnership, with the corollary that the partnership gradually moved into a "lock-in" effect wherein the partners cannot transcend their original terms and scope of engagement.

The "lock-in" effect over African agency deserves further explanation. Despite earlier pledges and rhetoric to allow the AU to set the agenda for the partnership, this only survived to an extent especially because NATO would only deal with the operationalisation of the ASF. As changes were introduced to the form and function of the ASF, and the project brought more political baggage, it became clear that NATO could not fully accommodate African agency. That is why the two organisations could not agree over Libya. These challenges also manifested in the last negotiations (i.e. between 2012 and 2015) over how NATO can better contribute to APSA projects. This suggests that African agency or enabling Africa to be a security provider is a strong causal variable in the present tensions or "lock-in" effect between the two partners. This partially explains the gradual increase in shirking as well as broader participation anomalies, including when NATO made limited contributions to the partnership.

The material and agential outcomes of the partnership are also attributable to the way the partnership was institutionalised. This institutionalization can be considered at two levels. The other partnerships were institutionalised in such a way that they accommodate dialogue between various structures, but that was not the case in this partnership. The anomaly in the institutionalisation of this partnership is the evident dwarfed political latitude. It is inconsequential that there was relatively lubricated collaboration between mid-tier structures of the AU and NATO. Conversely, the lack of direct dialogue between the NAC and the PSC or AHSG (and/or occasionally the NATO Parliamentary Assembly) grossly undermined NATO's potential to make bigger material and technical contributions to APSA. This omission manifested in the failed attempt to secure dialogue between the then Chairperson of the AU Commission and the North Atlantic Council regarding the Libyan political crisis. NATO intervened in Libya disregarding proposed AU interventions (through fledging APSA institutions). As a corollary, the AU refused to upgrade the status of the NATO Senior Military Liaison Team (SMLT), a critical liaison for NATO contributions to APSA, which had been under negotiation for years.

The role and design of the NATO SMLT, regarding APSA, also leave a lot to be desired. Indeed, the liaison office bridges cognitive and policy gaps between the partners. However, the office has not attained diplomatic status, hence lacking in legitimacy. On one hand, despite the timeline the AU had to operationalise all the main APSA institutions, it has done little or nothing to pressurise the Ethiopian government to grant the SMLT diplomatic status. On the other, NATO is not sombrely institutionalising the SMLT. First, for an institution dealing with APSA (as a broad and comprehensive security institution), there are no civilian members of the SMLT. For example, the office is not (or at least envisioned to be) led by an ambassador and has no civilian staff. Moreover, whereas the SLMT was initially staffed by very senior officials—led by a Brigadier General—it has been downgraded, such as to be headed by a Captain (in 2014). It raises questions as to how a Captain can fully appreciate the broad needs of APSA, as well as equally engage his peers from the African diplomatic corps (or the African Defence Association), the majority of whom are either at the rank of Brigadier General or Colonel. Moreover, by international standards, brigadier generals and colonels (or higher) are considered diplomatic ranks.

In contrast to other partnerships, networks played an important positive role in this partnership. This partnership was largely founded based on transnational policy networks. Former NATO secretary general, Jaap de Hoop Scheffer, a man with a confessed affinity for Africa, started his diplomatic career in Africa and cultivated extensive networks.[55] His career path had crossed with that of the then Chairperson of the AU Commission, Professor Alpha Konare (former Malian president). (His deputy also had a profound understanding of Africa.) These networks paid off in the early days of the AU–NATO partnership as these leading figures had a better apprehension of the actual needs of APSA (or African security).[56] This was demonstrated by their strong (albeit selective) engagement with the AU. Comparing the previous crop of senior NATO officials with those I encountered at the AU–NATO high-level symposium, the latter was a far cry from the old guard.[57] Not only was there little understanding of APSA, but a poor articulation of what a possible post-Libya AU–NATO strategic partnership should look like. I also observed that this new corps seemingly had no experience or understanding of Africa, as well as a convergence of views with their African counterparts. This suggests that without a strong network between policymakers, NATO and the AU will hardly transcend their present state of shirking.

The agential outcomes in this partnership are partly attributable to the type of agreement governing the partnership. The AU–NATO agreement, unlike the others, is rather loose. It is simply a Memorandum of Understanding (MoU) that has no depth and clarity on how the partnership should be governed and how APSA contributions should be implemented as well as monitored and reviewed. This is worsened by the fact that it is non-binding and without legal status. The NAC and PSC (or AUC Chair) could not engage each other on the verge of the NATO intervention in Libya because their agreement did not spell out the perimeters and mode of engagement. This suggests that it is not the existence of an MoU that matters, but the contents. For example, the previous AU–NATO agreement did not envisage the two as co-actors in global security. Characteristically, senior NATO officials claim that this is the case,[58] but it is inconsequential if such views are not included in the MoU. The framing of the agreement undermined the capacity to collaborate effectively. This implies that casually designed agreements left room for reneging and defection during engagement, with the result that the partnerships became dysfunctional.

The issue of interest and preference coordination between the AU and NATO had a causal role in the partnership shirking. The infamous NATO intervention in Libya is a result of poor preference coordination with the AU. The AUC/PSC and the NAC did not coordinate preferences prior or post the promulgation of UNSC Resolution 1979, even though NATO was already aware of the fledging APSA architecture, and the AU's then decade-old tradition of preventive diplomacy prior to intervention. When former AUC Chairperson, Jean Ping, pleaded with the NAC in 2011 it was akin to a dialogue with a tabula rasa. This was a result of poor or limited institutionalisation, wherein there was no dialogue between the chief decision makers. This implies preference coordination is closely tied to institutionalisation and engagement with a partnership. Moreover, this suggests that preference coordination is contingent on the type of institutionalisation. The pre-Libya type of institutionalisation was commendable but had no far-reaching impact.

Teetering on Slippage? AU–NATO Pre-Libyan Intervention

At this stage, the reader can infer that this is a different type of shirking. It seems that unlike the AU–UN partnership, this one was punctuated by several positive outcomes in its early phase. If anything, requested inputs were delivered on time in the manner in which they were requested, at least in the early phase of the partnership. Correspondingly, this would imply that this partnership was more accommodative of African agency which only relegated to shirking after the Libyan intervention. Far from it! Evidence suggests that this partnership was already gravitating towards (a different form of) shirking prior to the NATO intervention in Libya.

Presently, this case invites us to reconsider the measure used to determine shirking as a partnership outcome. Compared to the AU–UN partnership, this partnership was manifestly progressive—albeit only at an operational level but very complicated at a managerial level. Any manifestations of progress were attributable to the issues discussed below. It is imperative to retain this categorisation of shirking because this form of slack can manifest in different forms other than those introduced in the earlier part of this treatise. A helter-skelter manifestation of positive outcomes does not imply a healthy accommodation of African agency. If anything, this case, as argued below, may invite a reconsideration of the nature of shirking: is it a monolithic phenomenon or it has various degrees. This further invites one to perpend on related notions of the relevance of: the vertical latitude of institutionalisation, managerial complexity, agreement longevity, cross-institutional reciprocity and synergistic tautness of different elements of the partnership.

Partnership agreement longevity raises the question on whether this partnership could have reached a state where it could accommodate African agency—African ownership and leadership—instead of receding into agency slack. The AU–NATO, unlike that of the UN, is renewed on an annual basis. This has implications for both the contents and managerial complexity of the partnership. An annually renewable partnership

174   T. GWATIWA

agreement suggests myopia and parochialism. It means that the partnership is reduced to some sort of quick impact projects. It does not envision a long and broad prospect of collaboration. This is despite the fact that those at the operational level can see the (broad scope of) demands in the mission space. However, this does not mean much if the partnership is reduced to the status of quick impact projects. Such quick impact projects require specificity (or parochialism) and short-termism to thrive. This short-termism dwarfs the significance of the partnership in the shadow of equally senior partnerships such as the EU and UN. This is irrational and self-corrosive given the fact that the EU and NATO have a strategic agreement on their collaboration within and beyond Europe. What is the rationale for the AU to sustain [chronically] asymmetric partnerships with two bedfellows with the similar capacity to contribute towards APSA?

In the same measure, the managerial complexity of such a design also limited this partnership from reaching a state of full African agency. Typically, managerial complexity works better if it operates within the perimeters of a lengthy partnership agreement (of about five to ten years). This would stretch the managerial structure to include implementation, monitoring and review structures. This division of labour ensures a holistic but multipronged implementation of APSA projects (such as in the AU–EU partnership). However, in the AU–NATO partnership there is a small managerial clique that is predominantly preoccupied with renegotiating the renewal of the MoU of collaboration as opposed to the operational outputs towards key APSA projects. This suggests that there is little time spent on reviewing the quality of outputs of the partnership as well as its potential for expansion. Worse, the current managerial onus rests with mid-tier structures of this partnership.[59] This suggests that this partnership does not benefit from the [positive] managerial spillovers that accrue to other partnerships of the same rank. This managerial complexity, therefore, is humdrum because it remains dwarfed in its scope and intensity because it has no vertical reach to the echelons of both organizations.

The [structural] vertical latitude of the institutionalisation of this partnership failed to elevate this partnership to a state of full African agency. Changes in the managerial complexity means less if it has no vertical reach to the echelons of power in both organisations. If anything, the Libyan saga (of 2011) illustrates the significance of dialogue at the highest levels of two organisations. The AU–EU partnership suggests that sustained dialogue at the highest levels of partnering institutions can curb the recalcitrance of a powerful or irrational organisation. It suffices to argue that the AU–NATO could have experienced a different outcome (more African agency or a different degree of agency slack) if the level of institutionalisation had a higher vertical reach in terms of structural design. Moreover, although the literature suggests that organisations tend to assume life and cultures of their own, in spite of [overlapping] membership, it is safe to argue that a higher vertical structural reach would benefit from spillovers from the AU–EU partnership by virtue of the NATO–EU Strategic Agreement of 2003.

This partnership is failing in terms of cross-institutional reciprocity. This means that the two organisations are unable to positively if not progressively respond to each other's gestures. Indeed, there is more mutual suspicion than trust between the parties—especially on the part of Africans. However, it is important to realise that this partnership has failed to transcend whatever modicum of progress it bore prior to 2011 due to lack of reciprocity.

The Africans (or AU) did not reciprocate NATO's gestures towards institutionalisation. The initial staffing of the NATO SMLT portended a threshold for positive outcomes for the partnership. This can be inferred from the seniority of the officers deployed in Addis Ababa. It is usually the habit of committed states to deploy military officers at the level of brigadier generals as military advisers or attaches to Addis Ababa. Following on Segell's discussion of early AU–NATO collaboration, it goes to show that a brigadier general heading the SMLT brought greater access to senior military and political leaders at NATO HQ (indeed Brigadier General Andre Dewafe had access to the echelons of the NATO Command).[60] Moreover, the two lieutenant colonels were institutionally poised for peerage with their African and international counterparts in Addis Ababa. The Sergeant Major was also institutionally poised for operational synergy with Special Forces, intelligence and surveillance and other aspects of AU peace operations. The Africans failed to create a threshold for African agency in three respects.

First, the African group (or Union) did not capitalise on this opportunity to broaden the scope of NATO's contribution to APSA. Given the timeline set by the AHSG, the AU had about 15 years to fully operationalise APSA. At the time of the creation of the SMLT, this timeline was at seven years. Despite the slow pace of APSA at that point, the African Union officials were caught in the notion that "NATO is a military organization". Far from it! As the former head of the SMLT posited,

"NATO is both a military and political organization".[61] NATO had the ability to contribute to the development of the CEWS as well as initiate dialogue with the NAC. The CEWS coordinator's argument that the NATO approach is militaristic, and intelligence-based was myopic and puerile. He had the prerogative to choose only certain aspects of NATO's capacity instead of the whole approach. This signifies the chronic passivity and myopia in African institutional learning. The PSC and indeed the AHSG failed to capitalise on this honeymoon phase to initiate strong dialogue with the echelons of NATO structures.

Second, the African securocrats and diplomats did not put pressure on the Ethiopian government to grant diplomatic status to the SMLO. It would have been beneficial to capitalise on the initial design and structure of the SMLO. The seniority and high-level access of the initial SMLO (known as DIRLAUTH) portended to result in a triangulated institutional link between the NATO HQ in Brussels and the operational command in Lisbon. However, the two organisations had a major fallout over the diplomatic status of the NATO liaison office. Ethiopia has not ratified the Vienna Convention on diplomatic rights and privileges and thus holds prerogative of diplomatic acquiescence which it uses to tantalise different states and organisations.[62] For a long time, the NATO SMLT was sheltered by the Norwegian embassy in Addis Ababa, with the Norwegian ambassador doubling as the de facto NATO ambassador to Ethiopia/AU. This suggests that had the Africans approached the institutionalisation of this office with the same gusto, it would have been headed by an ambassador (possibly deputised by a Brigadier General) with access to Brussels political and military officials. When dialogue failed over the institutionalisation, NATO and its member states began diluting the SMLO, thus limiting the form and function of the liaison office, also curtailing its direct access to the HQ.

The foregoing submissions suggest that African agency is elusive without synergistic tautness between the various elements of the partnership. This means that the maximisation of one element, e.g. diplomatic engagement, has little effect if there is no corresponding efficiency in other aspects. Our star partnership (AU–EU) is emblematic of a partnership with a healthy synergistic tightness. The maximisation of efficiency is balanced across various aspects of the partnership, i.e. diplomatic engagement, institutionalisation, resource directionality and use, as well as preference coordination. Conversely, this partnership maximises only few aspects of the partnership, i.e. resource directionality and use, and dwarfs other elements such as institutionalisation, preference coordination and diplomatic engagement. That raises the probability of the partnership remaining in a state of shirking.

NOTES

1. Darren G. Hawkins, David A. Lake, Daniel L. Nielson and Michael J. Tierney, "Delegation Under Anarchy: States, International Organizations, and Principal-Agent Theory", in *Delegation and Agency in International Organizations*, eds. Darren G. Hawkins, David A. Lake, Daniel L. Nielson and Michael J. Tierney (Cambridge and New York: Cambridge University Press, 2006), 3–38.
2. Jide M. Okeke, personal interview, Senior Civilian Officer, AU Peace Support Operations Division, Addis Ababa: communication, June 2014.
3. United Nations, "Letter Dated 11 December 2006 from Secretary-General Addressed to the President of the General Assembly", (New York: 12 December 2006), A/61/630, 4, http://www. uneca.org/sites/default/files/uploaded-documents/NEPAD/ frameworkfor-thetenyearcapacitybuildingprogrammefortheafrican union.pdf.
4. Onuk, personal interview, AU Peace and Security Department, Addis Ababa: June 2014.
5. Terry Mays, *Africa's First Peacekeeping Operation: The OAU in Chad, 1981–1982* (Westport and London: Praeger, 2002), 9–10.
6. United Nations, "Somalia: UN Deploys new Special Force to Protect Staff in Mogadishu", (May 18 2014): http://www.un. org/apps/news/story.asp?NewsID=47820#.VsnFFbQrKUk.
7. United Nations, "Republic of Congo-ONUC Mandate", available at http://www.un.org/Depts/DPKO/Missions/onucM.htm.
8. Smith Hempstone, "Rebels, Mercenaries and Dividends: The Katanga Story", in *The Western Political Quarterly*, ed. Warren E. Tomlinson (New York: Praeger, 1963), 238.
9. Tatianna Carayannis, "The Democratic Republic of Congo", in *Dealing with Conflict in Africa*, ed. Jane Boulden (New York: Palgrave Macmillan, 2003), 253–303.

10. Katharina P. Coleman, *International Organization and Peace Enforcement: The Politics of International Legitimacy* (Cambridge: Cambridge University Press, 2007).
11. Peter Vale, *Security and Politics in South Africa: Regional Dimension* (Boulder, Colorado: Lynne Rienner, 2003).
12. United Nations, "Security Council Report: Briefings on the DRC: MONUSCO and Sanctions", January 21, 2015, http://www.whatsinblue.org/2015/01/briefings-on-the-drc-monusco-and-sanctions.php.
13. Tomaz Salomao, personal interview, former Executive Secretary of SADC Secretariat, Johannesburg: January 2016.
14. United Nations, n.d.
15. Alan Doss, personal interview, former head of MONUC, Geneva: October 2013; Lieutenant General (rtd.) Marc Caron, personal interview, former strategic advisor to MONUC, Geneva: June 2013.
16. Jide M. Okeke, personal interview, Senior Civilian Officer, AU Peace Support Operations Division, Addis Ababa: communication, June 2014.
17. Fiona Lortan, personal interview, Coordinator of AU-UN Partnership, AU Peace and Security Department, June 2015.
18. Lortan, personal interview, July 2015.
19. Okeke, personal interview, June 2014.
20. Linda Akua Darkwa, personal interview, AU Peace and Security Department consultant, Geneva: June 2013.
21. Mehari T. Maru, personal interview, former AU programme director and international security consultant, Addis Ababa: December 2015.
22. Sandra Oder, personal interview communication, Civilian Officer, AU Peace and Security Department, Addis Ababa: December 2015.
23. Tafa, personal interview, June 2014.
24. African Union Peace and Security Council, "Communique", PSC/PR/Comm (LXIX), (Addis Ababa: AU Commission, November 19, 2007), 1.
25. Oder, personal interview, December 2015.
26. Oder, personal interview, 2015.

27. Organization of African Unity, *Technical Report No.1 Prepared for African Negotiators by OAU Advisory Panel of Experts on ACP-EU Negotiations* (Addis Ababa: OAU, February 1999); Council of European Union, "The Africa–EU Strategic Partnership: p", 6. A Joint Africa-EU Strategy", Lisbon: 2007).

28. African Union and United Nations Development Programme, *Evaluation of the Africa's Strategic Partnerships* Draft Final Revised Report, UNDP/AU: Addis Ababa, (November 2014), 26.

29. The mandate of the UNOAU was to (a) provide capacity building to the AU; (b) support to AMISOM; (c) provide support to the AU commission, on matters including the budget and administration, including on structure and policies; (d) augmentation of the staffing capacity; and paramount focus was (e) to develop a strategic partnership.

30. Astrid Evrensel, personal interview, Head of Mediation Unit, UN Office to the AU, Addis Ababa: November 2014.

31. Boitshoko Mokgatlhe, personal interview, Head of AU Office to Khartoum, Addis Ababa: November 2014.

32. Abdel-Kader Harieche, personal interview, Head of Politics, UN Office to the AU, Addis Ababa: November 2014.

33. Benjamin Namanya, personal interview, Head of Police Component, UN Office to the AU, Addis Ababa: June 2014.

34. Colonel Mamadu Mbaye, personal interview, Coordinator of the African Standby Force, AU Peace Support Operations Division, Addis Ababa: June 2014.

35. African Union, "Communique", 2–3.

36. African Union, "Communique", 2.

37. The principle of subsidiarity implies that the UN would only participate when needed. This means that not every mission would be transferrable to the UN. This thinking is based on the experience in Burundi and Comoros.

38. United Nations General Assembly and United Nations Security Council, *Report of the African Union-United Nations Panel on Modalities for Support to African Union Peacekeeping Operations*, A/63/666—S/2008/813 (New York: United Nations, December 31 2008), 21–23.

39. Harieche, personal interview, November 2014.

180 T. GWATIWA

40. United Nations General Assembly and United Nations Security Council, *Support to African Union Peacekeeping Operations Authorized by the United Nations, Report of the Secretary General*, A/64/359—S/2009/470 (New York: United Nations, September 18 2009).

41. Bola Akinteriwa, "AU–NATO Collaboration: Defining the Issues from an African Perspective," in *AU–NATO Collaboration: Implications and Prospects*, ed. Brooke A. Smith-Windsor (Rome: NATO Defence College, 2013).

42. Marco Rimanelli, *The A to Z of NATO and Other International Security Organizations* (Toronto and Plymouth: The Scarecrow Press Inc., 2009), 282.

43. Colonel Vincent Alexandre, personal interview, Head of Military Partnerships Branch, NATO Command to the AU, Addis Ababa: November 2014.

44. Lieutenant Colonel (rtd) William Haag, personal interview, Former Lead Planner for NATO Missions to the AU, Lisbon: April 2014.

45. Haag, personal interview.

46. Mehari Taddele Maru, "'Resetting' AU-NATO Relations: From Ad Hoc Military-Technical Cooperation to Strategic Partnership", NATO Research Paper, no. 102 (June 2014) 2; Glen Segell, "The First NATO Mission to Africa: Darfur," *Scientia Militaria* 36, no. 2 (2008): 1–18 [7–8].

47. Captain Tongulac Hakan, personal interview, Head of the NATO Senior Liaison Team, Addis Ababa: June 2014.

48. AU–NATO High Level Conference, Addis Ababa: November 2014.

49. Oder, personal interview, December 2015.

50. United Nations Security Council, *Resolution 1973 (2011): Adopted by the Security Council at its 6498th meeting, on 17 March 2011*, (New York: March 17 2011).

51. Colonel William C. Wyatt, personal interview, US AFRICOM Strategic Advisor to the AU, November 2014.

52. Algerian Political Officer, personal interview, former Algerian Officer in the NATO Mediterranean Dialogue, Geneva: May 2014.

53. see Maru, "'Resetting' AU-NATO Relations".

54. Mihail Carp, telephone interview, Deputy Head of Operations, NATO Headquarters, Brussels-Geneva: May 2015.

55. Robert van de Roer, "Jaap de Hoop Scheffer: Diplomatic Long Distance Runner", *NATO Review*, Winter 2003, http://www.nato.int/docu/review/2003/issue4/english/profile.html.
56. Mehari T. Maru, "Rethinking and Reforming the African Union Commission Elections", *African Security Review*, 21, no. 4 (2012), 64–78.
57. I do not imply that Jaap de Hoop Schaeffer was saintly in the use of his network connections to Africa. (He failed to sustain dialogue between the NAC and the PSC). On the contrary, I suggest that at least the role of networks positively contributed to the outcomes in the early phase of the partnership. What the partnership was under him, is not under his successors.
58. Hakan, personal interview, 2014; Alexandre, personal interview, 2014.
59. Nyoyo, personal interview, August 2015.
60. Segell, "The First NATO Mission to Africa".
61. Hakan, personal interview, 2014.
62. Olive Tougan-Johnson, personal interview, Beninese Diplomat; Committee for the Rights of African Diplomats, (AU) Permanent Representatives Committee, Addis Ababa: August 2015.

CHAPTER 8

Slippage in AU Partnerships: The US Africa Command

The African Union's partnership with the US Africa Command (AFRICOM) also demonstrates *agency slack*. As stated in the previous chapter, this refers to an independent action by one party that is undesirable to other contracting parties. Agency slack takes two forms: "shirking" which is when an agent minimises the effort it exerts, or "slippage" when an agent shifts policy away from a preferred outcome to its own preferences.[1] The AU–AFRICOM partnership involves plenty of slippage.

INSTITUTIONAL DESIGN OF AFRICOM

AFRICOM is one of the US' seven combatant commands (CCDMs).[2] The idea of US commands is premised on the idea that the US has the primary responsibility for global and space security.[3] It is a self-imposed onus premised on US military capacity and strategic interests, and thus the geographic ambits covered by each CCDM are often called "Areas of Responsibility" (AORs). The idea of AORs does not derive from any solid acquiesce of the various world regions. (That is why all CCDMs are headquartered in the US—except for the European and Africa Command(s).[4]) Therefore, AFRICOM has the "responsibility" of all African countries, except Egypt which the Americans deem part of the Middle East.

AFRICOM has a unique institutional design which sets it apart from the rest of the CCDMs. It differs from other CCDMs in two ways.

© The Author(s), under exclusive license to Springer Nature Switzerland AG 2022

T. Gwatiwa, *The African Union and African Agency in International Politics*, https://doi.org/10.1007/978-3-030-87805-4_8

183

First, it is designed in an organisational format. Other CCDMs have a simple military structure without any organisational complexity. This design was meant to appeal to key continental actors, most probably the AU and the RECs.[5] Second, AFRICOM constitutively consists of an amalgamated services component. Its workforce consists of officials from the US Department of Defence (DOD), US State Department Bureau of African Affairs, US Agency for International Development and other government departments and agencies.[6] This was due to the underlying idea, promulgated both under the Clinton and Bush administrations, that the Command would take a "comprehensive" approach to security (discussed below). This unique design derived from the then major trends and changes in international affairs.

This unique design was influenced by both internal and external factors. First, there was a realisation within the US government that the nature of security threats in the twenty-first century had changed. According to Berchinsky, this realisation was first acknowledged by the Clinton administration. It experientially derived from the programmatic evolution of various US government agencies working in Africa: the DOD and State Department had many parallel programmes in various parts of Africa, although the latter leaned towards human security.[7] Second, an organisational outlook corresponded with the common ideas of "enabling Africans to bear their burdens" and the so-called "African solutions to African problems" promoted by the likes of Thabo Mbeki and Olusegun Obasanjo. This idea was not only highlighted by US Secretary of State Collin Powell's confirmation hearing in 2001 but was also discussed in earnest during Powell's first continental visit to Africa later that year.[8] Innately, such an approach reduced the transaction costs of dealing with 53 individual African states, especially that Collin Powell was already a proponent of the idea of dealing with the so-called regional hegemons. The ideas purveyed by Powell, who had briefly served in the Clinton administration, as well as the internal governmental changes, found synergy with early institutional fissures at the African Union and eventually shaped the design of AFRICOM.[9]

The structure of the Command also reflected synergistic correspondence with the abovementioned changes. AFRICOM is headed by a four-star general (full title of general). This rank carries political significance. A four-start general is directly accountable to a US cabinet as well as the US Senate and the US Congress. The first leader of AFRICOM was General William Ward, an African American. The four-star general is deputised by senior officials, a three-star (or lieutenant general) and a civilian ambassador (from the State Department). This gives the Command a modicum of cognitive and representational balance. However, this is betrayed by an overwhelmingly military mid-tier structure, which consists of nine military directorates, namely resources; intelligence and knowledge; operations and cyber; logistics; strategy, plans and programmes; C4S systems; joint training, readiness, and exercises; outreach.[10] The idea of integrating military and civilian structure seems to be a difficult one as the civilian element is still thin and undermined by its military counterpart.[11] This implies that the Command remained largely militaristic in design and function with a relatively thin civilian component. This was somewhat natural given the nascence of the organisational entity.

ORIGINS AND MOTIVATIONS FOR THE PARTNERSHIP

The origins of this partnership should be understood from two perspectives. The first perspective relates to the evolution of the US "Africa" [security] policy. The second perspective relates to the US's role in a post-hegemonic world. The two angles provide an understanding of the framing of the partnership as well as the level of engagement.

The origins of this partnership should be understood in the context of the US foreign and security policy in Africa. As the world's superpower, the US has several combatant commands responsible for security in each region. However, there was no specific command dealing with Africa.[12] This was because Africa was not a top strategic priority to the US. This can be traced to the historicity of the two institutions that form AFRICOM.

Historically, the US State Department and the US DOD—the main components of AFRICOM—had a lackadaisical policy approach towards Africa. The State Department established its Bureau of Africa Affairs in 1958. Schraeder argues that for a long time "the top echelons of the Africa Bureau...were dominated by European specialists who continued to approach the continent from a Europe-centric point of view".[13] The DOD faced similar challenges. Schraeder further argues that the word "Africa" was not introduced into DOD policy and structures until 1952. It is not clear whether the Europeanised approach was a result of a mere lack of strategic prioritisation of the then process of decolonisation. However, the foregoing anomaly did not prevent US involvement in African security and regionalism.

Early US activities in Africa largely took a subsidised approach. This meant two things. First, it meant that the US role was defined and driven by narrow interests. It mainly occurred within the rubric of anti-communism even where such concerns where in doubt. Second, such a pursuit did not involve full US involvement but was subsidised to regional or favourable domestic actors. It is imperative to note that much of post-War US activities in Africa was left to the CIA. The CIA was opaquely clandestine and not accountable to Congress. As a corollary, the CIA left a legacy of political destabilisation, entrenching several political stooges who favoured US or Western interests such as in the Belgian Congo (or Zaire) and Ghana.[14] The CIA also supported apartheid South Africa in its sub-imperial meddling in Angola and Namibia under the pretext of anti-communism.[15] This subsidisation correlated with questionable US military activities.

US military activities in Africa between 1980 and 2003 raised questions because of their apparent ambivalence to African security changes. They were largely characterised by parochialism. The first major US military involvement in Africa was the bombing of Libya in 1986 for its alleged sponsoring of terrorism.[16] In 1992, the US led the (UN) Unified Task Force to create a passage for humanitarian work during the Somali civil war. A few years later the US withdrew from Somalia following the killing of 19 US special forces in Mogadishu—ostensibly the crème de la crème of the US military.

In the ensuing years, the US hardly used its "combat-ready" troops which it often deployed in the periphery of large security crises. For instance, the US deployed combat-equipped troops in Burundi during the Rwandan genocide in 1994; deployed combat-equipped contingents to Sierra Leone and Liberia between 1996 and 2003; sent forces to Cote d'Ivoire in 2002—all of which were either to protect American personnel or military installations.[17] It was not until 2012, that the US deployed Special Forces to track Joseph Kony.[18] This trajectory not only entrenched a culture of parochialism but also created a corresponding lasting perception of US unilateralism and foreign security policy jingoism. This perception played into the response of the (AU) AHSG to its creation in 2007.

The idea of partnership in the US–Africa relations should be endorsed with a huge caveat. The actual motivation for the creation, or at least the operationalisation, of AFRICOM was owed to an amalgamated set of strategic considerations which were more inward than outward looking.

When the idea of an African combatant command was mooted under the Clinton administration it was mostly due to concerns about the rise of transnational terrorist networks that led to failed or weak states such as Somalia, Kenya and Sudan.[19] Moreover, by the time the Command became operational under the Bush administration there were economic motivations for a "partnership". By 2001 Nigeria, Angola and Algeria ranked as 5th to 7th largest oil suppliers to the US.[20] He also argues that the US had an incentive to monitor China's growing involvement in Africa. The foregoing suggests that the move towards a collaborative partnership was more of a self-help strategy that desires a mutually beneficial partnership in the mould of the Africa–EU partnership.

INSTITUTIONAL MAP OF THE PARTNERSHIP

The map below shows the structural or institutional links between the AU and AFRICOM (Fig. 8.1).

Much of the AFRICOM secretariat is based outside Africa. This is partly owed to the political resistance from African heads of state in the earliest days of the Command. To that end, the AFRICOM headquarters

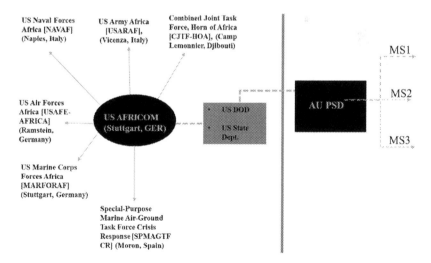

Fig. 8.1 Institutional map of AU–AFRICOM interactions

188   T. GWATIWA

are in Stuttgart, Germany. It is complemented by the following detachments all of which are assigned to operate in Africa—the US Army Africa [USARAF] (Vicenza, Italy); US Naval Forces Africa [NAVAF] (Naples, Italy); US Air Forces Africa [USAFE-AFARICA] (Ramstein Airbase, Germany); US Marine Corps Forces Africa [MARFORAF] (Stuttgart, Germany); US Special Operations Command Africa [SOCAFRICA] and the Special-Purpose Marine Air-Ground Task Force Crisis Response [SPMAGTF CR] used for crisis response (Moron, Spain) (AFRICOM, n.d.). The Combined Joint Task Force, Horn of Africa [CJTF-HOA], (Camp Lemonier, Djibouti) is the only component of AFRICOM based on African soil.

Two anomalies stand out in this institutional map. First, AFRICOM is strongly institutionalised outside of the continent, and has limited or (rather) weak links to the African Union. There is a liaison officer to the AU, often referred to as the "US AFRICOM strategic advisor to the AU". This is the most senior of about 32 AFRICOM officers attached to US Embassies all over Africa as "security cooperation officers [SCOs]".[21] Second, their Command is yet to sync previous State Department and Department of Defence operations without disruption of sustainable programmes. As shall be shown in the following assessment of AFRICOM support to APSA, this institutional map is comparatively not as effective as in other partnerships because of its loose relationship with the African Union.

Diplomacy and Engagement, 2007–2013

Slippage was most apparent in the high-level engagement between the AU and the US. In 2007, the US engaged the continent on the formation of the combatant. Part of the reason was to create buy-in for the Command and possibly land a partnership with the African Union. Employees of the DOD often distance themselves from those consultations, ascribing it to the State Department. According to Wyatt's veteran account, they often argue that the DOD never intended to relocate its headquarters from Stuttgart, Germany. That notwithstanding, most African states were opposed to the idea of hosting a US Africa Command. Even the scholarly community was very hostile to the idea.[22] The AHSG promulgated a solemn declaration that no African state should host AFRICOM, even though Liberia openly volunteered to host it. Nevertheless, the US, a superpower, could not be avoided and hence entered negotiations.

The initial set of (direct) negotiations between AFRICOM and the AU Peace and Security Department were not fruitful.[23] Prevailing negative perceptions of US motivations "coming to Africa" hampered (the then head of AFRICOM) General William K. Ward's efforts to engage the AU. Instead of an outright dismissal of the US, the AU settled for an informal agreement to collaborate in peace support operations. The informal agreement's legitimacy is derived from pre-existing US bilateral relations with most African states. This was inevitable because those bilateral arrangements were formally transferred to AFRICOM.[24] Between 2008 and 2011, the Africa–US relationship was largely an informal collaboration.

The slippage from perceived US imperialism evinced itself in the way peace and security were sequestered to the backwater of subsequent negotiations. To reduce the salience of security in the Africa–US strategic partnership,[25] the component was overshadowed by other components during major negotiations in 2011. It capitalised on trade, development and aid issues, making a skeletal reference to peace and security.[26] Apparently, AFRICOM wanted a separate agreement, at least like that with NATO.[27] The AU's persistent avoidance of an actual partnership with NATO reflected the fear of imperialism.

In 2013, the two parties held more negotiations. These negotiations also included RECs (i.e. SADC, ECOWAS, etc.). Negotiations reached a deadlock because the parties could not agree on the role and salience of African agency, especially regarding control of resources. For instance, the AU sought a drastic reform of the US' Africa Contingency Operations Training and Assistance (ACOTA) programme to meet AU training directives, which the US did not agree to.[28] Moreover, the RECs were not receptive to the prospect of an increased US military presence in Africa.[29] Although the Bush administration espoused more African agency, the Obama administration did not seem to share those views, at least in practice.

Contentious Preferences

To understand Africa's instance on a more daring form of agency slack, it is imperative to grasp the notion and position of preferences. Preference definition and coordination have been problematic in this partnership. This is partly caused by US unilateralism. Deservedly, AFRICOM is a branch of the US government and therefore more accountable to domestic audiences than other states. However, foreign relations either in bilateral or multilateral forms require periodic bargaining and adjustment of preferences, regardless of the stature of those involved.

Characteristically, the US has a unique approach to international and regional security. Empirical examples show that the US can (boldly) either support or undermine such processes, depending on perceived national interests.[30] As far as being a latecomer to AU partnership is concerned, US preponderance and relevance seemed curtailed, more especially that the US had not been heavily involved in AU-NATO engagement. As a corollary, the US approached the AU with scepticism and subsequently focused on an ambiguous form of expansion in Africa.[31] This expansion is meant to enable the US to act according to her own interests.[32]

This relationship deserves historical contextualisation. The US has a rich history of supercilious unilateralism and jingoism. It conducted more than 100 operations in Africa between 1952 and 2011, none of which showed intense, balanced and sustainable engagements with African actors except in the GWOT.[33] For instance, during the Rwandan genocide the US deployed "combat-equipped" forces in Burundi who were not authorised to intervene in the carnage. Furthermore, support to subregional organisations was no different. In 2003, the US deployed its Amphibious Ready Group (ARG), to "support" the ECOWAS Mission in Liberia (ECOMIL), under Operation Sheltering Sky: only 200 out of 5000 troops left the US marine pad. That this pattern continued to 2011—past the inception of an ostensibly reformed Command—raises questions about the US claims of a paradigm shift in its collaborative relationship with Africa. These precedents and continuity explain AFRICOM's failure around preference coordination.

As far as the findings show, this poor preference coordination is poised to continue because it is inhabited in the echelons of power in the US government. There is an enduring view among top decision makers that Africa is not a strategic priority to the US. Former US President George W. Bush , under whom AFRICOM assumed operational status, was the first leader to relay such a view. He argued that "while Africa may be important, it doesn't fit into [American] national strategic interests, as far as I can see them".[34] I also observed such myopia and parochialism in views expressed by DOD officials. Some observers posit that US national security strategy towards Africa is closely tied to its interests towards violent extremism, maritime security, oil and global trade. Unless and until there can be a bottom-up translation of understanding, this portends to dwarf the partnership or afflict it with a form of institutional rigor mortis that will limit the AU and AFRICOM ability to forge a healthy relationship.

The Western intervention in Libya in 2011 was a clear illustration that there is a failure of preference definition and coordination between the US (AFRICOM) and the African Union. This intervention took place five years into the inception of AFRICOM and at the height of US–Africa negotiations of the impending partnership. It, therefore, comes as a surprise that this was not seen as a golden moment to demonstrate goodwill for the partnership. However, the US did not engage the AU or its lead states (which were in the UNSC) prior to the intervention. However, even the so-called African lead states, South Africa and Nigeria, were for the most part divided on the Western intervention and the future of Muammar Gaddafi.[35]

In the run-up to the legitimation and execution of the Western intervention in Libya, the US overlooked African states and the AU.[36] The US sponsored and drafted the resolution that legitimated the Western (or NATO) intervention in Libya. Instead of engaging the AU or its representative group, it opted for the Arab League which already had a rough relationship with Muammar Gaddafi. By the time the UNSC resolution authorised a NATO no-fly zone over Libya, the US had AFRICOM troops on standby. The AFRICOM troops commenced Operation Odyssey Dawn in Libya days ahead of the NATO intervention. This deliberate circumvention of African interests was emblematic of the general failure of preference definition and coordination in the partnership.

SLIPPAGE BETWEEN ADDIS AND WASHINGTON

By indicating that this partnership is illustrative of slippage does not imply that it bears no lessons for the other types of outcomes. Indeed, this partnership is emblematic of slippage by the way the AU often shifts from strong engagement with AFRICOM. The outcomes could have been different had the collaborative relationship between the AU and AFRICOM followed a different trajectory.

This case suggests that the type of agreement governing a partnership determines outcomes of the partnership. The agreement governing the AU–AFRICOM collaborative partnership is thin and vague. Consisting of only three pages, it is the thinnest document in the AU partnership milieu. Precisely, the agreement is inimitably vague on peace and security. It is also heavily themed towards economic issues rather than peace and security. It also leaves the peace and security component open. In the absence of a clear articulation of the peace and security component of the partnership, there is no action plan as found elsewhere (in partnerships with the EU and UN). With the benefit of such precedence, I can safely posit that with no soft, binding or at least guiding, addendum to the agreement either partner does not see serious obligation. This creates room for any party, especially the stronger one, to act as it pleases including "breaking down" (atomizing) the partnership. Empirically, this incited a response in the form of agency slack.

The preceding factor invites the subject of African agency in this partnership. Did the lack of an elaborate agreement undermine African agency? When the Command took shape in the early years of the Bush administration there was a "perceived need for African to 'do more for themselves' in the realm of conflict resolution".[37] Did this mean the US would afford Africa the "agenda and priority setting" which the AU and its lead states vehemently sought? Indeed, the foregoing rhetoric (by the then US Secretary of State Collin Powell) seemed to resonate with Thabo Mbeki's rhetoric of "African solutions to African problems" which had gained ample buy-in in Europe. However, a closer look at Colin Powell's statement reveals that this was simply a hortatory rhetoric in what was an already changing political landscape. Evidence suggests that even when AFRICOM took shape, the CCMD had problems with either enabling or letting Africans "do more for themselves". It habitually overrode African preferences at the technical or operational level, especially considering the type of operations the US conducts in the periphery of African peace support operations in Somalia, North Africa and the Sahel. They have no regard for African preferences in those regions.

Africa's constant slippage was caused by the poverty of professional networks between the US and Africa. The role of elites is just as important as in other partnerships, as evinced by the case of NATO. The echelons of the CCMD as well as security elites in government had either no or limited networks in Africa.

Indeed, there were scores of people with experience of Africa who could have better articulated how the US could contribute to APSA, but they were replaced by several personalities with either corrosive or no actual experience on Africa. For instance, Jendayi Frazer who was the Assistant Secretary of State for African Affairs and the "Africa" focal point and advisor in George Bush administration, was often criticized for her one-dimensional and often embellished views, and hawkish rhetoric, and policies favouring US militarism in Africa.[38] She had no extensive policy networks with senior African policymakers who were working on APSA projects. This also applies to the inaugural commander of AFRICOM, General William Ward. Ward had no strong background on African security. How he failed to create lasting networks during his tenure also remains a mystery. Had these two elites created useful networks, they would have lobbied for better results between the two organisations.

This slippage is also attributable to the problem of historical longevity. The lack of a long history of engagement undermined the process of institutionalisation as well as engendering trust between US and AU/African elites. Other partnerships (in preceding chapters) show that longevity affects the institutionalisation of a partnership. However, in this case, the parties had and stuck to diametrically opposed approaches to security. Hell, the US failed to transform from realist approach to its touted "whole of government approach", which theoretically resonates with the AU's human security approach. Its failure to reify its aspirations caused tensions with the AU. As a corollary, the US often implemented its preferred programmes singularly or used a few African client states. This implies that the AU's slippage tactics were not sufficient to inhibit US activities in the continent.

Agency slack, in this case, is also a response to cognitive regionalism. To be fair, there was a desire for a paradigm shift towards comprehensive security to align with AU security doctrines. However, old perceptions and habits prevailed. Schraeder observed that the nucleus of the Bush administration consisted of a "realist-oriented foreign policy" triumvirate that "emphasized a more 'hard-headed' analysis of concrete US interests" and criticised the preceding Clinton administration for a "feel good" policy towards Africa.[39] This implies that there was a contradiction between rhetoric (earlier referred to) and practice. This hampered an actual shift in such a way that the Command could appreciate the efficacy of APSA.

The slippage in this partnership is also attributable to its form of institutionalisation. Unlike other partnerships, the CCMD's most important institutional structures are far removed from the African Union. It does not have a strong liaison in Addis Ababa. It is surprising why the US, with its capacity [in Stuttgart], did not assign more liaison officers to Addis given that it had more experts in areas related to APSA institutions. Perhaps the biggest problem was the US military focus, whereas

APSA had transformed in many ways to incorporate multidimensional designs. As a result, the CCMD often appeared overzealous and misdirected within this milieu. For instance, the US suggested a big project for the interoperability of ASF, but AU member states had deep suspicions for its motives. To further enable AU agency slack, the EU supported the AU resistance of the US offer.

Finally, there is a fear of militarisation of the continent. AFRICOM is still headquartered in Stuttgart (Germany) with nearly 600 military officers transferred from the US European Command plus another 600 civilians within the new amalgamated structure.[40] There are also more than 30 security cooperation officers attached to US embassies all over Africa. This overwhelmingly military formation creates unease. To the AU, formalising a partnership with such an actor carries risks.

SLIPPAGE OR ANOTHER DEGREE OF SHIRKING?

Is this slippage or simply another degree of shirking? This is a pertinent question given the implications raised in the preceding chapter. The reader must bear in mind that shirking is a form of agency slack where one actor minimises its activities, much to the consternation of the other. So, is this slippage or a different form of shirking? There are number of factors that need to be assessed when answering this question.

Resource disbursement directionality is an important indicator of slippage. Shifting away from preferred outcomes does not insinuate a cessation of collaboration. To the contrary, the resources (or projects) continue. However, it is the manner of implementation that becomes contestable to one of the parties. If this disbursement and directionality remain one-dimensional, without conjoined activity, the partnership is contestable and inadvertently elicit slippage or shirking. For instance, US security programmes, especially in Somalia and North Africa and the Sahel, are emblematic of this. There has been a failure to modify existing one-dimensional and heavily militarised programmes. Their overwhelming military character runs contrary to the multidimensional form and function of the ASF. That is why the AU constantly avoids entering a partnership that would suffocate and change its preferences. This avoidance is indicative of slippage. These would qualify as shirking if the AU participated in those programmes but minimised its efforts. However, in this case the AU shifted away from US offers, also partly because it had options from partnerships with the EU, UN and NATO.

The above mentioned closely relates to the issue of engagement and interaction which also illuminates whether this is slippage or shirking. The reader should not assume that US unilateralism in resource disbursement occurs in isolation. The AU and AFRICOM continue to interact through various forums such as the AU Partnership Group meeting in Addis Ababa, NATO, the United Nations and periodic meetings organised by the AU PSD. However, this interaction simply serves as surveillance not a platform for serious engagement. Despite the interactions, why are the two parties still unable to graduate to a higher level of trust and engagement?

Their interaction involves low-level meetings. There are not high-level summits between the two. This gives the impression that this partnership has no actual strategic importance. Other partnerships suggest that high-level meetings tend to result in stronger commitments and intensive dialogue over priority issue-areas. They also have follow-up meetings at the technical level to augment implementation. In other words, the scant and schizophrenic engagement means that there is no strong bond. A strong bond would have at least resulted in shirking because there would be commitments. However, since there are no commitments, it is easier for the vulnerable party to consistently exercise slippage.

In the absence of such type of summitry, there can be no expectation of serious outputs towards APSA. There are no joint-expert meetings to review and monitor partnership outputs to see whether they align to APSA as well as US interests, hence a slippage evinced by a further gravitation from common objectives. If it were a partnership which accommodate African agency, there would be more high-level summits that result in considerable resource outputs that, even if delivered occasionally or late, would be a conjoined implementation of peace and security projects. However, AFRICOM security programmes are increasingly either dictated to the AU or are heavily altered to serve parochial interests.

African Agency in AU and AFRICOM Strategic Futures

However, in the grand scheme of things, this partnership requires a review and wholesale paradigm shift in relation to Africa agency. There is no doubt that the two parties' security interests have meeting points. However, its potential efficacy requires further dialogue regarding the role of African agency. African agency does not imply a radical transformation of US security interests, but it implies the need for the US—especially as a relatively new player in the continent—to adjust its manner of engagement and aligning of security interests. The biggest failure in this partnership has been the US' inability to treat the AU as an equal partner. It has not been willing to abandon its unilateralism.

The stakes are not necessarily in favour of either party. To start with, the US already has its own agency. It is an agency built around force, political bullying and the dwarfing of other actors' efforts. The modern-day African security architecture involves multiple players: traditional and emerging powers, from which the AU and its member states can draw resources that AFRICOM is not willing to provide. China, Russia, Turkey, Brazil and others are ready to replace the role of the US in Africa, by pandering to African agency. Conversely, the AU cannot avoid the US either. Most AU member states are tied to US security in bilateral terms. As the world's most advanced security establishment, the US is unavoidable. The AU can only exercise slippage to a certain extent and for a certain amount of time. The AU's widest opportunity is to engage its member states to diplomatically persuade AFRICOM—which also deals with individual states—to formally adopt a position of accommodating African agency. This should not only be found in the rhetoric of senior political leaders (as was in the case of the Bush administration) but should be codified into official documents, including US–Africa Strategic partnership, which will most likely be reviewed in 2022. Moreover, the AU–AFRICOM partnership should be fully institutionalised beyond Addis Ababa. There are already ample avenues for further institutionalisation through AU diplomatic offices in Washington and Brussels (which is not far from Stuttgart). Above all, the AU should have liaison officers at the Pentagon and Stuttgart, the same way that AFRICOM, NATO and the EU have liaison officers at the AU Commission headquarters in Addis Ababa.

NOTES

1. Darren G. Hawkins, David A. Lake, Daniel L. Nielson and Michael J. Tierney, "Delegation Under Anarchy: States, International Organizations, and Principal-Agent Theory", in Delegation and Agency in International Organizations, eds. Darren G. Hawkins, David A. Lake, Daniel L. Nielson and Michael J. Tierney

(Cambridge and New York: Cambridge University Press, 2006), 7–10.

2. The other commands are United States North Command; United States Central Command; United States Southern Command; United States Pacific Command; United States European Command and the United States Space Command.

3. Colonel William C. Wyatt, personal interview, US AFRICOM Strategic Advisor to the AU, Addis Ababa: November 2014.

4. The US European Command (EUCOM) was based in Stuttgart, Germany due to the Cold War threat. It was felt that it had to be closer to the Soviet threat. The US Africa Command was eventually based in Stuttgart for two reasons: the first being a collective decision to not host AFRICOM in the African continent; and the idea that it was more sensible to base AFRICOM in Stuttgart which had a leading role in the previous arrangement where Africa was the responsibility of EUCOM, PACOM, CENTCOM and SOUTHCOM.

5. Wyatt, personal interview, November 2014.

6. Robert G. Berchinsky, "Africom's Dilemma: The 'Global War on Terrorism', 'Capacity Building', Humanitarianism, and the Future of US Security Policy in Africa" (Strategic Studies Institute Monograph, 2007).

7. Wyatt, personal interview, November 2014.

8. United States Senate, "Statement of Secretary of State-Designate Colin L. Powell Prepared for the Confirmation Hearing of the US Senate Committee on Foreign Relations Scheduled for 10:00 AM, January 17, 2001," http://www.senate.gov/%7Eforeign/tes timony/wt_powell_011701.txt.

9. See Ademola Abass, "African Peace and Security Architecture and the Protection of Human Security", in *Protecting Human Security in Africa*, ed. Ademola Abass (Oxord and New York: Oxford University Press, 2010), 247–283.

10. United States Africa Command, "About the Command", https:// www.africom.mil/about-the-command.

11. Lauren Ploch, *Africa Command: U.S. Strategic Interests and the Role of the U.S. Military in Africa*, Congressional Research Service, Report for Congress, July 22, 2011, 29.

12. David E. Brown, "AFRICOM at Five Years: The Maturation of a New US Combatant Command" (Strategic Studies Institute, The Letort Papers, August 2013).

13. Peter J. Schraeder, *United States Foreign Policy Towards Africa: Incrementalism, Crisis and Change* (Cambridge: Cambridge University Press, 1994), 197.
14. Lemarchand, "The CIA in Africa"; Devlin, "Chief of Station"; Assensoh and Alex-Assensoh, "African Military History and Politics". Rene Lemarchand, "The CIA in Africa: How Central? How Intelligent?" *The Journal of Modern African Studies* 14, no. 3 (1976): 401–426; Larry Devlin, *Chief of Station, Congo: A Memoir of 1960–67* (New York: Public Affairs, 2007); Akwasi B. Assensoh and Yvette M. Alex-Assensoh, *African Military History and Politics: Coups and Ideological Incursions* (New York: Palgrave, 2001).
15. Schraeder, "Forget the Rhetoric and Boost Geopolitics".
16. Bruce J. St. John, *Libya and the United States: Two Centuries of Strife* (Philadelphia: University of Pennsylvania Press, 2002).
17. Ploch, "Africa Command", 33–37.
18. Dan Roberts, "US Confirms Troops Hunting Joseph Kony Will Be Used Across Central Africa," *The Guardian*, March 24, 2014, http://www.theguardian.com/world/2014/mar/24/us-troops-uganda-joseph-kony.
19. Carl A. Le Van, "The Political Economy of African Responses to the US Africa Command," *Africa Today* 57, no. 1 (2010): 3–23 [5].
20. Berchinsky, "Africom's Dilemma".
21. Wyatt, personal interview, November 2014.
22. Laurie Nathan, "AFRICOM: A Threat to Africa's Security," *Contemporary Security Policy* 30, no. 1 (2009): 58–61.
23. This was prior to the formation of the Partnerships Management and Coordination Division [PMCD], and any aspiring partner had to negotiate directly with the concerned department.
24. Le Van, "The Political Economy," 6.
25. The US-Africa Strategic Partnership of 2013 which was signed by the Chairperson of the AUC Commission, Nkosazana Dlamini-Zuma and the then US State Department, by Secretary Hilary Rodham Clinton.
26. African Union and United States State Department, "US-Africa Strategic Partnership: Memorandum of Understanding" (Addis Ababa: AU Commission, 2013), 3.

8 SLIPPAGE IN AU PARTNERSHIPS: THE US AFRICA COMMAND   199

27. Elizabeth Choge, personal interview, Senior Political Officer, African Union Commission, Addis Ababa: July 2015.
28. Sandra Oder, personal interview communication, Civilian Officer, AU Peace and Security Department, Addis Ababa: December 2015.
29. See Le Van, "The Political Economy," 9–10.
30. Björn Hettne and Frederik Ponjaert, "Interregionalism and World Order: The Diverging EU and US Models," in *European Union and New Regionalism: Competing Regionalism and Global Governance in a Post-Hegemonic Era*, ed. Mario Telo, 2 ed. (London and New York: Routledge, 2013).
31. Nick Turse, "Tomgram: Nick Turse, AFRICOM's Gigantic 'Small Footprint'," *TomDispatch.com* (September 5, 2013), www.tom dispatch.com/blog/175743/tomgram/3A/nick-turse/africom's-gigantic-footprint.html.
32. US expansion in Africa contravenes an AU/AHSG declaration on the hosting of AFRICOM on African soil. Even the countries that host such bases have little awareness or control over US activities within these military bases (or "lily pads" as they are known). There has been complaints and friction about US activities in some lily pads such as Djibouti, Ethiopia and less so in the Seychelles. The only base to be closed was the US drone base in Ethiopia. While the official reasons were undisclosed, this incident followed an episode of disagreements between Ethiopia and the US on how to approach security issues in the Horn of Africa (see Maru (b), personal interview, 2015). Disagreements between Djibouti and the US have not led to closure of any bases because US, French, Russian, Chinese and Japanese military bases are strongly tied to the Djiboutian political economy. However, the friction has strengthened Djibouti's negotiating position vis-à-vis the US in the renewal of the lease of military bases.
33. Ploch, "Africa Command".
34. Berschinsky, "Africom's Dilemma", 4.
35. Mehari T. Maru, personal interview, former AU programme director and international security consultant, Addis Ababa: December 2015
36. AU interests in the UN system are represented by different African diplomatic corps, but the primarily role is ascribed to the "Africa Group" at the UN Headquarters in New York.

37. United States Senate, "Statement of Secretary of State-Designate".
38. Roland Marchal, "Somalia: A New Front Against Terrorism", Items: Insights From the Social Sciences, (February 5, 2007), https://items.ssrc.org/crisis-in-the-horn-of-africa/somalia-a-new-front-against-terrorism/.
39. Schraeder, "Forget the Rhetoric and Boost Geopolitics".
40. Tim Murithi, "The African Union Peace and Security Partnerships." Paper Presented at the Europe Africa Policy Research Network (EARN) (Cidade da Praia, Cape Verde: October 14–15, 2010), 5.

CHAPTER 9

Conclusion

This chapter provides a nuanced conclusion of this treatise. In its broadest strokes, this chapter concludes that the AU's agency slack is, first and foremost, a response to the internal pressures exerted by a huge, complex and constitutively irreconcilable regional security order. In this instance African shortcomings compromise its own agency in international politics. These factors (discussed below) are understandable but inexcusable. Yet, they do not occur in a vacuum. Those pressures are also a limiting factor in the AU's ability to project intentionality and configurative power in international affairs. The AU's agency slack is also a response to the interconnectedness of African states to imperialism which grossly affects African multilateralism considering the partnerships. This also implies that Africa's continuing positionality in the subaltern place in international politics drives it into a state of perennial agency slack. International politics occasionally tempts the AU, and Africa as a continent, to escape this subaltern position. Making "African ownership and leadership" a sine quo non of the partnership was indicative of this attempt. It sought to exercise the freedom and citizenship associated with agency. However, the spectre of imperialism and postcoloniality is abiding, persistently rearing its ugly shadow of various agential efforts.

The argument in this treatise posits that the two forms of agency slack—shirking and slippage—are evident in these key partnerships of the

© The Author(s), under exclusive license to Springer Nature Switzerland AG 2022
T. Gwatiwa, *The African Union and African Agency in International Politics*, https://doi.org/10.1007/978-3-030-87805-4_9

201

AU. One partnership stands out as emblematic, but it is not without challenges. Its state as the yardstick is threatened by its own politics. These partnerships are representative of the overall partnership milieu. Indeed, the partnerships appear skewed towards the West, yet they are illustrative of a trajectory that has been in play for more than half a century.

For discursive purposes, it is imperative to conclusively highlight the critical factors that cause, shape and facilitate the manifestation of agency slack, in its various forms—or its supposed lack thereof—in the different partnerships.

Diplomatic Engagement and Partnership Outcomes

The manifestation and role of agency slack rests on the fulcrum of diplomacy and high-level engagement. The practice of diplomacy is undoubtedly better in other parts of the world, where nation-states existed without interruption for centuries. While the history of the nation-state is in doubt, the quality of diplomacy and internationalism was interrupted by colonialism. Thus when the new "independent states" arose there was doubt about their ability to negotiate a new partnership with Europe. There are indications that non-Africans were surprised by Africans' diplomatic prowess in negotiating what resultantly became the Lomé Agreement of 1974. However, the quality of diplomacy was not matched by other levels of engagement such as to accentuate the partnership (and those with other regions) to levels that could transform the continent. Even though there was a twinkle in African diplomacy at the twilight of African regional diplomacy, this was not necessarily matched by similar capabilities and aspirations at the national or sub-national level. Uneven development, divergent capabilities, starkly opposed strategic outlooks and different histories and aspirations did not adequately match the continental aspirations lent by collective diplomacy. This is something that still persists, although more African countries have acquiesced continental regional integration: continental aspirations are not necessarily aligned with national aspirations. However, continental diplomacy can create a threshold for African agency.

Diplomatic and high-level engagement with partners remains a critical element of the partnerships and international cooperation. Thus, the quality of diplomacy determines the agential gains that Africa can make in international partnerships. Better diplomacy, which seems to be sporadic but aptly timed, often results in better gains. The quality of diplomacy in the run up to the inception (early 1970s) and renewal (late 1990s) of the partnership with Europe cannot be understated. It was aptly timed and accentuated to potent levels. To be sure, African negotiators were still somewhat outdone in numbers, but not so much in terms of tact. Their biggest achievement was to secure an inscription of African agency in the partnership, often highlighted as "African ownership and leadership" in most documents, or "agenda and priority setting" in most AU publications. It is also imperative to highlight why diplomatic engagement resulted in higher gains in those partnerships.

The greater agential fortunes in early African international diplomacy benefited from the input of skillful heads of state and government. This entailed the fortitude of Presidents Thabo Mbeki (South Africa), Olusegun Obasanjo (Nigeria), Abdelaziz Bouteflika (Algeria) and Muammar Gaddafi (Libya) and often with the input of Abdoulaye Wade (Senegal). Interestingly, most of these had previously been formal or informal diplomats in their different capacities. Mbeki, Obasanjo, Bouteflika and Gaddafi interacted during the 1970s through the early 1990s over various issues. By the 1990s, these figures were in power in their states, which are also the wealthiest. They resuscitated their networks to revamp African regionalism. More importantly, they used their networks to reach out to their counterparts in Europe and Asia, who also reciprocated, especially throughout the 1990s. Their efforts benefited from corresponding diplomatic developments within African multilateralism.

African diplomacy benefited from the efforts of the chief of the last chief of the OAU secretariat and first chief of the AU Commission. This treatise did not explore the role of Salim Ahmed Salim, who played a key leadership role when the OAU renegotiated its emblematic partnership with the EU; but it explored the role of former AU Commission Chairperson, Alpha Konare. Konare, a former head of state, played a key role in these negotiations and bargaining. The then nascent AU augmented its capacity through the use of skillful diplomats from Africa's major states: primarily Nigeria, South Africa, Algeria, Libya, Ethiopia and others. The AU also made an extensive use of consultants during its early days, to fill in other structures of engagement especially where institutionalisation was in place and in earnest.

What is evident in the foregoing submission is that African diplomacy and high-level engagement made agential gains in as far as it benefited from key personalities, their networks, and the response from their counterparts in other world regions. However, this only responds to African agency, but not agency slack in the AU's partnerships.

The AU's diplomacy gradually incurred hiccups and institutional paralysis, thus limiting its freedom and ability to project its diplomatic function. This owed to three main factors. First, African negotiating teams, at different periods, are often understaffed. When negotiating its partnerships with the EU, NATO and UN, the AU only had a handful of experts. These often faced more endowed counterparts whose diplomatic prowess often limited Africa's gains. Second, there persisted the problem of international ambitions lingering without supporting structures in the AU Commission. Different partnerships were managed by divergent departments and offices in the AU. For instance, the EU partnership itself was split between the Department of Economics and the Peace and Security Department—and with a focal bias towards the latter. The US–Africa partnership was managed by the office of the Deputy Chairperson of the AU Commission. The partnership with the UN was perhaps the most scattered: UNESCO dealt with more than two departments at the commission; the UNDP dealt with various departments; and other units also picked their preferred partners without any coherence. It was not until 2013 that the AU created the Partnerships Management and Coordination Division (PMCD) with the objective to provide some form of strategic guidance. The division was not a panacea either: it struggled to control partnerships which were already entrenched in various departments, offices and units. Third, the AU had difficulty in getting member states to act in unison to project a singular voice with various partners. The attempt to align the continent with the Banjul Formula (of 2006) which guides African states' collective diplomacy has not been successful. These three factors, limits the freedom and ability of the AU as an African agent, thus keeping it in a subaltern position. Even it finds itself in a subaltern position, the AU still has an agential imperative to the continent. The need to balance between a heightened aspiration and limited empirical capacity incites recourse to agency slack.

African Strategic Citizenship

The status of strategic citizenship—regional role playing and burden sharing—affects Africa's agential fortunes. When African states play their roles and adequately share burdens [of various nature] this results in better gains for African agency. The impact of strategic citizenship in the partnerships can be illustrated using two partnerships. For instance, in the emblematic partnership with the EU, the roles and burdens of various African states were clearly outlined in various components of APSA. These were effectively used in the various test of the ASF as well as other components of the APSA. This, unfortunately, did not exist in the case of partnerships with NATO, the UN and AFRICOM. Without clarity on this notion, two phenomena occurred. First, African states either competed for roles and prominence or outright rescinded their resources for various reasons. Second, some partners, especially AFRICOM and NATO, often preferred working with certain African states over others—something that did not always align with AU objectives. However, given that the AU largely depended on external support, it had limited freedom and control of outcomes in these partnerships. Often times when the AU found itself at odds with partner preferences, it would often resort to shirking and slippage. The former was more evident in the UN and NATO partnerships while the latter was evident in the partnership with US AFRICOM. However, this was a problem that was limited in imperialism, coloniality and forum shopping.

Imperialism, Coloniality and Forum Shopping

Although African agency is a laudable strategic aspiration, it is imperative to highlight how Africa's efforts are railed against an international order steeped in imperialism and coloniality. The AU often touted the notion of "African ownership and leadership" and "African solutions to African problems". The findings in this treatise suggest that although Africa occasionally secured positive outcomes in various partnerships, the continent eventually has to contend with the spectre of imperialism and coloniality. When this does not emanate as a challenge in inter-regional cooperation, it emanates from the tentacles of neo-imperialism within the continent where erstwhile colonizers such as France have entrenched themselves in African affairs. Similarly, African agency has been a source of tension in the negotiations with NATO and US AFRICOM, which are unashamedly characteristically emblematic of Western imperialism. The US, in particular, has no qualms declaring its mostly one-dimensional interests and thereafter accosting African agents to accept them. In the post-OAU, African agents appear less concerned with intimidation because their scope of bargaining has broadened since the advent of new or emerging powers—particularly from the East and from within the G77—with whom they can forum shop for different preferences.

However, this has not deterred Western partners from using forum shopping to limit African agency. After all, the West still controls a substantial part of the world economy and the assets needed for Africa's regional security integration. The West, as any other self-interested international actor has used forum shopping to obtain favourable gains. For instance, the West used an opportunity to forum shop for its interests between the UN Security Council, NATO and AFRICOM during the Western intervention in Libya. Similarly, forum shopping also takes place within the EU and the UNSC, by Western states, on issues relating to peace support operations in Africa. This has created tensions, especially in the AU partnerships with the UN, NATO and AFRICOM. This forum shopping inadvertently puts the AU in a position of limited power, freedom and ability to project its preferences. The AU innately recourses to agency slack where it exercises shirking and slippage as a means of survival.

THE HISTORICAL AND CHRONOLOGICAL INFLUENCE ON AGENCY

The history of a partnership has a significant bearing on whether a partnership yields better outcomes for either party. The preceding chapters have demonstrated that the strength, maturity and benefits vary with each partnership. The partnership with the EU, which accommodates African agency the most, benefits from historical longevity. That is followed by the partnership with the UN, NATO and AFRICOM in that order. The latter is relatively the newest, and the weakest in terms of accommodating African agency. That is because the historical significance of each partnership does not rest on longevity alone but the constituent major events within the partnership.

The longevity of a partnership portends efficacy in so far as the formality of the partnership goes. The partnership between the European Union and the African Union is difficult to pinpoint on a chronological scale. It can commence in the 1600s, or 1885 when colonial borders were entrenched. However, it is reasonable to consider the time when the then European Economic Community signed the Lomé Agreement of 1974 with the Africa, Caribbean and Pacific (ACP). The better agential outcomes in that partnership are attributable to nearly three decades

9 CONCLUSION 207

of deep political and diplomatic engagement. This is not evident in any other partnership.

Yet, it is imperative to note that longevity has yielded somewhat different agential outcomes in other partnerships. The AU–UN partnership has not yielded better agential outcomes despite a collaborative relationship between the OAU and UN dating back to the 1960s. This is attributable to two factors. First, although this was a lengthy period, the interaction involved weak engagement where neither party had a strong approach to African security. Thus, longevity did not amount to much. Second, in the post-OAU period, the parties had an opportunity to augment their collaboration, but they were preoccupied themselves with non-issues of supremacy and leadership politics, which ostensibly pruned African agency. Moreover, the UN as an organisation redirected their efforts to the institutionalisation of the United Nations Office to the African Union (UNOAU). Indeed, it may appear that the inception of the UNOAU was a good investment, but it mainly created another agency within the UN system—not a neutral liaison platform.

The AU–NATO partnership may be relatively new but its accommodation of African agency is caused by similar factors. This partnership, when new, was institutionalised at a faster pace by incepting the NATO SMLT. However, this jettisoned process created more problems similar to those found in the AU–UN partnership. Indeed, this got a lot of projects done. Most importantly, the team was instructed to accommodate African agency without limit. The partnership remained unproblematic for almost five years. However, the short period created problems. The dwarfed diplomatic latitude of the SMLT and its unsustainability created problems for the partnership. Some NATO member states rescinded citizens seconded to the SMLO, thus undercutting expertise. NATO also diluted the diplomatic clout of the SMLO when it reduced its leadership from a brigadier general to a captain. The host nation, Ethiopia, also decided not to give the SMLO any diplomatic status. This limited NATO's ability to make contributions to African security and the augmentation of APSA. Without the benefit of the rich history brought by longevity, this potentially important liaison link was aborted. In this case, Africa contributed to the erosion of its own agency.

The short span of the AU–US AFRICOM collaborative relationship robbed the parties of their potential. There was no lengthy period during which to institutionalise the partnership. The main reason was Africans' suspicions of the US motives for seeking what appeared to be a one-dimensional partnership.

What appears in both partnerships is the extent to which lack of longevity between parties can frustrate the partnership. It is worth noting that, as the case studies in this treatise show, lack of longevity and a rich history is often a threshold for agency slack. In both cases, NATO and AFRICOM are undoubtedly more powerful than the AU. They do not necessarily need the AU for their strategic ambitions, but it needs their support. The AU is also aware of this. However, longevity in itself is not an apogee for the AU to make any gains. It is what occurs within a partnership or relationship that can prepare for greater gains.

Major Events in the History of the Partnerships

During the span of such relationships, a number of major events occur that either shaped or altered the relationship to different agential outcomes. A partnership, as evident in the AU–EU partnership, can be shaped by a number of events in the area of peace and security. First, improved relations between political leaders can accentuate prospects for greater African agency. Landmark summits, such as the Cairo Summit of 2000, can create a threshold for negotiating an equitable partnership. Once assurances are given for each party to play their part, it gives impetus to mid-level and low-level negotiations to follow until a partnership is fully institutionalised. This would also depend on the extent to which the other party is willing to see it through. This becomes easier when the other party is eager to establish itself as a promoter of certain values or regional models. However, the most defining aspect in the span is the significance of learning curves.

Learning curves often lead to a better or worse accommodation of the other party's agency. In the case of the Africa–EU partnership, there were several learning curves which widened the accommodation of African agency. Surprisingly, this was not the case with the UN, even though the two parties had a long history punctuated with a battery of grotesque events. The UN rarely had any successful projects in Africa, yet it still seeks to overshadow the AU's corrective efforts by limiting the AU's agency. The UN failed to stop the Rwandan genocide; failed to effectively handle the two ECOMOG missions in Sierra Leone and Liberia which were transferred to a UN mandate in the 1990s; failed to

9 CONCLUSION 209

manage a UN mandate in the Congo and has bared managed any security crisis unless it was an AU–UN hybrid mission. Yet, the UN insists on its seniority without any historical legitimacy to support its preferential demands. The UN even refused to implement the recommendations of the Prodi Commission of 2004 which were favourable to the AU's desire for equality and complementarity in the partnership. As a result, the AU resorts to shirking in most cases when it is unable to agree with the UN. By shirking it does not entirely disengage from the UN, but it keeps certain elements of the partnership which are essential for the existence of security institutions and architecture in the continent. Similarly, there are fewer major events that upset relations between the AU on the one hand, and NATO and AFRICOM, on the other: mostly around one major case study—Libya. More importantly, those events are quite recent. This implies that these partnerships have fewer learning curves, which could otherwise improve Africa's bargaining position for better agential outcomes.

The Nature of Agreement and Partnerships

The type of agreement for each partnership determines the extent to which a partnership accommodates and enables African agency. Generally, there is a preference towards political agreements because they are not binding but rely on the political will and commitment of the parties. The case studies show that the efficacy of an agreement rests in both their wording and structuring as well as the rate of interaction; although that is not necessarily uniform.

The proper wording of a partnership agreement is a good start. Partnerships which clearly spell out a commitment to African ownership and leadership often incite correspondingly positive diplomatic efforts. That commitment is a clear acquiescence to African agency. The AU often responds accordingly, even though it may have limited diplomatic resources. However, that is a sign of goodwill. If there is goodwill the other parties often provide various forms of support. However, it is the level and frequency of interactions that make the difference.

Agreements with thorough wording mostly provide operational guidance. Such agreements clearly outline the terms of engagement between the parties. The agreements, such as in the case of the EU, also involved clear timelines as well as action reviews. This enables the parties to measure progress over years. By contrast, in some partnerships such as

210 T. GWATIWA

the AU–UN case study, the type of agreement in place accommodated African agency sporadically. This was largely because the wording was neither thorough nor precise. Between the first agreement and its renewal in 2015, the wording became more elusive. However, the difficulties that actually limited African agency in this partnership had more to do with inter-organisational politics than with the wording of the agreement. It suffices to state that while the partnership agreement wording might provide some strategic guidance, its agential capacity should not be overstated. It works much better when this guidance results in more interaction.

Multilevel and more frequent interactions also often produce better results for agency. These produce more engagement and dialogue over contentious issues. This was evinced by the Africa–EU agreement. However, in case where there is less frequent interaction there will be no ample room for dialogue over contentious issues. For instance, the AU–UN case study entails regular interaction without multilevel engagement. The meetings seem mostly limited to the two security councils. In the case of NATO, there is a similar challenge where there is sporadic interaction between the two councils. The US–Africa partnership also suffers from the same maladies. This partnership is further compounded by the disparity of interests. The inability to interact frequently in these partnerships has often resulted in contention over various preferences. There is often no thorough follow-up and lessons learned between the parties, often reducing conjoined action. These partnerships gradually relegate the AU to a subaltern position, which elicits agency slack.

COGNITIVE REGIONALISM, SECURITY AND AGENCY

Cognitive regionalism, a perception of regional security policy in relation to others, creates an important threshold for agency. This applies for both the AU and partners. For the AU, the reification of APSA as a step to Common African Defence Security Policy (CADSP) is a pivotal issue. It is also aware of its subaltern position. However, its freedom and potential to reify the CADSP depends on how different partner perceive the project's impact on theirs.

The evidence in this treatise shows that a strategic partner is more likely to accommodate greater African agency if there is a perceived closer linkage between their notion of security and that of the AU. For instance, the case of the EU affirms the foregoing notion. European security is

9 CONCLUSION 211

perceived as closely linked to peace and stability in Africa. Instability and insecurity generates illegal immigration which is considered a security issue in Europe. These also threaten European economic interests in the extractive and petroleum industries. The foregoing provides an incentive as well as an imperative for the other partner to accommodate more African agency.

However, if a partner perceives African security as less crucial for its security, they will be less willing to accommodate African security. The foregoing notion has a greater variation than the one highlighted prior. In the case that a partner may consider AU security somewhat important but less central to its interests, they may accommodate African agency somewhat less consistently. The ensuing accommodation—i.e. the AU's freedom and ability to project its preferences—may only be a result of protracted contention. Even then, the accommodation will be highly selective. The UN case study exhibits these traits. Yet, when a partner similarly views African security as somewhat tangentially tied to its security, it will occasionally accommodate African security only to the extent that those agential elements are peripheral to its core security concepts or projects. When the AU attempts to negotiate for greater accommodation, the demands may be met with hostility, especially when they seem to require a significant shift in perspective and doctrinal approach. The cases of NATO and AFRICOM are emblematic of the aforementioned. But these cases exhibit another dimension to the impact of cognitive regionalism on African agency. It is neither a case of US policy singularity and preponderance in NATO, but a question of doctrine and security approach. Partners rooted in traditional approaches to security seem less willing to accommodate a comprehensive approach to security. Even if the partner such as AFRICOM may deem security interests intertwined, it may be less willing to adjust its security approach to accommodate more African agency.

When the foregoing occurs, the AU thus resorts to agency slack. Regardless of how long and how much effort is required to find common ground, it is not willing to lose the partnerships. Granted, any partner is able to transform its security approach. After all, the AU's primary influencers—the EU and the UN—have survived significant shifts in global security. Yet, the AU's need to remain a relevant actor even when it infringes on its agential liberties and capabilities, is not entirely sacrificed, but cushioned in slippage and shirking depending on the overall nature of a given partnership. After all, both parties, in each case, are aware that there is an abiding entwining of security interests.

Interest and Preference Linkage and Agency

Preference and interest linkage is an important aspect of each partnership. Security interests are the *raison d'etre* and basis for each partnership. African and non-African security interests may not be identical, but the desire to protect them is a primary push factor. Yet, more importantly, for a partnership to be as accentuated as those under study the strategic interests should be intertwined to an extent (and perhaps more than those of partnerships not included in this study).

The interests of the AU, as the main contracting party, form the central consideration. Interests are tied to agency to the extent that they are the centripetal force around which it revolves. Agency is meant to guarantee the survival of African security interests in their entirety. As argued in the substantive chapters, African actors are not unaware of the other parties' motives and their desire to project as well as protect their interests. Consequently, African actors measure the success of their agential manoeuvres on the basis of their ability to ultimately secure their interests. Even the decision to resort to agency is on the basis of the extent to which African interests seem compromised or under threat.

In the grand scheme of things, parties accommodate a much wider latitude of African interests if they deem them more proximate to theirs. This is not a direct cause in itself: it is also dependent on other factors as well. For instance, historical longevity offers parties an opportunity to gradually reconcile their preferential differences. As demonstrated by the case of the EU, the preferential confluence that is ascribed to this partnership is not miracle. It is a result of historical and multilevel engagement. Agency slack is very rare and largely ephemeral where it exists. This is because the partnership is sufficiently institutionalised. Moreover, economic interests also play a key role. These are more salient in the case of the EU, where member states' economic interests are closely tied to Africa.

When an organisation has less closely entwined interests to Africa, it is less likely to accommodate African agency. The security interests of an organisation such as NATO have a limited scope in Africa. In an attempt to redefine itself, it slightly extended its mandate to its immediate neighbourhood. Through its so-called Mediterranean Dialogue, with North Africa, NATO is largely concerned with the Sahel and adjacent areas where threats of terrorism and piracy emanate. Beyond this narrow scope of threats, NATO has not shown keenness to adjust its preferences around its common collaborative projects with the AU. Apart from the debacle in

2011 (i.e. in the Mediterranean region), NATO has remained somewhat accommodating of African interests in so far as they do not directly challenge their core interests. The same applies for the AU. As the initiator of the partnership, there was the view that the contracting party (also as some sort of an invitee) was expected to adjust its approach. After all, the contracting (partnership) document clearly highlighted the sanctity of African ownership and leadership in the partnership.

Conversely, when a partnership is characterised by a narrow congruence of interests, there will be less ability to balance agential outcomes. Given the dynamics of the global economic, geopolitical and historical dynamics and power dynamics, some parties may find that their interests are only tangentially related to African security issues. This is the evidence in the case of AFRICOM. The US is preoccupied with terrorism, patronage and global surveillance; and less concerned with institution building in African—especially institutions that are not modelled in American similitude. Deservedly, the AU is embarking on a continental project based on a more equitable philosophy and comprehensive approach to security. However, scope and magnitude is not a major issue. After all, AFRICOM is only part of a global architecture. However, it is the subsequent position that the US adopts after calculating the vitality of its interests in Africa as a fraction of its global security which influences the stance of AFRICOM on various agential issues. The disagreements and unwillingness to resolve them which is reflected in the relevant chapter does not emanate from a tabula rasa. It is a by-product of a broader strategic calculus in which other regions hardly challenge US preponderance or the manner of cooperation. Yet, in all this, the AU is aware of the importance of a partnership with the US, which is also a salient actor in both NATO and the UN. Thus, instead of disengaging from the US, the AU and its member states resort to slippage as a useful tactic.

CAVEATS ON THESE CONCLUSIONS

There are three anomalies that emerge from a close examination of the abovementioned conclusions. It is imperative to address the exigencies of these by providing commentary to avoid negating the validity of the argument of this treatise.

Two causal variables stand out from the preceding section. These are diplomatic and multilevel engagement and preference linkage. Deservedly, these are the most paramount. However, this does not imply that the other variables are less important. Institutionalisation, African strategic citizenship, partnership agreement and configuration, cognitive regionalism and historical longevity are as equally important. However, it is imperative to highlight the extent to which they shape agency. Multi-level [and diplomatic] engagement and preference linkage are "make or break" variables in each partnership. They stand out as the two fulcrums of the partnership. First, the presence, scope and viability of agency are dependent on the extent to which both party's interests and preferences are identifiable and measurable. Without preferential congruence, especially in favour of African ownership and leadership, there are lesser prospects for a thriving partnership. As a matter of fact, the less congruent the preferences, the more likely the parties are to diverge on agential issues and most likely paralyze the partnership. Second, multilevel engagement is a constant and reiterative process that constantly shapes the prospects of African agency. The prospects of African agency improve if there is mutual engagement. The case studies have shown that there are better agential outcomes when there is multilevel and frequent engagement between parties. On the contrary, less frequent and single-level engagements limit the dialogue that is necessary to facilitate the presence and scope of African agency. Whither are the other variables?

The salience of these two variables does not negate the other variables. The case studies have demonstrated that other variables often result in casual chains. Some of the variables such as history and agreement type are important on their own, but they also shape other variables. For instance, history and coloniality could be considered antecedent variables which predate the partnerships; while cognitive regionalism and strategic citizenship could be considered intervening variables, yet the analytic position and role of these variables are interchangeable. This implies that all the variables are important depending on where the viewer or analyst places them.

On the other hand, some analytic variables were not given enough attention in the case studies. The substantive chapters seem biased towards history, multilevel engagement, as well as interest and preference linkage. Other variables such as imperialism or coloniality, African strategic citizenship, agreement type and cognitive regionalism were not given thorough attention in each of the case studies. However, strategic

9 CONCLUSION 215

citizenship, imperialism and collective diplomacy are given more attention in the fourth chapter. In retrospective consideration, the substantive chapters would have benefited more from greater treatment of these variables.

Wither Agency Slack in the Partnerships

The case studies in the substantive chapters prove the conclusions prove the centrality of agency slack in the partnerships. There is no denying that African agency is a critical aspect of Africa (and the AU) in international politics. However, these chapters have proven that in the case of the AU, the attempt to secure African agency has been compromised and challenged by the partners to the extent that the AU has resorted to agency slack as a defence mechanism. The recourse to agency slack implies that the AU seeks to balance the importance of these partners/ships and the various threats that they pose to African security. These threats are not static nor are they always obvious. They are generated by an isomorphic process that involves evolving dynamics from either side.

There is little evidence that African preferences and interests have evolved quickly. For the most part, the AU and their member states have remained consistent in their security preferences. These preferences predate the formation of the AU by at least twenty-six years and their current form finalised between 1980 and 1990. Africa has remained constant. The reification of the APSA architecture is predicted to remain relevant and a sine quo non in the stabilisation of Africa. Africa has not deviated from these preferences. What Africa sought through and within the partnerships was "African ownership and leadership" often manifesting in the form of "agenda and priority setting". This is a sign of the freedom and capacity to act which was highlighted as the most important aspect of African agency. Unfortunately, the partners have challenge of these core principles in various ways.

The various partnerships have challenged African agency in various ways that drove the AU into a position of agency slack. The chapters have shown that the partners generally have different attitudes and approaches to African agency. This manifests in the way the partners engage the AU; how they disburse support; and how they engage on the issue of preferences. The European Union has been a relatively better partner. The high-level engagement between the partners created an environment where differences are dealt with via dialogue. Moreover, the disbursement of support largely accommodates African ownership and leadership. The preferences are also intertwined. As a result, the partnership has largely remained conflict free and encouraged Africa agency; hence there has been little need for agency slack. The partnerships with the United Nations and NATO have elicited different forms of shirking. While both of these partnerships were initially institutionalised to sufficient degrees, they dwindled with successive leaderships. The succeeding leadership in the partner organisations did not prioritise high-level engagement as their predecessors. The partnerships were also not sufficiently institutionalised at various levels, especially the technical and middle level where most interactions occur. When tensions arose with NATO, especially following the NATO debacle, there were no longer credible structures to address the issues that were deemed an affront to African leadership and ownership as well as agenda and priority setting. The inability to reconcile interests and preferences resulted in a situation where the AU eventually shirked on various efforts wherein NATO sought to have more dialogue as well as renew and upgrade the partnership.

Similarly, the UN partnership was subject to shirking. The partnership started well under the leadership of Kofi Anan and Alpha Konare. The AU considered the UN an important partner circa 2006 when the first partnership was signed. The disbursement progressed well without interference. The UN made massive contributions in the early design of APSA institutions. Although most institutions were designed by Africans in line with the empirical exigencies of the continent, there was a desire to align them with UN institutions for obvious reasons: AU member states are also UN member states, and most AU missions eventually end up as UN missions. However, tensions arose between the UN Security Council and AU Peace and Security Council. The UNSC seeks to entrench the principle of subsidiarity in the partnership, which would mean that the AU plays second fiddle to the UN; while the AU prefers the principle of complementarity, which seeks to balance competences—which would actually protect African ownership and leadership or agenda-priority setting. The politics between the two councils may seem like a tiny fraction of the partnership given the size of the UN as an organisation and multiplicity of the UN agencies supporting the APSA, but this must be put into perspective. The UNSC is the most powerful of all UN bodies. Its decisions can affect the viability of all other streams of collaborations. That is why, for example, the contentious politics have affected the effectiveness of the UN Office to AU (UNOAU). That is why the AU has minimised efforts in this partnership and often watered down the involvement of the UN as a way of reducing their influence in the overall Africa security project.

Finally, the partnership with the US is the most ironic. On paper, the strategic partnership blurs the security component giving the impression that it is the least potent. Yet, in reality—as the substantive chapters have shown—the US involvement in Africa exhibits more security involvement than in other spheres, although that is done in utmost secrecy. AFRICOM's preference of the shadows has created a problem in terms of partnerships. The partnership is the least institutionalised despite the fact that US security presence in Africa has grown in leaps and bounds over the years. The security interests and preferences of the US hardly align to those of the AU. As a result, AFRICOM provides highly selective support to African security. In some instances, some of the two parties disagree on the design and functions of security institutions which they both seem necessary. In some cases, the US already has similar institutions as part of AFRICOM or NATO, but the AU prefers a different model. In most of these cases AFRICOM officials seek to convince their AU counterparts to adopt their perspective, including on how to disburse financial support, but the latter are unrelenting. As of the 2010s, this partnership is characterised by slippage wherein the AU avoids certain suggestions or departs from previously tenable positions in order to protect its interests. After all, there are more platforms from which to obtain favourable outcomes which ensure African leadership and ownership.

In the grand scheme of things, the AU manifestly contests the limiting of its freedom to formulate and reify certain preferences in the partnerships. This is likely to endure as long as the spectre of imperialism and postcoloniality are not dealt with. There are simple glaring deficiencies. For instance, all partners have got liaison officers at the AU Commission headquarters, yet the AU does not have liaison officers in any of the partner organisations. The starting point could be to accredit the AU Permanent Representative to Brussels to NATO and AFRICOM. Security experts who are permanent employees of the AU (not on secondment) should be accredited as liaisons or observers in all those organisations. Furthermore, the UNOAU needs to be rolled back. As it stands it is a UN office (in the similitude of an embassy) and does not represent any equitable status where the AU can have liaison representatives. This would be a useful step after the UN's adoption of the Prodi Report's recommendation that the UN lean towards the principle of complementarity, which improves African agency without compromising UN efficiency. The EU also needs to prepare for a winding down of its influence at the AU Commission. It is only in the case of a crippled child where there is an unending need for an au pair. If the EU meant to help the AU become a capable actor, it must prepare for a draw down (as indicated in the reduction of troop allowances) and a substantial retreat from African security. In that case, the EU can retain its delegation to the AU, and the latter also creates its liaison teams in Brussels. All of the foregoing implies that African actors must also heighten their involvement in international politics. The nimbus and centrality of African strategic citizenship is long overdue. The lack of political will to use resources that already exist in the continent is a self-corroding exercise that must be terminated instantly. If the AU does not wean itself from global donor support, Africa agency will ultimately be compromised. After all, in the words of Chinua Achebe, "charity is the opium of the privileged".

INDEX

A
Ababa, Addis, 3
Active Zone, 45
Africa Conflict Prevention Pool (ACPP), 44
African Capacity for the Immediate Response to Crises (ACRIC), 47
African Centre for the Constructive Resolution of Disputes (ACCORD), 105
African Chiefs of Defence Staff (ACDS), 107
African Development Bank (AfDB), 57
African-led Mission in Mali (AFISMA), 87
African National Congress (ANC), 111
African ownership and leadership, 5
African Peace and Security Architecture (APSA), 4, 5
African Peer Review Mechanism (APRM), 84
African solutions to African problems, 184, 192
African Standby Force (ASF), 83
African Union (AU), 1, 2
African Union Mission in Somalia (AMISOM), 82
African Union Mission in Sudan (AMIS), 82
Africa Peace Facility, 81
Afro-pessimists, 41
agency, 1–11
agency slack, 1, 4, 7–11
agential, 17–19, 21–25, 29, 32
Algeria, 56–59
AMANI, 115, 127
Amphibious Ready Group (ARG), 190
Angola, 72, 81, 87
Annan, Kofi, 53
Arab League, 9, 55–57
Areas of Responsibility (AORs), 183
Assembly of Heads of State and Government (AHSG), 28, 32

© The Editor(s) (if applicable) and The Author(s), under exclusive license to Springer Nature Switzerland AG 2022
T. Gwatiwa, *The African Union and African Agency in International Politics*, https://doi.org/10.1007/978-3-030-87805-4

220 INDEX

AU Peace Fund, 109, 116, 121, 124, 126
AU Peacekeeping Support Team (AU PST), 119
AU reforms, 104
authenticity, 30

B

Ben Bella, 122
Botswana, 72, 82, 84
Bouteflika, Abdelaziz, 8
BRICS, 111
British, 42, 55
British Peace Support Teams (BPST), 44
Burundi, 68, 73, 80, 82, 84
Bush, George W., 190

C

capacity, 20, 24
capacity building, 114
Casablanca Group, 46
Central African Republic (CAR), 90, 94
Central Intelligence Agency (CIA), 186
Central Organ of the Mechanism for Conflict Prevention, Management and Resolution (Central Organ), 104, 119
Centre for Conflict Management (CCM), 106
Chairperson of the AU Commission/Chairperson, 8
China, 1
coercion, 142, 148
Cold War, 21
colonialism, 26, 29, 30
combatant commands (CCDMs), 183–185

Combined Joint Task Force, Horn of Africa (CJTF-HOA), 188
Common African Defence and Security Policy (CADSP), 27, 30
common African positions, 28, 30
the Commonwealth, 51
Comoros, 73, 80, 82
Comprehensive Crisis and Operations Management Centre (CCOMC), 124
concept of operations (CONOPS), 92
Conference on Security, Stability, Development and Cooperation in Africa (CSSDCA), 6
Constitutive Act, 1
Continental Early Warning Systems (CEWS), 104, 106, 120
contingent-owned equipment (COE), 74
contributions, 71, 72, 74–79, 81, 83, 84, 86, 88
Cotonou Agreement, 138, 139

D

Darfur, 84–86, 88
decolonisation, 42
De Gaulle, Charles, 44, 45
Delany, Martin, 50
Department of Peacekeeping Operations (DPKO), 156
Deutsche Gesellschaft Für Internationale Zusammenarbeit (GIZ), 148
diplomacy, 26, 27, 32, 78, 94

E

Economic Community of West African States (ECOWAS), 52
Economic Community of West African States Monitoring Group (ECOMOG), 75

INDEX

egalitarian, 73
Egypt, 53, 56, 58
elites, 26, 27, 31
Empire, 5
empirical, 17, 18, 20–23
Eteki, William, 57
Ethiopia, 67, 72, 73, 77, 84, 85, 87, 90, 93
European Development Fund (EDF), 109
European External Action Service (EEAS), 25
Europeanisation, 43
European Security Defence Policy (ESDP), 30
European Union (EU), 18, 22, 25, 32
EURO RECAMP, 44
Executive Council (EXCO), 28
expertise, 17
extraversion, 21
Ezuwlini Consensus, 53

F
Fanon, Frantz, 24
Fertile Crescent, 55
Force Multinational d'Afrique Centrale (FOMAC), 94
Foreign policy, 25, 26, 28

G
Gaddafi, Muammar, 27, 31, 32
Gambari Report, 141
General Ward, William, 184, 193

H
hegemony/hegemonic, 69, 72–75, 78, 81, 87, 89, 92–94, 110, 111
Henri Sylvester-William, 49

I
identity, 21, 23–25, 27, 29
imperialism, 18, 30
influence, 20, 21, 23, 26, 29, 32
institutionalisation, 9
Inter-Governmental Authority on Development (IGAD), 52
international partners/partners, 18, 23
intervention, 110, 111, 115, 124

J
Japan, 9
Joint Africa-EU Strategy (JAES), 139, 146
Joint African High Command (JAHC), 46, 47
Joint Combatant Command (NATO JCC), 166
Joint Defence Command (JDC), 46
Joint Financial Arrangements (JFAs), 142
Joint Research Centre (EU JRC), 106, 117

K
Kagame, Paul, 31, 33
Kampala Movement, 58
Kenya, 80, 81, 84
Konare, Alpha, 27, 32, 154–156, 165, 166, 171

L
Lagos Plan of Action, 109
Liberia, 157
Libya, 68, 74, 79, 87, 90, 94
Lomé Agreement, 138
Lomé Convention, 43
lumpy goods, 70

222 INDEX

M
Maghreb, 49, 57
Mamdani, 22
Mandela, Nelson, 50
Mbeki, Thabo, 3, 8
membership, 23, 24
Military Attachés Association (MAA),
    83
Mimicry, 145
minimization, 18
Mixed Zone, 45
mobility, 20, 23–25
Monrovia Group, 46
multilateralism, 41, 48, 52

N
NATO Mediterranean Dialogue
    (NATO MD), 168
NATO Senior Military Liaison Office
    (NATO SMLO), 166
New Partnership for African
    Development (NEPAD), 30
Nigeria, 27, 30–32
Nkrumah, Kwame, 46, 47
North African, 49, 56
North Atlantic Treaty Organization
    (NATO), 2
Norway, 32

O
OAU Defence Force (OAU-DF), 48
OAU Secretary General, 52
Obama, Barack, 6
Obasanjo, Olusegun, 8
Office of Defence Cooperation
    (ODC), 46, 47
Operation Artemis, 116
Operation BOLEAS, 157
Operation Odyssey Dawn, 168
Operation Sangaris, 90
Operation Serval, 91

Operation Shaba, 165
Operation Sheltering Sky, 190
Operation Sovereign Legitimacy, 157
Organization for Security Cooperation
    in Europe (OSCE), 148
*Organization Internationale de la
    Francophonie* (OIF), 45
Organization of African Unity
    (OAU), 21
Organization of Islamic Cooperation
    (OIC), 168
Organization of Islamic Countries
    (OIC), 91

P
PAMPA, 44
Pan-Africanism, 23, 30
Panel of the Wise (PANWISE),
    104–106, 117, 118, 120–122,
    124, 126, 127, 129
participation, 23
Passive Zone, 45
Pax-Nigeriana, 111
Peace and Security Committee (EU)
    PSC, 45
Peace and Security Department
    (PSD), 7
Peace Support Operations Division
    (PSOD), 107, 122
peace support operations (PSOs), 81,
    84, 86, 87, 91
Permanent Representatives
    Committee (PRC), 28
phantom(s), 21, 41
political will, 75, 82, 83, 86, 89, 94
Portugal, 44, 47
postcolonial condition, 10
postcoloniality, 10
post-conflict reconstruction and
    development (PCRD), 89
Powell, Collin, 184, 192
power, 21–23, 26, 29, 31

INDEX

preferences, 17–20, 24–26, 28
private military and security
  companies (PMCs), 159
Protocol on the Peace and Security
  Council (PSC), 32

Q
quick impact projects (QIPs), 82, 89

R
RECAMP, 44, 45
Regional Economic Communities
  (RECs), 28
Regional Mechanisms (RMs), 28
rights, 22
Russia, 2

S
security, 17, 18, 25, 29–32
security cooperation officers (SCOs),
  188, 194
shirking, 4, 11
Situation Room, 117, 120
slippage, 4, 11
Somalia, 113, 115, 116
South Africa, 27, 30–32
Southern African Development
  Community (SADC), 48, 52
Soviet, 69
special forces, 186
strategic airlift, 75–78, 81–84
Strategic Military Mission Order
  (SMMO), 166
subaltern, 20, 23, 30

T
ten-year capacity building agreement
  (TYCBA), 154

transregional, 24
Treaty of Rome, 42
Tubman, 46
Turkey, 9
Tutu, Desmond, 50

U
UN Force Intervention Brigade
  (UNFIB), 157
UN Guard Unit, 159
Unified Task Force (UNITAF), 186
unilateralism, 138, 144
United Nations Economic
  Commission for Africa
  (UNECA), 161
United Nations Office to the African
  Union (UNOAU), 161, 162
United Nations Security Council
  (UNSC), 68, 79
United Nations Support Office to
  AMISOM (UNSOA), 158, 163
United Nations (UN), 1, 21, 26
United States Africa Command
  (AFRICOM), 3
UN Stabilization Mission in the DRC
  (MONUSCO), 157
US Department of Defence (US
  DOD), 184

W
W.E. Du Bois, 50

Z
Zenawi, Meles, 60
Zuma, Nkosazana Dlamini, 32